Toward Community-Based Learning

Urban Education, Cultures and Communities

Series Editors

Christopher Emdin (*Teachers College, Columbia University, USA*)
Edmund Adjapong (*Seton Hall University, USA*)

Editorial Board

Amil Cook (*Visual Artist/Educator, Pittsburgh, USA*)
Michael Dando (*University of Wisconsin, USA*)
Hodari Davis (*Teaching Artist, Oakland, USA*)
Reenah Golden (*Teaching Artist, Rochester, USA*)
P. Thandi Hicks Harper (*Youth Popular Institute, Maryland, USA*)
Awad Ibrahim (*University of Ottawa, Canada*)
Timothy Jones (*FreeStyle Artist/Public Speaker, District of Columbia, USA*)
Tina Kahn (*Toronto School District Board, Canada*)
Gloria Ladson-Billings (*University of Wisconsin, USA*)
Ian Levy (*Manhattan College, Bronx, USA*)
Lauren Kelly (*Rutgers University-New Jersey, USA*)
Emery Petchauer (*Michigan State University, USA*)
Elaine Richardson (*Ohio State University, USA*)
Courtney Rose (*Teachers College, USA*)
Yolanda Sealey-Ruiz (*Teachers College, USA*)
Sam Seidel (*Stanford University, USA*)
Terri Watson (*City College of New York, USA*)
Vajra Watson (*University of California – Davis, USA*)
Torie Weiston-Serdan (*Claremont Graduate University, USA*)

VOLUME 1

The titles published in this series are listed at *brill.com/uecc*

Toward Community-Based Learning

Experiences from the U.S.A., India, and China

Edited by

Eija Kimonen and Raimo Nevalainen

BRILL
SENSE

LEIDEN | BOSTON

Cover illustration: Photograph by Raimo Nevalainen

All chapters in this book have undergone peer review.

The Library of Congress Cataloging-in-Publication Data is available online at http://catalog.loc.gov

Typeface for the Latin, Greek, and Cyrillic scripts: "Brill". See and download: brill.com/brill-typeface.

ISSN 2666-2167
ISBN 978-90-04-42448-7 (paperback)
ISBN 978-90-04-38976-2 (hardback)
ISBN 978-90-04-42449-4 (e-book)

Copyright 2020 by Koninklijke Brill NV, Leiden, The Netherlands.
Koninklijke Brill NV incorporates the imprints Brill, Brill Hes & De Graaf, Brill Nijhoff, Brill Rodopi, Brill Sense, Hotei Publishing, mentis Verlag, Verlag Ferdinand Schöningh and Wilhelm Fink Verlag.
All rights reserved. No part of this publication may be reproduced, translated, stored in a retrieval system, or transmitted in any form or by any means, electronic, mechanical, photocopying, recording or otherwise, without prior written permission from the publisher.
Authorization to photocopy items for internal or personal use is granted by Koninklijke Brill NV provided that the appropriate fees are paid directly to The Copyright Clearance Center, 222 Rosewood Drive, Suite 910, Danvers, MA 01923, USA. Fees are subject to change.

This book is printed on acid-free paper and produced in a sustainable manner.

Contents

Foreword   VII
   Linda Hargreaves
Preface   x
Notes on Contributors   xv

PART 1
Foundations for Community-Based Learning: An International View

1   Ideals for Community Engagement from the East and West   3
       Eija Kimonen and Raimo Nevalainen

PART 2
The Research and Evolution of Community-Based Learning

2   Community-Based Learning: An Exploration from Philanthropy to Praxis   95
       Thomas L. Alsbury, Suzan Kobashigawa and Mary Ewart

3   Community-Based Learning and Student Outcomes: What Research Reveals   124
       Thomas L. Alsbury, Suzan Kobashigawa and Mary Ewart

PART 3
Community-Based Pedagogical Strategies with Students and for Educators

4   Community-Based Pedagogical Strategies with Students   149
       Lakia M. Scott, Karon N. LeCompte, Suzanne M. Nesmith and Susan K. Johnsen

5   Connecting Learning to the Community: Pedagogical Strategies for Educators   172
       Suzanne M. Nesmith, Lakia M. Scott, Karon N. LeCompte and Susan K. Johnsen

PART 4
Global Approaches for Community-Based Learning

6 Toward Learning in the Community: Insights from the U.S.A., India, and China   197
  Eija Kimonen and Raimo Nevalainen

  Afterword   259
  Eija Kimonen and Raimo Nevalainen

  Index   263

Foreword

This book offers promising pedagogical solutions to fundamental questions that have long haunted educators. As life inside school has become increasingly disconnected from life outside school, this internationally informed *re-vision* of community-based learning promises several approaches to *re-connection*. Through community-based learning, children can find meaning, experience agency, and see purpose in the process of schooling beyond the mere instrumental. Community-based learning could even preempt employers' complaints about new employees' (alleged) lack of practical everyday skills. But, as Eija Kimonen, Raimo Nevalainen, and their contributors make clear, fulfillment of this potential is not a foregone conclusion. This book, through numerous examples set in diverse cultural and political environments, draws attention to cautionary research findings concerning the nature of student involvement and the optimal pedagogical approaches. That said, community-based learning can make a major contribution in reforming classrooms that are so often out of step with community lives.

Kimonen and Nevalainen bring unique insight to this field. This is not surprising given their previous publications. Their opening chapter, which occupies the first part of the book, provides a deep foundation for the chapters to follow. In it, Kimonen and Nevalainen present, compare, and contrast historical, philosophical, and practical perspectives on community-based learning from East and West. They identify the pioneers of community-based learning, noting, in particular, the international influence of John Dewey. Working with a broad conceptualization of community, they conduct a meticulous analysis of the complex relationships between classical philosophies, educational aims, and social, moral, and ethical values, and how these have changed through time in the United States, India, and China. They then make connections between community-based learning in the former Soviet Union and these disparate jurisdictions and examine the cultural differences in the interpretation and practice of community-based learning in each location. Ultimately, the contributors to this book celebrate the many positive outcomes of community-based learning, while also identifying shortcomings and offering pedagogical strategies to preempt such outcomes from these limitations. Through it all, the chapters acknowledge the increasing influence of technology in the various forms of community-based learning.

Parts 2 and 3 focus on community-based learning in the United States. Thomas L. Alsbury, Suzan Kobashigawa, and Mary Ewart pursue the evolution of community-based learning in the United States, dating it back to Jane Addams in 1889 and John Dewey's recognition of the potential of community-based learning to nourish democratic society. In Chapter 2, they recognize the many ways of defining community-based learning, but helpfully draw out three common forms, namely, service-learning, work-based learning, and community service. In Chapter 3, these authors review relevant contemporary research and examine student outcomes. Part 3 moves on to critically examine research on the pedagogy of community-based learning *with* students and *for* educators in Chapters 4 and 5, respectively. Lakia M. Scott, Karon N. LeCompte, Suzanne M. Nesmith, and Susan K. Johnsen provide critical, research-informed insights into significant pedagogical strategies, including student involvement in creative problem solving, performing independent investigations, or engaging in action civics that entails researching and campaigning for a community cause. Salient here is the teacher's sensitive encouragement of constructive reflection in connecting action with thought.

In Chapter 6, the concluding chapter, Kimonen and Nevalainen integrate the implications of the preceding chapters with their own comparative, historico-hermeneutical research project on the relationships between education and society in the 20th century and beyond. Using numerous examples, they focus on the pedagogical practices shown to build community-based relations. They chart developments through axes of social change and the associated prominent learning environments (such as Naturalistic, Productive, Ecological, and Scientific-Technical). In the three very different contexts of community-based learning, the Scientific-Technical dimension emerges in the later 20th century as principal secondary socializer in pursuit of intellectual aims. In conclusion, Kimonen and Nevalainen perceive a generation arguably deprived of the natural and the community worlds as students "live" through their screens: a deprivation to be remedied through renewed emphasis on community-based learning. Finally, the Afterword synthesizes the learning of the whole volume into a succinct typology of ideals about community-based learning for the future.

Community-based learning can be restricted to examples of the school going into the community to help tackle local issues. For me, this prompts the question of reciprocal action, in which the community becomes involved in the school and its problems, such as declining rolls or social conflicts. The Finnish reforms of 1994 called for parental and community involvement in curriculum building (Nevalainen, Kimonen, & Hämäläinen, 2001) and the present book reveals authentic historical examples of mutually supportive community-based learning, especially in the villages of India and China. As Kimonen and Nevalainen suggest in their Afterword, an ideal community-based learning curriculum involves all voices—community, students, educators—planning and participating collaboratively in their projects. This book shows how, with appropriate pedagogical strategies, community-based learning has the potential to rekindle school and community relations at the local level and renew that intrinsic motivation for learning so badly eroded by the present-day obsession with global competition.

References

Nevalainen, R., Kimonen, E., & Hämäläinen, S. (2001). Curriculum changes in the Finnish comprehensive school: The lessons of three decades. In E. Kimonen (Ed.), *Curriculum approaches: Readings and activities for educational studies* (pp. 123–141). Jyväskylä, Finland: Department of Teacher Education & Institute of Educational Research, University of Jyväskylä.

Linda Hargreaves
Reader Emerita
Faculty of Education
University of Cambridge

Preface

1 Prospects for Connecting Schools and Communities

This volume intends to provide an articulated overview of the manifestations of community-based learning in school pedagogics. Approaches to community-based learning are geared toward meeting the following educational challenges: How do educators connect learning with the authentic community environments, where learning is linked to life, experiences, and practical problems? How do educators make learning more functional and holistic for students and enable them to work in new situations and analyze the complex world around them?

Putting community-based learning into practice requires that educators expand their professional orientation from a restricted one to an extended one. The extended orientation of teacher professionalism is associated with educators who view their responsibility as something that extends beyond classroom activities to include cooperation with members of the surrounding community (see Hoyle & John, 1996). Hargreaves and Shirley (2009) stated that educators can learn to engage with and benefit from parent activism and community development as a core part of their professional identity. Connecting schools more to their communities increases schools' influence in the community (pp. 78–79). In such a school culture, educators emphasize professional cooperation and are willing to be engaged at the school and community levels. They must be holistically conscious of the factors influencing school activities and be able to critically analyze their own instruction. Furthermore, they must be aware of both the schools' and their own roles in developing the community. Consequently, it is important for teacher education to develop forms of instruction which offer prospective teachers an opportunity to build fully functioning thought and action patterns and to adopt the strategies necessary to change school practices.

Approaches to community-based learning have many positive influences on the school culture and the surrounding community. This volume describes how a school curriculum can emphasize life-centered issues in school pedagogics in the United States, India, and China. Many schools encourage community members to participate in realizing the school curriculum. In schoolwork, cooperative activities are essential for effective community-based projects when students are learning to access information from various sources using different methods. These types of experiential activities are based on initiative work, cooperative learning, and service, and give rise to material consequences when combined with the performance of work.

Schoolwork can also create organic relations with interest groups in the surrounding community. These schools help community members to achieve their common goals and solve problems. Moreover, many schools actively work to maintain the school by cooperating with members of the community while, at the same time, breathing life into the neighborhood. This can enhance processes so that education uses all the human, physical, and financial resources of the community's learning networks. Similarly, various groups within the community can utilize the learning networks to develop different partnerships based on cooperation.

2   Overview

The purpose of this book is to outline the complex character of community-based learning in schools and their communities. This type of learning is observed in the light of research findings regarding innovative approaches and reforms. The process of concept formation proceeds in a contextual manner with the source material aiming to be as close to the original as possible. The book chapters intend to reflect various topics and processes for community-based learning in an approachable and theoretically grounded form.

Part 1 explores the foundations of community-based learning within social change. It interprets the nature of the philosophical views, educational aims, and associated values from an international perspective. The first chapter, "Ideals for Community Engagement from the East and West," by Eija Kimonen and Raimo Nevalainen, discusses the main philosophical background views as well as the aims of education and the value dimensions of community-based learning, most specifically in the United States, India, and China. It attempts to identify the essence of developmental trends in the history of ideas in the field of education and the value-oriented aims intertwined with them using data from these socially different countries. The focus of interest is on the interplay between changes in educational policy and society in these countries at different times and how this interplay has been reflected as various ideals, aims, and values of community-based learning. Additionally, it attempts to identify possible philosophical connections between the three countries and one former country, the early Soviet Union. The study is based on a research project that examines the interrelationship between education and society during the 20th century and beyond.

Part 2 discusses the evolution of and research about community-based learning. It focuses on how the evolving definition, purpose, and design of community based learning contributed to disparate outcomes and limited use of this learning approach across the United States. Chapter 2, "Community-Based

Learning: An Exploration from Philanthropy to Praxis," by Thomas L. Alsbury, Suzan Kobashigawa, and Mary Ewart, provides a historical overview of the development of community-based learning approaches in the United States, from its philanthropic origins to more pragmatic vocational skills development. It examines current pluralistic definitions and program purposes, ranging from service-learning to social activism. Instructional and classroom applications are reviewed, including second language, newcomer, and place-bound programs. The chapter concludes with remarks on how this reform's dichotomy of purpose has persisted from its inception to the current day, contributing to the lack of widespread adoption and program clarity.

Chapter 3, "Community-Based Learning and Student Outcomes: What Research Reveals," by Thomas L. Alsbury, Suzan Kobashigawa, and Mary Ewart, provides research findings on the effectiveness of using community-based learning, which are reviewed with a focus on substantive student outcomes, including improved community orientation, cultural capital, social advocacy, work ethic, and classroom achievement. Research found outcomes primarily in student social and cultural competency and sensitivity, although the findings vary based on program purpose and design as well as on the level of relationship development between school and community mentors and students participating in the community experiences.

Part 3 examines pedagogical strategies used with K–16 students and in teacher preparation programs that build community-based relationships in the United States. The strategies contribute to involving students and educators in the community and teaching them to value its resources. Chapter 4, "Community-Based Pedagogical Strategies with Students," by Lakia M. Scott, Karon N. LeCompte, Suzanne M. Nesmith, and Susan K. Johnsen, presents an overview of community-based learning opportunities for students to increase their community engagement, make curriculum meaningful, and strengthen their connection between learning in schools and in the community. This chapter highlights student-led independent investigations, action civics where students engage civically and behave as citizens, justice-oriented citizenship using the Freedom Schools model, and transdisciplinary learning experiences that bring together university faculty, staff, and students in developing innovative ways to promote human fulfillment. Each pedagogical strategy is clearly defined using characteristics and tangible examples with K–16 students. The chapter concludes by emphasizing the importance of using community-based learning to enhance critical inquiry and civic engagement.

Chapter 5, "Connecting Learning to the Community: Pedagogical Strategies for Educators," by Suzanne M. Nesmith, Lakia M. Scott, Karon N. LeCompte, and Susan K. Johnsen, presents an overview of community-based pedagogies and the benefits, outcomes, and challenges of community-based learning. Specific to the ways in which community-based pedagogies may be used to confront cultural disconnects, the authors include specific community-based learning pedagogical strategies utilized for and with educators. The authors provide descriptions of four pedagogical strategies, including creative problem solving in community learning, field-based environmental education, action civics, and service-learning, along with depictions of the ways in which the strategies were shared with preservice and in-service educators. The chapter concludes with a comprehensive summary highlighting how community-based pedagogies have the potential to empower students and transform school settings.

Part 4 is devoted to global approaches for community-based learning through a qualitative comparative study. It shows how, using available data, community-based learning in three socially different countries has been theorized and practiced in the 20th and 21st centuries. The final chapter, "Toward Learning in the Community: Insights from the U.S.A., India, and China," by Eija Kimonen and Raimo Nevalainen, examines the pedagogical procedures and practices of community-based learning at different times. The authors view community-based learning as pedagogical processes taking place in authentic learning environments, such as the natural world, social life, and the world of work. The most significant function of this process is that the various approaches to community-based learning are linked to dimensions of learning environments, such as Naturalistic, Sociocultural, Productive, Economic, Martial, Ecological, or Scientific-Technical Dimensions. The study applies the historico-hermeneutical approach to comparative education and follows the developmental trends of educational policy at different times in the context of social change.

Acknowledgments

We would like to express our gratitude to all those who, in one way or another, contributed to the realization of this book. Our special appreciation is due to our coauthors for their inspiring and creative contributions.

We are grateful to the Emil Aaltonen Foundation, the Finnish Cultural Foundation, and the Alfred Kordelin Foundation for their financial support. The editing process for this volume was carried out in the RICEI Project at the University of Jyväskylä, Finland. We would like to take this opportunity to extend our sincerest thanks in particular to the following colleagues from the University of Jyväskylä for their support and encouragement in this project: Ms. Päivi Seppä, Director of Administration; Ms. Hanna Sahinen, Financial Planning Coordinator; Ms. Tuija Koponen, Head of the International Office; and Dr. Pekka Ruuskanen, Head of the University Teacher Training School.

We express our warmest thanks to the following colleagues for their valuable support and advice over the years: Professor Congman Rao and Associate Professor Xin Chen from Northeast Normal University, Professor Weiping Shi and Associate Professor Meilu Sun from East China Normal University, Professor Emerita Shakuntla Nagpal from the National Council of Educational Research and Training in New Delhi, Professor Dhruv Raina from Jawaharlal Nehru University, and Professor Emeritus Robert F. Arnove from Indiana University. We are thankful to the reviewers who kindly commented on this volume's chapters and provided constructive feedback. We are also indebted to Ms. Lea Galanter for her invaluable contributions in performing the language and copy editing of the entire text. We express our sincerest appreciation to Mr. Joed Elich and Mr. Marti Huetink, Publishing Directors, Ms. Evelien van der Veer, Assistant Editor, and Ms. Jolanda Karada, Production Editor, for making publication of this book possible.

References

Hargreaves, A., & Shirley, D. (2009). *The fourth way: The inspiring future for educational change.* Thousand Oaks, CA: Corwin Press.

Hoyle, E., & John, P. D. (1995). *Professional knowledge and professional practice.* London, U.K.: Cassell.

Notes on Contributors

Thomas L. Alsbury
is Professor of Educational Leadership at Northwest University. His research interests include school board governance, organizational theory, and school district reform. Recent publications include an article in the journal *Research in Educational Administration & Leadership* (Vol. 3, 2018). He is editor of the volume *The Future of School Board Governance: Relevancy and Revelation* (Rowman & Littlefield, 2008) and coeditor with Phil Gore of the book *Improving School Board Effectiveness: A Balanced Governance Approach* (Harvard, 2015). Prior to his academic career, Alsbury served almost 20 years as a high school teacher, K–12 principal, and district administrator.

Mary Ewart
is Assistant Professor of Education at Northwest University. Her research interests include culturally responsive teaching, instructional design, and STEM education; her proposed doctoral research will focus on pedagogical strategies to strengthen mathematics understanding and combat mathematics anxiety in preservice elementary school teachers. Her master's thesis centered around teacher leadership, specifically how to create and maintain cross-departmental professional learning communities, with an emphasis on collaboration between secondary mathematics and English departments. Prior to joining higher education, she taught mathematics and science for 13 years in secondary schools.

Linda Hargreaves
is Reader Emerita in the Faculty of Education at the University of Cambridge in the U.K. Her background is in psychology and primary education, and her research interests include educational provision in small rural schools and classroom interaction in various contexts. Relevant publications include "Theory as the Source of 'Research Footprint' in Rural Settings" with Rune Kvalsund in *Doing Educational Research in Rural Settings* (Routledge, 2014), edited by Simone White and Michael Corbett, and "Turning Talk Around: Time for Children to Talk and Teachers to Listen in Primary Mathematics" with Rocío García-Carrión in *Promoting Academic Talk in Schools* (Routledge, 2018), edited by Robyn M. Gillies.

Susan K. Johnsen
is Professor Emerita in the Department of Educational Psychology at Baylor University. She is editor in chief of *Gifted Child Today* and the author of more

than 300 articles, monographs, technical reports, chapters, and other publications related to gifted education. Johnsen has written three tests used in identifying gifted students: Test of Mathematical Abilities for Gifted Students, Test of Nonverbal Intelligence, and Screening Assessment Gifted Students. She has received awards for her work in the field of education, including the National Association for Gifted Children's Ann F. Isaacs Founder's Memorial Award and the Council for Exceptional Children's Leadership Award. Her research interests focus on assessment, standards, and serving gifted students from diverse populations.

Eija Kimonen

is Senior Researcher with the RICEI Project at the University of Jyväskylä, Finland. This project studies international educational reforms carried out in the United States, Russia, China, and India in a comparative context. She is also Adjunct Professor of Intercultural and Comparative Education at Northeast Normal University in China. Her research interests include the interplay between education and society generally, and reform pedagogics, outdoor education, and work-based education more specifically. Kimonen most recently authored the book *Education and Society in Comparative Context* (Sense Publishers, 2015) and coedited the volume *Reforming Teaching and Teacher Education* (Sense Publishers, 2017) with Raimo Nevalainen.

Suzan Kobashigawa

is Professor of Education at Northwest University. Her research interests include English language teaching, teacher development, intercultural communication, and language revitalization. Her research in language revitalization focuses specifically on generational use of the Hawaiian language and the context needed for continued growth. An outgrowth of this research has centered on schools and the role they play in Indigenous language education, both in Hawaii and in Washington State. In addition, Kobashigawa conducts training for English language teachers in the United States and globally in pedagogy, teacher reflection, and intercultural communication.

Karon N. LeCompte

is Associate Professor in the Department of Curriculum and Instruction at Baylor University. She teaches courses with an emphasis in social studies education, where she involves preservice and Texas teachers in civics education and law-related education. Her research interests include social studies education and leadership theory. She has authored or coauthored over 25 book chapters and articles on topics related to civics education and leadership and has presented at state, national, and international conferences. LeCompte was named a Baylor iCivics Fellow in 2012 and spent six weeks in Washington, D.C., working with the national iCivics team established by retired Supreme Court Justice Sandra Day O'Connor.

Suzanne M. Nesmith
is Associate Dean of Undergraduate Education and Associate Professor in the Department of Curriculum and Instruction at Baylor University. A specialist in science and environmental education, she has published extensively on the ways in which content, instructional strategies, and instructional contexts work together in the construction of meaning and understanding. Her recent studies include exploring elementary preservice teachers' perceptions toward using literature in science, educators' design and implementation of environmental education curricula, and the influence of professional development experience on how educators apply green chemistry concepts. Nesmith is also director of the Wetlands Environmental Academy for Educators.

Raimo Nevalainen
is a Lecturer in the University Teacher Training School and a researcher at the Research for International Comparison of Educational Innovations (RICEI) Project at the University of Jyväskylä. Along with his research work, he has presented his studies around the world, particularly in the United States, India, and China. His research interests include active learning, curriculum change, teacher professionalism, teacher competencies, and teacher social participation in the process of community education. He is a coeditor with Eija Kimonen of the recent volumes *Transforming Teachers' Work Globally* (Sense Publishers, 2013) and *Reforming Teaching and Teacher Education* (Sense Publishers, 2017).

Lakia M. Scott
is Assistant Professor in the Department of Curriculum and Instruction at Baylor University. She teaches courses in elementary reading methods and diversity issues to preservice teachers and has over 10 years of combined experience teaching at the elementary, secondary, undergraduate, and graduate levels. She is a recognized scholar in the field of urban education and has coauthored and coedited books, book chapters, and educational evaluation reports. Most recently, she coedited the book *Culturally Affirming Literacy Practices for Urban Elementary Students* (Rowman & Littlefield, 2016) with Barbara Purdum-Cassidy. Scott is currently conducting research on national reading and language intervention programs for urban students with a particular focus on the urban dialect.

PART 1

Foundations for Community-Based Learning: An International View

∴

CHAPTER 1

Ideals for Community Engagement from the East and West

Eija Kimonen and Raimo Nevalainen

Abstract

The aim of this chapter is to globally analyze the foundations of community-based learning with a focus on the philosophical views, educational aims, and associated value dimensions in the United States, India, and China. The previous research in comparative education leading to this analysis utilized a historico-hermeneutical approach. This chapter shows that the American philosophical tradition of community-based learning is founded on the ideas of progressive education and is based on the tradition of pragmatism and the naturalistic view of the human being held by functionalism. In India, the philosophical tradition of such learning is related to the ideas of neo-traditional education and relies on a tradition that insists on truth, as included in the philosophy of *satyagraha*. The Chinese philosophical tradition of community-based learning is rooted in the ideas of revolutionary education, which rely on the radical social theory of dialectical materialism. These traditions in the United States and India gave particular importance to sociomoral aims and socioethical and universal values, and in China to moral-political aims and values. The study concludes that development in the countries started to stress school-centered intellectual aims and science- and technology-related values, and community-based learning allowed experts to be trained for an advanced society in which mental work is performed in modern production.

Keywords

philosophy – aims – values – community-based learning – pedagogical progressivism – essentialism – neo-traditionalism – neocolonialism – postcolonialism – revolutionism – postrevolutionism

1   Introduction

This chapter addresses some philosophical views, educational aims, and associated values for community-based learning in the context of social change. The examination focuses on the philosophical background of community-based learning and the changing quality of value-oriented aims of this form of education, specifically in the United States, India, and China. Additionally, the study presents some of the philosophical connections between these three countries and the former Soviet Union. Finally, the main philosophical background views and the aims of education and their value dimensions are compared from the perspective of social change.

This chapter analyzes the processes of educational policy borrowing and lending. Previous studies have indicated that the ideas underlying an international school of thought can be adapted or assimilated to a national philosophical tradition as they cross national borders (see, e.g., Steiner-Khamsi, 2016). Phillips (2004) concluded that this kind of assimilation is possible if the new current of ideas is experienced as philosophically or ideologically fascinating and the national context is also receptive for political, economic, or social reasons. The specific national conditions in one country thus create the need to experimentally utilize the experiences offered by others (Phillips, 2004, pp. 56, 58). The philosophical background of community-based learning in the countries studied here can be considered to rely both on national philosophical traditions and on the reformist ideas represented by international schools of thought. This study also shows that over the course of time strong opposition to the influence of certain international pedagogical ideas has surfaced in these countries.

The present study is part of a broader research project, the purpose of which is to examine the interplay between education and society (see Kimonen, 2015). The overall aim is to document the existence of profound social and educational policies and patterns. A historico-hermeneutical approach is applied while making use of the comparative educational method. The interpretive process used in this epistemological tradition utilizes the canons of textual interpretation set down by Betti (1962) and the rules and phases of textual interpretation proposed by Danner (1979).

1.1   *Pedagogical Approaches to Community-Based Learning*
Pedagogical approaches to community-based learning are commonly applied in various parts of the world for the purposes of building strong school–community relationships and creating profound learning experiences. Prast and Viegut (2015) viewed "community-based learning" as an educational

strategy that educators can use to increase student engagement, make the curriculum more relevant and experiential, and strengthen school–community connections (p. 2). The present study regards community-based learning as a broad framework that includes a wide variety of instructional methods educators use while making connections between experiences obtained in the community and the different subjects in the curriculum. These methods offer various out-of-school and work-related approaches.

We can distinguish universal, reformist, and radical trends in the development of community-based learning. Different roles have been attached to the educator in these three versions of community-based learning. The universal life-centered form of such education, the reformist movement that highlights processes, and the awareness-raising radical version all differ with respect to the emphasis of the educator's role.

The American universal version of community-based learning can be seen as resting upon the educational theory and sociocultural practice of John Dewey (1859–1952). This approach regarded the educator's role as being based on the ideas of both the progressive education movement and the life-centered community school movement. The Deweyan progressive school was to be part of the larger whole of a functional social life in such a way that teaching was based on the social activities of the surrounding community. Through various kinds of work-related activities and projects, schoolwork could become part of the child's immediate experiences (Kimonen, 2015, p. 197). In the early 20th century, these progressive ideas in education also inspired many other educationists to conduct experiments in education. Among them was Elsie Ripley Clapp (1879–1965), Dewey's distinguished adherent. She worked as the director of school and community affairs in the village of Arthurdale in West Virginia and documented her experiences in the book *Community Schools in Action* (1939). Her successful work in Arthurdale reveals Clapp as a major contributor to the development of life-centered community-based learning. This approach extended the educator's role further toward the community, with the focus on improving living conditions.

The reconstructionist educational ideas that underlie reformist community-based learning proposed that education must alter the prevailing social and financial structures in order to make the world a better place to live in. The theory of reconstructionism requires the educator to promote processes that enhance social transformation. The following brief list details that these types of processes sought to:
- recognize societal problems by critically analyzing the prevailing conditions;
- promote human growth and development by trying to analyze and solve social problems; and

– be actively involved in initiating social changes and reforms (Gutek, 2009, pp. 371, 375, 384–387).

Process-centered, reformist community-based learning requires that the educator have a broad understanding of the concepts of education and familiarity with the educational system. The educator is in charge of accelerating, facilitating, and coordinating the school–community process by identifying the problems, needs, and resources in the community.

Radical community-based learning has been influenced by Ivan Illich's (1970) ideas related to learning networks and grassroots communities of local people. Furthermore, Paolo Freire's (1970) pedagogy of the oppressed and the closely related process of awareness-raising have also impacted the approach. The educator who uses the ideas of radical community-based learning in practice assumes the role of an animator who enhances awareness among community residents regarding local problems and assists them in developing the knowledge and skills that can help solve these problems (see Brookfield, 1990, pp. 177–178). This approach sees that schools and their educational methods are intimately related to the communities in which they are embedded (Gutek, 2011, pp. 459–460).

1.2 *Traditions of Educational Aims*

An understanding of educational aims, purposes, and values, and their philosophical and historical bases is one of the central elements in the teaching profession (see Shulman, 2004, p. 227). Aims and values, which give reform-minded educators direction in terms of what they hope to accomplish, are influenced by changing economic, political, and social forces as well as by educational philosophies and theories. This could be interpreted as meaning that the process of teaching in community settings is linked with the broader development of educational policy within a particular social context.

1.2.1 Functionalist and Pragmatistic Approaches

The nature of educational aims can be examined in relation to certain distinctive traditions of thought. This study interprets the aims of community-based learning from the perspective provided by the functionalist and pragmatistic traditions, as well as through a global approach, based on the framework presented by Rizvi (2007, pp. 65–67, 88).

Durkheim (1922/1956) approached the aims of education from the standpoint of the functionalist tradition, attaching a central role to a systematic socialization process through which young people are socialized to a particular society (p. 71). The instrumental aims of education reflect the processes that provide a foundation for society, as the educational system is a historical output constructed by society. A society attempts to reproduce commonly accepted beliefs, norms, and traditions through the school system. Even though school is intended to be developed in compliance with the requirements of the day, an educational system is always influenced by the society's earlier developmental stages (Durkheim, 1922/1956, pp. 72, 89, 94–95). According to Durkheim, one of the key pillars of any national educational reform is analyzing and understanding the historical characteristics of a society, and only then reflecting on how to develop the society by restructuring the educational system (Durkheim, 1922/1956, pp. 152–153). Following this approach, the aims of education express the social needs of a particular era and location. Society constructs the educational system by promoting and reproducing social ideals (Durkheim, 1938/1977, pp. 11, 14).

In turn, if the aims are viewed from the perspective of a pragmatistic tradition, it is understood that education refers to continuing growth, which is a goal in itself. The value of school education can be determined based on how well it can generate the willingness to continually grow and provide the means to realize these efforts (Dewey, 1916/1950b, p. 62). Dewey suggested that the aim of education is to provide individuals with opportunities to continue their own education. Education is thus both the end and the means. Nonetheless, Dewey admitted that although certain aims also apply to teachers' practical work, they must be linked to the educational activities in a natural manner so that they are flexible and arise from the circumstances. Moreover, they must be based on activities and needs that are typical of the individual being educated. Ultimately, the teacher bears the responsibility for translating the aim into a method that suits the learning situation (Dewey, 1916/1950b, pp. 117, 121–124, 126).

The functionalist and pragmatistic traditions, however, can also be analyzed critically. It has been argued that the pragmatistic tradition presents the aims at an overly general level, and that the functionalist interpretation of goals leaves little room for social critique or radical change (Rizvi, 2007, pp. 66–67). Conflict theoreticians have found that functionalism does not recognize the ideological supremacy of the dominating class, which is why society regards its values as natural.

1.2.2   A Global Approach

Education has become a global issue, and this imposes new pressures on educational systems and their functioning. Rizvi (2007) argued that traditional approaches to the aims of education are no longer sufficient, as they are not fully engaged with the new global, transnational economic, political, and cultural interdependencies. Traditional approaches cannot be used to develop broader educational outlooks that aim to prepare students to be critical and committed to meeting the new challenges, threats, and opportunities of globalization. The global economy requires a new kind of employee who is multiskilled, service-oriented, adaptable to changes in the nature and conditions of work, and able to function in global, multicultural environments. Such an employee must also possess the ability to utilize new information and communication technology (Rizvi, 2007, pp. 64–65, 88).

1.2.3   Aims and Their Value Dimensions

This study explores the aims and values of community-based learning in the United States, India, and China within the context of social change. The aims and value dimensions of this form of education are compared in light of the main currents of educational philosophies and ideologies as well as related pedagogical approaches that prevailed at different times. The aims of education and the value dimensions intertwined in them are analyzed in these three countries from the standpoint of society- and school-centered community-based learning. Such an analytical process makes use of a framework for classification compiled on the bases of the value theories for this study (see, e.g., Spranger, 1914/1966; Allport, Vernon, & Lindzey, 1970; Schwartz, 1992).

1.3   *Educational Reforms in a Changing Social Context*

Reforms involving an entire society usually lead to major changes in the nation's social, economic, and political structure. Social reforms can also bring about gradual or abrupt changes in educational principles and their implications. Fullan (1993) stated that school reform is a continuous process of change that can be characterized by dynamic, complex, contradistinctive, and unpredictable features (p. 20). This chapter observes that the term *reform* is closely related to the concept of *educational change.*

The change processes at different schools can vary significantly. The foundations of formal education services may remain relatively unchanged if the teaching methods, curriculum, and learning environments are considered. The school system may gradually adapt itself to the prevailing demands of society. Such a process of change can be regarded as an incremental adaptation (see, e.g., Hawkins, 2007, p. 143). Cuban (1992) argued that changes in schools have often been merely gradual attempts to develop the current system in order to eliminate insufficiencies manifested in operating principles and practices. The aim has been to make the operations of the organization more effective and to develop its special characteristics without actually addressing operational principles. Educational reforms that focus on changing the central structures and processes of school organizations have generally been unsuccessful.

A challenge for the future school is to develop change efforts that fundamentally affect school culture through such means as identifying new objectives, structures, and roles (Cuban, 1992, pp. 218–219).

A straightforward, rational, and systematic change process reflects an approach in which the reforms school administrators propose are meticulously and thoroughly followed. The change process can also be characterized as eclectic when the teacher implements only part of the reform, guided by individual practical ethics, but does not change the basics of practical theory. Alternatively, the school reform may cause profound and radical changes in teachers' thinking and action models if the changes represent a view in which the teachers accept the principles, educational philosophies, and beliefs behind the reform (Snyder, Bolin, & Zumwalt, 1992, p. 402). Waks (2007) observed that such fundamental educational change is "primarily about change in educational ideas, norms, organizational arrangements, and frameworks that constitute education as a social institution" (p. 294).

A reform based on particular educational thinking can be used in an effort to adapt education to new social requirements. For schools, such policy could mean that teachers should familiarize students with the reality of what a society needs. This study notes that during major social changes, the education system can be required to accelerate large national reforms. Under these circumstances, attempts can be made to have schools increase economic productivity through such measures as promoting the developmental trajectory of scientific and technological modernization. Characteristic of this type of change is a deterministic belief that school reform could be the key to effectively achieving social goals (for more details, see Kimonen, 2015, pp. 174–177).

Hopkins (2013) concluded that although we understand a great deal about school reform, we do not systematically realize its potential. This lack of understanding has not had any positive impact on students' learning and achievement. The ultimate mission would be to formulate relevant information for the purposes of creating theories of action within a comprehensive plan for school reform (Hopkins, 2013, p. 317).

This dilemma Hopkins presented could be approached by leaning on the ideas of Botkin, Elmandjra, and Malitza (1979), which state that an answer to the prevailing problem must be sought through a new type of learning that diverges from everything previously used (p. 10). This educational reform is characterized by something innovative and societal.

The following section treats the essence of community-based learning in three socially different countries from the standpoint of their philosophy of education. The point of the analysis is to obtain an understanding of the thoughts of John Dewey, Mahatma Gandhi, and Mao Zedong, along with their Soviet connections.

2 Early Ideals for Community-Based Learning

2.1 *Pragmatism in the American Philosophical Tradition*

The present analysis sees the educational philosophy of community-based learning in the United States as related to the principles of pragmatism, which is traditionally considered to be the earliest independent American philosophical trend. Philosopher Charles S. Peirce (1839–1914) initially presented the epistemological ideas of pragmatism regarding the relation between meaning and action in his 1878 article "How to Make Our Ideas Clear." Peirce (1868/1960c) concluded that thinking is based on signs or conceptions that are produced through experience (pp. 151–152). The meanings of the conceptions can be ascertained by studying their practical consequences, and human consciousness and beliefs thus develop in close association with action (Peirce, 1877/1960a, 1878/1960b). The beliefs in reality, however, are not, in Peirce's pragmatistic view, based on personal experience, but rather develop in connection with such objective action that is related to an infinitely continuing process. Therefore, action is the prerequisite, aim, and guarantor of knowledge.

Peirce also presented a three-category classification of experience that is applied here to interpreting human experience (Peirce, 1931/1965, pp. 148, 152–153, 161–162, 170–171). When analyzing Peirce's classification of experience formation from the perspective of community-based learning, it could be argued that the first category of human experience (firstness) consists of feelings related to an authentic experience and its properties, while participating in activities within different learning environments. The second category (secondness), in connection with the first category, consists mainly of conscious observation as the individual participates in activities in and outside the school. The third category (thirdness) combines action with thinking, with the experiences obtained in different learning environments thus gaining a conceptual meaning.

Peirce's contemporary William James (1842–1910) interpreted the principles of pragmatism specifically from the perspective of an individual's experiences, expectations, and feelings. James (1891) stated that the source and origin of reality is subjective, and therefore knowledge also expands on the basis of an individual's practical and esthetic interests (pp. 295–297, 344–345). The significance of an idea is determined by its value and usefulness in the experience of the individual. Practice reveals truth, which is manifested as something good (James, 1907/1963, pp. 31, 36, 98). Practical activity consists of valuable experiences to which new incentives are linked through action. Images in a stream of consciousness are also linked together in a similar fashion (James, 1899/1983, pp. 48, 55–60). Consequently, according to the pragmatism-based functionalist approach to psychology, humans are primarily practical, thinking, and active creatures. It has also been stated that such creatures are capable of adapting to social transformation in a democratic culture (Garrison & Neiman, 2005).

2.2   India's Ancient Philosophical Tradition

India was developing a philosophy of education based on an inherited philosophical tradition at the same time as the Indigenous inhabitants of the American continent were building their societies in what is now the United States. Indian philosophical tradition is generally understood to have arisen from the original Indus Valley culture, which flourished between 3000 B.C. and 1500 B.C., as well as from the Indo-European culture that later spread into India over a long period of time (for a closer examination of the peoples speaking Indo-European languages, see, e.g., Doniger, 2010, pp. 81, 90–92). The roots of the written sources in the philosophical tradition extend to the *Vedas* (from approximately 1500 to 1200 B.C.) and the *Upanishads* (from approximately 800 to 600 B.C.).

The *Mimamsa* school, one of the earliest trends in Indian philosophy, based its thinking directly on the *Vedas*, in particular, on the first two parts of each of them (Raju, 1992, p. 40). According to Raju (1992), the adherents of this school believed that the purpose of life is unending activity and doing; a person performs activities and enjoys their fruits in a continually alternating process in this life and the next (pp. 82–83). The *Mimamsa* doctrine concerning the validity of knowledge (*pramanyavada*) is based on the assumption that every piece of knowledge or a process relating to cognition can reveal only its own truth and the falseness of some other cognitive process. Pragmatic action can confirm the truth of such a cognitive process that has already revealed its apparent truth. It has also been claimed that the meaning of every word or sentence is associated primarily with action (Raju, 1992, pp. 75–77).

The *Mimamsa* texts (from approximately the 400s B.C.) and their later elucidations (from the early 700s A.D.) offer interpretations that can be compared to the aforementioned basic ideas of pragmatism when analyzing the connection between meaning and action, even though they differ with respect to their philosophical foundations. The earliest Indian philosophers have been characterized as focused primarily on the human ego—as the Indian philosophical tradition is ultimately based on religious practice—rather than on the material world, external to humans, and its explanations (for more on the earliest philosophical schools in India, see, e.g., Doniger, 2010, pp. 504–505).

2.3   *Confucianism in Traditional Chinese Culture*

Chinese educational philosophy is related to Confucianism. Although more than two millennia old, the Confucian school tradition has had a strong influence on the Chinese and on Chinese educational philosophers. The philosophical foundations of Confucius (551–479 B.C.) and his followers are set out in the *Four Books*, which for centuries contained the basic writings of Chinese teaching and education. One of the *Four Books*, the *Analects,* includes a collection of thoughts and dialogues attributed to Confucius. The *Analects* has been one of the most widely read and studied books in China for the last 2,000 years, and it continues to have a substantial influence on Chinese thinking today (Collinson, Plant, & Wilkinson, 2000, pp. 217–218, 221). Confucius believed that social reform could be implemented through education, and he aimed to create an ideal social order by cultivating ideal individuals. In his ideal society, which is the state of Great Harmony, both individual and social rights are perfectly developed and harmonized (Chen, 1990, p. 459).

The *Doctrine of the Mean*, another of the *Four Books,* allegedly written by Confucius's grandson, elaborates the way of harmony. The goal of the Mean, or the Middle Way, is to maintain balance and harmony by directing the mind to a state of constant equilibrium (Collinson et al., 2000, p. 218). The Confucian *harmony* is a philosophy that can be understood as defining the relation between the self and others and among the elements of the unity. It is a way of living and behaving that leads to modesty and flexibility. Furthermore, it is a moral process starting from the self and reaching the Mean. The way of harmony is not only theoretically important to Confucian philosophy but also practically significant for Chinese culture, and it gradually became central to the doctrinal foundation on which all philosophical schools operated (Yao, 2013, pp. 252–268).

As early as possibly 1000 B.C., Chinese philosophers formulated a dualistic belief system that examines the universal interplay of two opposing forces, yang and yin. Each of these cosmic principles represents the whole of certain characteristics. Yang is a masculine principle that makes itself known in everything that is active, radiant, hot, vigorous, strong, and aggressive. Yin is a feminine principle that is expressed as passive, moist, cold, docile, yielding, and gentle (see, e.g., Liu, 2006, p. 7). Yang and yin together gave birth to the heaven of the universe, which mainly has yang characteristics, and the earth, which is reigned by yin characteristics (see, e.g., Zhang, 2002, p. 88). According to this interpretation, these two opposing forces are in permanent conflict with each other, which leads to constant struggle and change.

The Chinese view of nature is based on the interaction of yang and yin as well as on the certain systematic connection between five elements: water, fire, wood, metal, and earth (Zhang, 2002, p. 96). Chinese tradition considers this interplay as creating the Great Harmony, a part of which also includes humans (see, e.g., Liu, 2006, pp. 37–38). This belief is especially evident in

Confucianism, in which ethics, ideology, and the sciences all belong to a vision of a common mental foundation. According to Western philosophy, humans are the actual goal of the creation of the world and the master of nature, but in Chinese philosophy humans are only a part of the world process. Where Western individuals aim to subjugate nature to be their servant, the traditional Chinese have tried to live in harmony with the universe.

3   The Foundational Thinkers

3.1   *John Dewey and the Progressive Educational Movement*
3.1.1   Life and Ideals

Pedagogical progressivism, when it emerged in the United States at the turn of the 20th century, became a new philosophical mainstream of education. This powerful branch of pragmatism was connected to the American philosophical tradition, particularly with regard to experimentalism and, consequently, also constituted a national philosophical foundation for community-based learning. The progressive education movement was essentially related to school experiments by its major figure, the philosopher John Dewey, as well as to his publications on reforming teaching methods (see Dewey, 1897/1940, 1902/1950a, 1916/1950b, 1899/1953; Dewey & Dewey, 1915).

Dewey's thinking in the philosophy of education developed within the context of the philosophical trend of pragmatism and the social and economic changes taking place in the increasingly industrialized United States. After studying philosophy at Johns Hopkins in Baltimore (from 1882 to 1884) with George S. Morris (1840–1889), Dewey moved to the University of Michigan in 1884 to teach philosophy (Dewey, 1939/1971, pp. 14, 16, 19). By this time, he had been strongly influenced by the ideas of his colleague George H. Mead (1863–1931) and German philosopher G. W. F. Hegel (1770–1831) (see Dewey, 1930/1960, pp. 3–11). After familiarizing himself with the psychological ideas of James in particular, however, Dewey gradually adopted the epistemological tradition of pragmatism (Dewey, 1930/1960, pp. 12–16), an American system of thought that he applied to his studies, as he also discovered an interest in educational sciences and the societal significance of educational procedures.

Dewey's thoughts in the philosophical field of education could be interpreted as a combination of Hegel's view on dialectical change in society and the naturalistic evolution theory represented by Charles Darwin (1809–1882), to the extent that Hegelian social development is seen to take place gradually. Here, the absolute idealism Hegel developed is replaced by the constant reconstruction of situations implemented by individuals and groups (for the influence of Hegelianism on Dewey's thought, see, e.g., Hickman, 1996). In this analysis, Dewey was convinced that the individual is a unique living being who, through education, cannot only reach his or her latent abilities but also contribute to society while actively adapting to the demands of the environment in a new industrialized and urbanized America (for more on neo-Darwinism, see Garrison & Neiman, 2005). In essence, Dewey's pragmatism could be described as a material counterpart to Hegel's absolute idealism. The following brief summary illustrates the significant role of Dewey's school experiments on the construction of his philosophical thinking in the field of education:

> John Dewey was one of the most influential educational philosophers and progressive educators in the United States. After becoming interested in education and the social significance of educational principles, Dewey accepted an offer from the University of Chicago in 1894 to head the combined departments of philosophy, psychology, and pedagogy (Dewey, 1939/1971, p. 27). Inspired by the atmosphere of pedagogical reform in Chicago (see Parker, 1894, pp. iii–vi), he founded a laboratory school for his own teaching activities that served as a workshop for his students' personal observations, experiments, and research. It eventually became an experimental school for progressive educational ideas (see, e.g., Mayhew & Edwards, 1966, pp. 42–52). During this period, Dewey wrote his first significant works on education, which were based on combining teaching with activity and school with life (see Dewey, 1897/1940, 1902/1950a, 1899/1953). While professor of philosophy and education at Columbia University in New York City from 1905 to 1930, Dewey published, in addition to innumerable philosophical essays, his main pedagogical work, *Democracy and Education* (1916). He visited the early Soviet Union and was invited to lecture in China and other countries (for more detailed information on Dewey's impressions abroad, see Dewey, 1929, pp. 27–28, 32, 160–161, 238–239; for biographical details, see Cremin, 1988, pp. 165–173; Gutek, 2011, pp. 351–358).

Dewey's progressive pedagogic ideas are based on the epistemological tradition of pragmatism and the naturalistic conceptions of the human expressed by functionalism. Dewey claimed that reality is evolutionary, as it is constructed through interaction between humans and the environment. Knowledge is not related to absolute truth but evolves from experience generated by active effort (see Dewey, 1933, 1916/1950b, 1938/1951). It is constantly being corrected by new theories more in accordance with experience. Theory is thus an instrument for organizing experience and evaluating activity. The reconstruction of experiences proceeds by means of problem solving based on reflective thinking. This involves recognizing and defining the problem and testing the hypotheses developed for solving it (Dewey, 1916/1950b, pp. 89–90, 188–189, 192). An essential characteristic of reflective thought is the suggestion of possible solutions, the intellectualization of experienced difficulties, the proposing of hypotheses, the mental elaboration of ideas, and the verification of hypotheses by action (Dewey, 1933, pp. 107–115). Thinking is consequently a means of mastering experience that furthermore promotes adaptation to the surrounding world (Dewey, 1916/1950b, pp. 192, 401). Such an interpretation, that of instrumentalist and experimentalist pragmatism, sees learning as occurring best in connection with doing and the associated immediate experiences. For this reason, school teaching should also be combined with practical work.

3.1.2 Aims and Values

The ideal progressive school offered the opportunity to articulate reality in such a way that connects teaching and education with situations of social reality, in which learning can be connected to the student's life and experiences. Dewey (1899/1953) stated that an individual's uniqueness and initiative are expressed as a desire to interact socially as well as to create and construct. These instincts also form the foundation for the need to investigate and invent as well as to express oneself artistically. The essential function of school is to provide students with the opportunity to develop their specific functional traits, but in close contact with the reality prevailing in society (Dewey, 1899/1953, pp. 42–45). In this manner, progressive pedagogy intended to combine motor, sociomoral, and intellectual education, an essential component of which is mental and moral consciousness (Dewey, 1899/1953, pp. 131–132).

The aim constituting the background for this type of work-related pedagogy was to teach children personal responsibility and to provide them with practice for the physical realities of life. To some degree, practical work would contribute to the school itself becoming a genuine manifestation of active community life (Dewey, 1899/1953, pp. 9–11). The ultimate socioethically value-oriented goal for child-centered progressive education was to teach students to understand the social meaning of work and, therefore, to help them to cope with the demands of a capitalist, early industrial state. The following describes more thoroughly the features of the aims of community-based learning in light of the progressive pedagogical approach Dewey presented:

> During the 1920s and 1930s, society-centered pattern of community-based learning in the United States can be seen as emphasizing motor

and sociomoral aims. These aims had been designed to educate a real American, a citizen who has internalized "the American dream" for an early industrial, classical liberal society. The goal of the progressive school, rooted in pragmatism, was to educate individuals in a way that took their interests and needs into account while socializing them into the requirements and values of the society at that time.

In light of an approach to progressive education based on experientialism, the observation can be made that community-based learning emphasized the learning experience with active involvement. Pedagogical progressivism was, by nature, a universal pedagogical approach that, in a down-to-earth manner, strove to narrow the gap between education and society. Dewey (1899/1953) suggested that by performing different work-related activities, students could familiarize themselves with the skills, current procedures, and principles needed in society (p. 11). The central idea in this process was that resolving problem situations through active efforts in cooperation with others would prepare students for life outside the school. As referred to by Dewey (1899/1953), this form of community-based learning aimed to:
- integrate the curricula of the various subjects and grade levels;
- teach manual skills so that students can utilize the experiences of their daily life in school, where they acquire experiences that they can, in turn, apply outside school;
- teach students the ideology of classical liberal democracy, that is, to act as members of the embryonic society of the school and in the real life of society; and
- unite school directly with life, work, and activities in the community (pp. 11, 27, 72–76, 80).

The strengthening of the progressive education movement in the United States also revived the camping education movement. Both organized and public school camping placed an emphasis on motor and sociomoral aims and their value dimensions. As a reform-pedagogical implication of progressivism, the school camping movement was based on closeness to nature. This approach had only infrequent connections to school curricula. In the early days, the purpose of organized and public school camping was to offer students outdoor life experiences under camp conditions. An attempt was made to develop camping skills in order to promote virtues related to nature as well as to promote the students' character, health, work, love for their fellow people, and citizenship. The following expresses the nature of the aims of organized camping:

Organized camping intended to offer city children experiences with open spaces and sunshine. Sharp (1941) wrote that camping represented "a way of life" that was to be based on the past struggles of the people and on the role of nature in life as a whole. It was to relate to the way people used to live and still do in the open, close to nature. The aim was the development of the whole child involving, in addition to character-building, the advancement of aspects associated with physical fitness, spiritual balance, and health (pp. 4–6). Organized camping is seen to have aimed to:
- teach the knowledge, skills, and attitudes that are necessary for a simple and healthy life;
- develop camping skills and leisure activities;
- teach respect for work, that is, to adopt a conscientious attitude toward work and to appreciate work as a joy in life;
- develop character by music, books, play, and worship;
- promote love for nature and fellow human beings;
- raise national spirit; and
- offer experiences in the great outdoors (Gibson, 1939, pp. 2, 5–6).

The relatively few public school camps that existed in the 1930s and 1940s intended to offer students real-life situations under such conditions. In addition to offering regular outdoor activities, these camps also provided opportunities to observe nature in order to learn about it and understand it better. These were just the preliminary intentions for integrating school camping with school education. Emphasizing the universal values associated with nature and life also represented an aspiration for socioethical values related to the individual's inner self, fellow people, and national spirit. The following illustrates the features of the aims of early public school camping:

By 1950, there had been no significant increase in public school camping, particularly regarding school camps functioning during regular school hours. The early public school camps were, to a great extent, based on progressive ideas of education. Vinal (1936) observed that school camps provided a learning environment "of realism where human and natural values" were to be more important than academic ones. "The materials of camp" were to be "the materials of life." Working "in the laboratory of life" led to the socialization of the individual (p. 424). This method of education aimed to:
- integrate camping with school teaching;
- teach camping skills and knowledge of nature;

- enhance initiative and independence;
- develop social skills;
- promote national spirit; and
- provide real-life situations under camp conditions (Sharp, 1935, pp. 26–29; Sharp & Osborne, 1940, pp. 236–237).

No doubt exists that Dewey's thought represented an understanding of education and its practices that differed completely from prevailing traditional and mentalistic education of the time. The traditional school was based on formalism, verbalism, and authoritarianism, whereas pedagogical progressivism can be seen as resting upon the ideology of an American early industrial society. The ultimate goal of education was to promote the students' sense of responsibility, thus leading them to membership in a free, democratic society. Dewey (1899/1953) held the view that the school itself was to be "a genuine form of active community life, instead of a place set apart in which to learn lessons" (p. 11). A progressive school of this type aimed at familiarizing the students with skills and courses of action needed in society. The integration of school education with activities and real life in the community was consequently a prerequisite for progressive, experiential education.

3.1.3   Summing Up

The conceptual features of experimentalism can be analyzed from the perspective of community-based learning by applying the three-level classification represented by Hlebowitsh (2007, p. 107). There the ideal relationship between education and society is outlined from the standpoint of the student, the educational program, and society. Experimentalism sees the ideal student as a problem-solver who is socially conscious, democratically inspired, and capable of thinking while actively participating in experiential activities based on collaboration in different learning environments. Similarly, the ideal educational program must contain problem-centered and goal-directed activities, this being consistent with authentic personal and communal experience. The student is oriented toward an ideal democratic society, the strength of which is based on public social discourse and mutual consensus, and the citizens of which work in early industrial production and, increasingly, in the service sector.

The progressive school reform continued its path to success in the United States during the period between the two world wars. Surprisingly, however, the popularity of progressive education diminished rapidly soon after the end of the Second World War. During the most intensive phase of the "great debate" about education in the mid-1950s, the progressive education movement suddenly crumbled; progressive education no longer had any supporters (Ravitch,

1983, p. 78). Cremin (1968) concluded that the collapse of the progressive trend in education was primarily the result of the professionalization of the movement, the rise of a new political trend, and far-reaching changes in American society. Being connected with these contextual factors, progressivism in education encountered the following process-related obstacles:

– The progressive education movement could not be revitalized, but rather it became professionalized and drifted into internal contradictions. The previously popular movement became vulnerable to criticism leveled at its policies and practices. Some of progressivism's ideas were adapted in schools with no commitment to its overall pedagogical thinking (see also Dewey, 1952, p. x), nor could the supporters of progressivism revamp their program.
– The conservative political and social thinking of the postwar period accelerated criticism of the school revision movement. Many educationists imagined that they would be able to preserve the progressive school as it had been without change, although nobody could predict with certainty what kind of institution would ultimately arise to replace it (see also Dewey, 1891/1970, p. 3).
– The progressive education movement did not keep up with the continuing transformation of society. The major technological innovations of modern society revealed the school's ultimate responsibility for organizing and transmitting knowledge. The ideas that the progressive school in education offered, which were devoted to traditional activity-oriented learning, seemed outdated (Cremin, 1968, pp. 348–351).

3.2 *Borrowing and Lending Educational Ideas*

The progressive trend in education developed within the sphere of influence of international reform-pedagogical ideals. The representatives of progressive pedagogics, such as Dewey, Clapp, William Heard Kilpatrick (1871–1965), Helen Parkhurst (1887–1973), and Carleton Wolsey Washburne (1889–1968), were influenced by the national scientific tradition. The following compilation describes in detail the progressive pedagogics of Kilpatrick and Parkhurst:

> Kilpatrick and Parkhurst made significant efforts to relate learning activities to the needs of the student. Kilpatrick emphasized the comprehensiveness of teaching. His project teaching method was based on concrete activities chosen by students. These were projects in which students were required to participate in the planning, investigation, and assessment related to many school subjects in order to solve the problem in question (Kilpatrick, 1922, pp. 16–17; Kilpatrick, 1940, pp. 102–103; Kilpatrick, 1949, pp. 17–24). Parkhurst developed an educational program

that gave importance to students' independent activities in special subject classrooms. Her Dalton Plan, as it was termed, was based on a range of curricula, for a day, a week, a month, or a semester, according to students' abilities. The curricula were implemented alone or in groups, the teacher's function being that of a counselor, supervisor, and facilitator (Parkhurst, 1930, pp. 28–46).

Undoubtedly these progressive educationists were also influenced by European philosophers and pedagogues such as Herbert Spencer (1820–1903). Spencer's work *Education* (1861), which talked about a school that prepares children for life (p. 8), attracted many enthusiastic readers in the United States. This book emphasized educational ideas pertaining to freedom, independence, creativity, and activity propounded by Jean Jacques Rousseau (1712–1778), Johann Heinrich Pestalozzi (1746–1827), and Friedrich Fröbel (1782–1852).

Spencer (1861) proposed that school should, above all, teach the knowledge and skills required to cope with life. School should also provide guidelines for educating future generations, help in developing social conditions, and introduce means for acquiring educative interests (pp. 8–10, 37). Teaching, which follows the child's developmental level, proceeds from the particular to the general and is based on immediate experiences that the child obtains while solving problems independently in his or her own fields of interest (pp. 73–80).

Romantic naturalism, best represented in Rousseau's writings, grew into a well-known modern philosophical approach to education in the early 20th century. Examining the conceptual features of romantic naturalism using Hlebowitsh's (2007) classification, from the perspective of American community-based learning, allows for the interpretation that the ideal student has an innate proclivity for self-education. This proclivity can be subjected to minimal adult guidance only by giving students an opportunity to engage in free activities within the context of open learning environments. The ideal educational program must also be content neutral, with an emphasis on free activity. The student is oriented toward a fragmented, ideal society where various kinds of individual efforts occur in the communities of an early industrial country.

Ideas created by American educational reformers also influenced European and Asian educators. Just as American progressives utilized European ideas when elaborating educational practices, American ideas soon found inspired followers in Europe and Asia. For example, Georg Kerschensteiner (1854–1932) in Germany, Pavel Blonsky (1884–1941) in the former Soviet Union, and Tao Xing-zhi (1891–1946) in China developed their own activity-based work school in the spirit of reform pedagogy (see, e.g., Danilchenko, 1993, pp. 118, 121–122; Darling & Nordenbo, 2005, p. 292; Xu, 1992, pp. 54, 59–60). The application of the philosophical ideas and reform-pedagogical methods associated with progressive education in the early Soviet Union is outlined in greater detail in the following summary:

> Ballantine and Hammack (2009) argued that the writings of progressive educators "have been interpreted, misinterpreted, and modified, but they have influenced all movements in education since the turn of the twentieth century" (p. 49). Similarly, copies of the pedagogical works of such Western reform educators as Dewey and Kerschensteiner were widely distributed in the Soviet Union after the Russian Revolution (Mchitarjan, 2000). Russian school reformers visited Europe and the United States in the early 1900s (see, e.g., Brickman, 1960; Skatkin & Tsov'janov, 1994, p. 50). Dewey himself visited the Soviet Union in 1928, discussed progressive ideas in education with Soviet educators, and learned about the aims and teaching methods used in the Soviet school system (see Dewey, 1929).

The decade following the Russian Revolution saw a range of school experiments, and in this era of reform pedagogics, the unification of the country's dispersed school system into a labor school (*trudovaya shkola*) was planned with the support of the New Economic Policy. Between 1919 and 1920 the People's Commissariat for Education (Narkompros), which corresponded to the Ministry of Education, undertook several labor school experiments that followed reform-pedagogical principles in terms of the content and timing of studies and the freedom and self-government of children in the Marxist spirit (see, e.g., Holmes, 1991, pp. 9, 32–35). By 1925, the school experiments had been established as a seven-year factory school, from which it was possible to continue studies in apprenticeship training at factories and in technical schools (*teknikum*) (Löfstedt, 1980, p. 54).

The writings of Western reform educators impacted the educational ideas of the school reformists of the People's Commissariat, in addition to Marxist polytechnical education and Leo Tolstoy's (1828–1910) Rousseauean child-centered pedagogy. One of the school reformers, Blonsky, also developed his own unified labor school, which followed Western reform-pedagogical ideas. These included the active-learning methods of instruction, experiential learning processes based on problem solving, practical and everyday activities for learning, and students' self-reliant attitude during educational processes (Blonskij, 1919/1973, pp. 70–71, 78–79, 220–221). Kilpatrick's project method and Parkhurst's Dalton Plan were applied to teaching as the "complex method." The teacher's role became that of an instructor, organizer, or older comrade (see, e.g., Mchitarjan, 2000).

A radically different process of change in educational philosophy, compared to the course of events in the early Soviet Union treated above, was carried out on the Indian subcontinent. In addition to the ancient philosophical tradition, Indian school reformers were deeply influenced by the various peoples who had conquered the country over the centuries. After the long period of Islamic rule (1206–1858), European colonial policy (starting in the 16th century) eventually brought the country under the subjugation of Great Britain (1858–1947). The expressed goal of the British administration was to instill Western culture in the Indians, including their educational philosophers. Among those who utilized various syntheses of Western and Indian ideas was philosopher Rabindranath Tagore (1861–1941). Tagore based his thoughts concerning the freedom of the mind and will, that is to say, the world of human intelligence and morals, on Indian tradition, but he also wanted to derive benefit from Western culture and some of its educational practices (Tagore, 1921, pp. 82–85; Tagore, 1961, pp. 222–223). At *Brahmacharya Ashrama*, his boarding school in *Shantiniketan*, Tagore combined music, excursions, nature study, and sports in his teaching in the British sense; the esthetic and religious piety of festivals; and activity in the surrounding community (see Pearson, 1917, pp. 16–53). Western progressive educational ideas also made their way to India. Documentary evidence demonstrates that many schools were already following Parkhurst's Dalton Plan in the early 1920s (Olsson, 1926, p. 46).

The influences of international ideas in China were comparable to that of India, especially during the first decades of the 20th century. In addition to the Confucian philosophy, Chinese school reformers were influenced by ideas from many European countries, Japan, and the United States. Innovative ideas were introduced by Chinese who had studied abroad and by foreigners, mostly American missionaries. Additional influences also came through translated literature. Berry (1960) mentioned that Chinese intellectuals became acquainted with the ideas of Tolstoy, Darwin, Spencer, and Rousseau. Knight (2015) reported that a significant number of works by Karl Marx (1818–1883), Friedrich Engels (1820–1895), Vladimir I. Lenin (1870–1924), and other Marxists became available in China in the 1920s and early 1930s.

Dewey, invited by Chinese students, visited China from 1919 to 1921 (see Keenan, 1977). In addition to progressive ideas on education, Dewey gave lectures in universities on Western political philosophy and radical empirical philosophy. Several of his works were translated into Chinese, among them *How We Think*, *Schools of To-Morrow*, and *Democracy and Education* (see Berry, 1960). Hundreds of experimental schools following Dewey's and Parkhurst's progressive educational ideas were founded in the country (Olsson, 1926, p. 46).

Soon after these processes, China experienced the beginning of the Chinese Civil War (1927–1950), along with new international ideals. Many different schools competed with each other until several useful alternatives were seen in the political practice of the Russian Bolsheviks. After the unsettled era of the Guomindang (1927–1948)—after the power struggle between the Nationalist Party of China, the Communist Party of China (C.P.C.), and Japanese intruders— the Communist Party, led by Mao Zedong (1893–1976), rose to power. In 1949, the People's Republic of China was founded (see, e.g., Moise, 1986).

Chinese communists took the central fields of economy under their control. Agriculture and private industry were nationalized. The planning and reconstruction of the economy were based on the Soviet system of a planned economy aimed at heavy industry. Assisted by Soviet experts, the Chinese government drew up a plan for a specialized and technically oriented school system in 1951 (see State Council, 1998b, pp. 105–106). Price (2005) reported that higher education institutions had some 600 Soviet experts between 1950 and 1958 (p. 102).

3.3   Mahatma Gandhi on National Education
3.3.1   Life and Ideals

The first decades of the 1900s witnessed a struggle for independence in India that was also connected with the national reform-pedagogical trend. This struggle arose in response to the further consolidation of British power and the consequent spread of Western culture. Compared to the revolutionary processes in China previously discussed, India chose a completely different path for its social development after the Hindu lawyer Mohandas Gandhi (1869–1948) became the leading figure in the struggle for independence.

Gandhi's social reformist ideas must be seen within the context of Indian cultural historical tradition, along with his sociopolitical activity, first in South Africa and then in India under British rule. During Gandhi's efforts in South Africa to achieve social and political improvements for the Indian minority, he developed a nonviolent form of civil resistance, literally the idea of "insistence on truth" (*satyagraha*). This ideal was based on Hindu phrases that he had long remembered, on the message of the Christian Sermon on the Mount, and on the ideas of the Russian writer Tolstoy (Gandhi, 1927/1959, pp. 25, 48–49, 99, 115, 194–195; Gandhi, 1928/1961, pp. 109–110). *Satyagraha* was highly characteristic of the struggle for independence in India and involved aiming for self-sufficiency through truth (*satya*) and nonviolence (*ahimsa*). This was the basis for a national program of self-sufficiency, a program that eventually also included a national basic school system.

The development of a national school system was crucial to the idea of obtaining independence from the British raj, which was not only invincible but also benevolent in offering its Indian elite a Western education considered superior to anything India could offer. Urban and Wagoner (2009) reported that a comparable context had prevailed in the United States between the 1890s and the 1930s, when government programs attempted to assimilate Native Americans by moving their children from reservations to boarding schools. There, the children were openly taught to despise their traditional Native American cultures, including the languages, customs, and values, since these were all seen as inferior to European culture (Urban & Wagoner, 2009, p. 244).

From the viewpoint of conflict theory, such a government process forced the Native Americans to abandon the ideals and beliefs of their own identities in order for the conquerors to maintain their domineering relation toward the earlier inhabitants. The different views were deeply contradictory, as they were linked to different life-sustaining value objectives and associated conceptions of being human. In this context, we can easily understand that national educational thought in India naturally formed a vital cornerstone for the independence struggle, as its philosophical background of education relied on the national legacy of Indian traditional society. The following summary, based on Tähtinen (1970, pp. 13–20), provides a background for Gandhi's thoughts on nonviolence and self-sufficiency:

> Gandhi, the father of Indian independence, is universally known and renowned as a proponent of nonviolence. Gandhi's convictions have to be seen within the context of both Indian cultural tradition and his own sociopolitical activity in South Africa and India. After qualifying as a lawyer in England and failing in his career in India, Gandhi traveled to South Africa in 1893 to practice law. Experiencing firsthand the oppression to which nonwhites were subjected in South Africa, he gave up his law office and embarked on a struggle to improve the social and political rights of the local Indian minority (see Gandhi, 1927/1959, 1928/1961). Realizing that efforts to work in the midst of the Indian population were futile, Gandhi developed a nonviolent form of civil resistance, literally the idea of "firmness of truth" or "adherence to the truth" (*satyagraha*), from the old Hindu phrases, the discourse of Jesus of Nazareth, and Tolstoy's writings (Gandhi, 1927/1959, pp. 25, 48–49, 99, 115, 194–195; Gandhi, 1928/1961, pp. 109–110; for the letters, see, e.g., Gandhi, 1909/1991; Tolstoy, 1969). As a base for his social and political activity, and encouraged by the ideas of John Ruskin (1819–1900) on work, Gandhi first established the Phoenix Settlement and, later, the Tolstoy Farm, with between 50 to 70 members.

In this work center (*ashrama*) devoted to a common goal and household, Gandhi edited a newspaper, worked on handicrafts, cultivated land, and ran a school. He simplified living, eating, and clothing (see Gandhi, 1927/1959, pp. 220–222; Gandhi, 1928/1961, pp. 233–258; for Gandhi's biography in Africa, see also Fischer, 1986, pp. 53–154).

Gandhi returned to India as a well-known social reformer in 1915. Within three years he had become a religious, social, and political reformer, a national leader to whom people turned for help with a wide variety of problems. After determining that India's most difficult problem was its status as a colony, Gandhi began his public struggle for independence in 1916 using the philosophy of truth in action and a philosophy of nonviolence as his weapons (see Tähtinen, 1964, pp. 11–16; Tähtinen, 1979, pp. 83–96; Tähtinen, 1982, pp. 47–50). He established *Satyagraha Ashram* for his activities, in which the existence of a traditional religious settlement was combined with political activity. In 1920, nationwide nonviolent opposition to cooperation with the British authorities began. Boycotting everything foreign as a means of achieving self-sufficiency was an essential element of Gandhi's campaign. The boycott covered imported products, schools, and the legal system as well as the law and the power that it granted. People held meetings and strikes in different parts of the country in addition to fasting and praying. Gandhi reformed traditional village industry and offered everyone a simple spinning wheel so that the villages could attain self-sufficiency (see Gandhi, 1948c, pp. 73–74).

Gandhi believed that putting himself at the disposal of politics and business was his moral responsibility. He believed that political and economic institutions could include violence and exploitation. In his view, centralized heavy industry is immoral because, in becoming mechanized, it furthers the interests of only a few people and necessarily results in the exploitation of the working class (Gandhi, 1958, pp. 38, 42, 45). Industrialism results in unnecessary needs, unemployment, social alienation, and moral degeneration (Datta, 1953, pp. 113–114). Social freedom is based on decentralizing political and economic power. Social justice prevails in a decentralized economy: the individual can influence economic decision-making by monitoring the system and refusing to cooperate (see Gandhi, 1947, p. 7; Gandhi, 1948b, p. 35). This natural law, truth, which is above laws and social systems, is to be achieved without violence. A requirement for truthfulness is harmony between thought and deed, thus doing away with all exploitation (see Gandhi, 1948a, p. 14; Gandhi, 1948b, pp. 33, 35). Democratic decision-making is possible only in an economically self-sufficient society, the ideal being a self-sufficient village community, the economic basis of which is handicraft production (see Gandhi, 1958, pp. 36, 45; for more details on Gandhi's economic strategy discussed above, see Tähtinen, 1970, pp. 94–95; Tähtinen, 1986, p. 27). Such a program for self-sufficiency was also firmly linked to the Indian basic school.

The Gandhian reform-pedagogical ideal was related to the tradition of Indian philosophy, and thus formed the national philosophical foundation for Indian approaches to community-based learning. The present study sees Gandhi's educational thinking as being founded on a tradition in the theory of truth, that is to say, the philosophy of truth in action, *satyagraha*. Gandhi (1947) noted that social freedom in the form of self-government is achieved by acquiring the ability to resist authority when it uses its position wrongly (p. 7). This ability to resist is internal strength that is achieved by character-building, which includes developing the courage, resilience, virtue, and unselfishness that are needed in goal-directed activity (Gandhi, 1948d, p. 254). Consequently, the central function of education is to change the heart. It is essential to learn to feel what the soul is and what hidden powers it contains. Equally essential is internalizing the fact that, in the struggle of life, hate may be conquered by love, lies by truth, and violence by one's own suffering (Gandhi, 1958, p. 140). Such a process of spiritual awakening should also be part of the development of the body and mind.

A balanced education requires the holistic integration of physical, moral, and intellectual activity, which is best achieved through the teaching of handicrafts. For this reason, a central responsibility of the school is to offer students the opportunity to develop attributes of personal character through handicraft production or other lines of work available in the area. The students familiarize themselves with the vocational activities required in the community, such as spinning, carpentry, and agriculture. They undergo in-depth studies concerning the fundamentals of these crafts and the different phases in the relevant working processes (Gandhi, 1948d, pp. 257–259; Gandhi, 1962b, p. 59). They develop themselves holistically in vocational work, the results of which they use to finance their education; the knowledge they derive from education they use outside the school (Gandhi, 1937/1950, 1951/1962a, 1953/1963). Gandhi (1948d) believed that vocationally productive education provides practice in being responsible for doing one's own share and ushers in the silent revolution. This will do away with the contradictions between social classes, thus laying the foundation for a just social order in a traditional Indian society (pp. 259–260).

3.3.2   Aims and Values

India carried out educational efforts in the 1940s and 1950s that rested upon traditional cultural values. The society-centered pattern of community-based learning can be seen as emphasizing the physical and sociomoral aims that endeavored to educate spiritually and morally fortified citizens for a preindustrial agrarian society. In this manner, physical, sociomoral, and intellectual education was intentionally integrated. The aim of neo-traditional education, based on the Gandhian theory of truth, was to apply universal life values in developing attributes of personal character, that is, character-building, in order to train self-sufficient, independent citizens for a traditional society. The ultimate goal associated with socioethical values was national reconstruction through Gandhian basic schools. The following outlines the essential nature of the aims of community-based learning in light of the pedagogical trend inspired by Gandhi's ideas:

> The purpose of the ideal Indian school was to be a self-sufficient school that can essentially be seen as a spinning and weaving institution with a cotton field attached to it. Gandhi (1948d) described that the instruction that it provides should be wholly linked to village handicraft production or other lines of work, since a person can develop best within a village community in which a balance exists between individual and social development (pp. 258–259). A school of this type, based on Indian tradition, sought to familiarize students with the vocational activities required in the community, such as spinning, carpentry, and agriculture. Here, in-depth learning of different ways of working and the phases involved could lead to a higher level of development of the body, mind, and soul (Gandhi, 1951/1962a, p. 11; Gandhi, 1962b, p. 59). Teaching was to progress scientifically, emphasizing the interpretation of the bases of the work processes (Gandhi, 1948d, p. 257). This form of community-based learning aimed to:
> - correlate the curricula of the school's various subjects with the world of work;
> - provide training in a craft or other local work;
> - make learning without books possible so as to decrease educational expenses;
> - promote the beneficial use of what is learned at school in practice to everyday life;
> - teach respect for manual work in an effort to erase the inequality between manual and intellectual work as well as between workers;
> - increase self-sufficiency and thus do away with unemployment;
> - promote social development, that is, raise the morals of the nation and work to nonviolently achieve a democratic social order; and
> - combine teaching with the village community, its traditional means of livelihood, and manual occupations (Gandhi, 1948d, pp. 259–260;

Gandhi, 1937/1950, pp. 30–31; Gandhi, 1951/1962a, pp. 11–12, 65, 89; Gandhi, 1962b, p. 193; Gandhi, 1953/1963, pp. 36, 44–45).

Within the context of an approach to neo-traditional education, rooted in *satyagrahaism*, community-based learning could be said to draw attention to life-centeredness in pedagogy. This constituted the neo-traditional approach of craft-related education, which was a means of searching for ways to link school education as closely as possible to practice in real-life learning environments. The purpose of craft-related education was to integrate instruction into students' lives and communities, their local productive work, and crafts. The aim was to help them utilize what they learned at school in practice to their daily life in order to promote self-sufficiency and independence in a preindustrial agrarian community. The following clarifies the characteristics of the aims of craft-related education:

> The Zakir Husain report (1938) was based on the final resolutions made at the highly esteemed Wardha National Education Conference in 1937 and thus conformed with Gandhi's thoughts on education. The report proposed that teaching should be closely connected with local productive work, since this was seen to be the best means of effecting integrated, diversified education. Some local craft, such as spinning and weaving, carpentry, agriculture, fruit and vegetable gardening, or other work belonging to the life of the community, was to be chosen as the basis for craft-related education in the school (Zakir Husain Committee, 1938, pp. 12–14, 19). Based on the 1938 report, craft-related education aimed to:
> - create a uniform curriculum for the entire school through handicraft;
> - provide all students with vocational training in handicraft in order to enhance national self-sufficiency;
> - teach respect for manual work in order to break down the prejudice between manual and intellectual workers;
> - teach democratic civil action, that is, to carry out responsibilities and use civil rights in a cooperative community;
> - promote social development without violence, that is, work to achieve solidarity between people and democracy in the various areas of culture; and
> - integrate into the child's life teaching about one's own community and its local productive work and crafts (pp. 12–17, 19).

Gandhian economics can be seen as related to spiritual and socioeconomic principles. Economic values were prioritized in education by stressing schools' self-maintaining activities and instruction without books, even though the teachers tried to correlate all of the various subject curricula around work. However, guided by social and traditional values, the most essential thing was the attempt to break down the prejudice between manual and intellectual workers in order to help implement civil rights and duties in a cooperative community. Character-building was a means for achieving the various virtues needed in goal-directed activities, such as courage, resilience, and unselfishness, that arise from universal values. The ultimate end of education related to socioethical values was to contribute to societal development without violence in order to attain a democratic social order that accentuated solidarity between the people. The following illustrates the role of the aims of craft-related education in the pursuit of a righteous society:

> The dawn of Indian social modernization saw that community-based learning remained society-centered until the mid-1960s in accordance with Gandhi's views, with continuing emphasis on physical and sociomoral aims. The handbook for teachers at basic schools (1958) suggested that productive, creative, and socially useful work was to be the core of teaching, since the schools were to offer education for, as well as through, life. This would make the achievement of a nonexploitative and nonviolent society possible (Ministry of Education and Scientific Research, 1958, p. 6). The syllabus for postbasic education (1961) held that the purpose of education was to further the construction of a new and just social order that presupposed the integration of education into the crafts pertaining to the village community's handicraft production and agriculture (Education Department, 1961, pp. 42, 44). As a part of this process, craft-related education aimed to:
> – integrate teaching in the school's various subjects through the crafts;
> – develop the ability to coordinate sensory activities and apply such experience in real situations;
> – lead to investigation of the processes, tools, and arrangements relevant to the craft;
> – enable higher education by continuing to practice the craft in question in a self-reliant manner;
> – help attain a livelihood through the craft after schooling;
> – provide the opportunity to become a good guide in the development of the crafts practiced by the community; and
> – advance the development of the school and the community, that is, to make the school a center for comprehensive social service and reconstruction for the community, as well as to make the latter as

self-sufficient and cooperatively functioning as possible, as an example for the surrounding region (Education Department, 1961, pp. 43–46; Ministry of Education, 1956, p. 7).

3.3.3 Summing Up

The conceptual features of Gandhian neo-traditionalism can be examined from the perspective of community-based learning by applying Hlebowitsh's (2007) classification. Neo-traditionalism interprets the ideal student as being self-reliant, community-minded, spiritually and morally fortified, and insisting on truth, while also being familiar with the vocationally productive activities needed in the community and participating in social service. The ideal educational program is built around craft-related productive work linked to the child's entire social and physical environment. The student is oriented toward an ideal democratic society, the citizens of which live in self-sufficient village communities and work in traditional crafts and the agricultural production offered by them.

Such a philosophical trend in education undoubtedly represented an exceptionally radical idea about education and its practices with regard to a human society based on tradition. Since productive crafts were assigned to the lowest groups in the caste system of colonial India, the argument has been presented that Gandhi's reform reversed the hierarchy, thus causing a conflict between the social classes (Kumar, 2005, p. 179). However, Gandhi's philosophy also justifies the opposite interpretation. Neo-traditional, vocationally productive education that is aimed at being responsible for doing one's own share could bring about a silent revolution that could eradicate the contradictions between social classes and provide a setting for a just social order in a traditional Indian society. Therefore, school education had to be integrated with work and life in the surrounding community.

3.4 *Mao Zedong and the Revolutionary Movement*

3.4.1 Life and Ideals

National philosophical thinking on education can be strongly influenced by international currents of thoughts concerning society as well as by educational trends connected to them. These new ideas can lead to radical national reforms that include periods of major pedagogical shifts, meaning that development proceeds in a contradictory manner. Such radical education reform was associated with the communist revolution in China, which began in 1946 and was the culmination of the Communist Party's drive for power since its founding in 1921.

The present study shows that the Chinese socialist revolution stressed the ideas of labor-related education, also referred to as revolutionary labor education, when analyzed in the context of community-based learning. Such an educational consciousness was in accord with the view of dialectical materialism. The following section briefly examines the basis for this view and its relationship to education and offers a background for Mao's thinking in the field of the philosophy of education.

The first ideas about dialectical materialism were formulated in central Europe a few decades before the basic ideas of pragmatism were developed at Harvard University in the United States. Dialectical materialism is a socialist theory that concentrates on political economy and the development of society. It offers a revolutionary alternative to capitalist ideology, which is based on a free-market economy. Marx and Engels, both German philosophers, developed a theory in which dialectics expresses the regularities of economic development and, consequently, the regularities of all other historical development. The theory Marx and Engels expounded combines Hegel's conception of dialectical change in society with Ludwig Feuerbach's (1804–1872) view of materialism so that a society's historical development is seen within the context of its materialistic conditions (Gutek, 1997, p. 232). In terms of its starting point, Marxism represents a material counterpart to Hegel's absolute idealism. From the perspective of materialism, reality is objective, notwithstanding the observer's experience.

Critical to the dialectical and historical materialism of Marx and Engels is the assumption that historical conflict in society reflects the struggles between social classes. Here, the classes and their mutual contradictions are fundamentally determined by the degree of development in economic conditions as well as by the prevailing mode of production and the respective method of exchange (Engels, 1852/1926, p. 22). This radical theory of social development was also associated with the idea of polytechnical education, which Marx and Engels originally wrote about in the 1840s. In Marx's writings, the term *polytechnical education* can be understood as referring to instruction in the general principles of productive processes as well as in the methods and instruments of work utilized in socially useful labor (Marx, 1866/1968, p. 195). The goal of polytechnically combining work and education is to provide individuals with all-around skills and knowledge for a new socialist society in which the nature of work and its duties change as a consequence of technical development (Marx, 1867/1974, pp. 436, 438–439). According to Marx (1927/1978), all human activities are determined by the general laws of economy. This view stresses the essential importance of training young people to understand and evaluate phenomena in accordance with the social laws in prevailing economic relations (Marx, 1927/1978, p. 250). It is thus logical that polytechnical work education, which was later applied in China, called for integrating theory and practice, school and life, teaching and production.

In 1917, about the same time that Gandhi was launching the struggle for Indian independence, the Bolsheviks, the representatives of the left-wing majority group of the Russian Social Democratic Workers' Party, successfully carried out a revolution in Russia. A direct consequence of adopting a Marxist materialistic view of history in the Union of Soviet Socialist Republics, established in 1922, was including productive work in the Soviet school curriculum. The following detailed summary demonstrates how the ideas of Engels and Marx were applied to educational reforms in the early Soviet Union:

> Georgi Valentinovich Plekhanov (1856–1918) was the forerunner of Russian dialectical materialism. Inspired by the works of Engels and Marx, Plekhanov formulated his own Marxist principles. Many Sovietologists have interpreted that views on dialectical materialism, militant nationalism, socially useful labor, and polytechnical education were prevalent in Soviet educational philosophy after the Russian Revolution (see, e.g., Zajda, 1980, p. 2).
>
> Lenin, the Bolshevist leader who rose to power after the October Revolution, emphasized Marx's belief in the tight bond between the three areas of education: mental, physical, and polytechnical. Lenin (1929/2013) argued that the essential function of a school is to provide young people with profound knowledge of scientific disciplines and, in this process, to educate them in the spirit of communist ideology and morals (pp. 533–534). Polytechnical education in this type of labor school consists of practical teaching about the principles of current industry and agriculture (Lenin, 1920/2012, p. 289).
>
> Lenin's spouse, Nadezhda K. Krupskaya (1869–1939), the organizer of the People's Education Program in the early Soviet Union, developed further the pedagogical ideas of the polytechnical labor school. Krupskaya (1927/1957b) pointed out that the most important aim of education is to guide students to work for the benefit of society (p. 121). The central element of schoolwork is polytechnical education in socially meaningful activities that combine school and labor. Krupskaya (1930/1957a) stated that all school subjects should be integrated with work-related activities that allow students to experience the various phases of industrial and agricultural production and to perceive the entire process. In this manner, the polytechnical school transmits appropriate knowledge to

students and teaches them to apply it in the different fields of production (Krupskaya, 1930/1957a, pp. 189–191). An essential element of polytechnical education is social education, which includes activities to develop one's own social instincts, awareness, and customs (Krupskaja, 1922/1965, p. 145). The aim of Soviet upbringing is to educate young people with the help of collectives that operate in the spirit of communist morals. The ultimate idea is to train citizens with a wide range of skills and abilities, who are members of the collective, not individualists who seek their own advantages, as in Western schools (Krupskaya, 1927/1957b, pp. 119–120). The purpose of this type of labor school was collective-based synthesis of school and life, and of learning and work.

The successful Bolshevik Revolution and its implications strengthened Marxist-Leninist thinking in China. Soviet advisers were invited to the country to help organize a revolutionary program and activities and to provide guidance in founding the c.p.c. in Shanghai in 1921. Chinese socialist literature was as yet largely reformist instead of revolutionary, and the works of Marx and Engels had not been completely translated into Chinese. The ideas of socialist thinkers were difficult to understand in China because its cultural history differed so greatly from that of the West. To alleviate the situation, Marxist study groups were founded; one participate was Mao, future Communist Party leader (see, e.g., Grasso, Corrin, & Kort, 2004, pp. 87–89). The following is a brief account of the main development steps in Mao's system of political beliefs:

> Mao's ideas concerning the function of an ideal society developed within the context of the Chinese philosophical tradition and a Marxist materialistic view of history as well as the social crisis that took place in China during the early decades of the 20th century. After studying at the First Provincial Normal School in Changsha from 1913 to 1918, Mao moved to Beijing, where he worked as a library assistant at the Peking University Library. At this point, he had been strongly influenced by the ideas of Li Dazhao and Zhen Duxiu, the future founders of the c.p.c. After also familiarizing himself with the social views of Hegel, Marx, and Lenin, Mao started to develop his own philosophy based on dialectical materialism. Between 1940 and 1945, the Chinese form of Marxism-Leninism began to crystallize, with Mao as its originator. At the first plenary session of the seventh Central Committee of the c.p.c. in 1945, Mao's thinking was canonized as the leading ideology of the Communist Party (see, e.g., Collinson et al., 2000, pp. 307–308, 310; Pantsov with Levine, 2012, pp. 340–341, 583). His speeches and writings have been published in many

collections; probably the most well-known volume is the *Quotations from Chairman Mao Tse-tung* (1964), which is often called The Little Red Book. In October 1949, Mao proclaimed the foundation of the People's Republic of China, which he led until the end of his life (for Mao's biography, see, e.g., Pantsov with Levine, 2012).

The influence of traditional Chinese philosophy on Mao's ideas is perhaps best expressed by the similarities that exist between the views of Confucianism and dialectical materialism regarding the concept of conflict and its importance in the development of society. Mao (1937/1966a) argued that social development requires a continuing revolution because conflict is inherent in society, both between different classes and between forces and production relationships. The development of these conflicts propels society forward and provides the driving force for replacing an old society with a new one. Conflicts are the prerequisite for all existence and development (Mao, 1937/1966a, pp. 26–27). The function of a school in this battle is to serve the proletarian politics and the socialist model of production.

In addition to the Chinese philosophical tradition, Mao's philosophical thinking on education is based on Marx's dialectical and historical view of materialism and Lenin's practical educational thinking. Marxism is for Mao (1956/1965) a means of solving problems: he studied Marx's and Lenin's theories in order to adapt them to China's conditions and circumstances. He put his ideas firmly into practice and applied the Marxist-Leninist theory to China's current conditions (Mao, 1956/1965, pp. 208–210). In the battle for social equality, Mao (1961/1975) believed in the power of the masses because an individual can easily make a mistake, whereas the nation and the party as a whole never can (pp. 241–242). He trusted a strategy known as "walking on two legs," which could support heavy industry along with light industry and agriculture (for more details, see, e.g., Mao, 1956/1977, pp. 284–285). This policy also allowed work-study schools to be established beside academic ones. Like the Soviets, Mao (1991/1998a) was convinced that a citizen develops best as a member of a collective. He proposed in 1958 that all schools should have contracts with local factories or agricultural cooperatives in order to combine theory with practice (Mao, 1991/1998a, pp. 796–797).

According to Mao (1937/1966b), human knowledge is generated during the process of consciousness, which takes place when performing practical activities. The first phase of consciousness involves sense perceptions and impressions, during which the citizen is unable to form profound concepts or make logical conclusions. The continuation of societal practice leads to a process that repeats the phenomena caused by the sensations and impressions (pp. 4–5). During the second phase of consciousness, the rational phase, the citizens use concepts when they make judgments and conclusions. Mao discovered that concepts are formed when a sudden change takes place in the human mind. This is a leap in the process of cognition. These concepts no longer reflect just the phenomenal character of things and their separate aspects and external relations but encompass the essence of the phenomenon, the phenomenon as a whole, and the various internal relations of phenomena (p. 5).

Mao (1937/1966b) interpreted that the function of consciousness is to proceed, with the help of perceptions, to the thinking phase and to gradually continue until insight into the inner contradictions of objective things occurs, along with comprehending the relationships between different processes. Logical consciousness is capable of understanding the surrounding world as a whole within an inner relation of all its aspects (pp. 5–6).

The two phases of the process of consciousness, sensory and rational, have different qualities but are not actually distinguishable from each other when they integrate in the course of practical activities. As Mao (1937/1966b) contended, "All genuine knowledge originates in direct experience. But one cannot have direct experience of everything; as a matter of fact, most of our knowledge comes from indirect experience" (p. 8). However, theoretically, during the first phase of the consciousness process, through their senses, people are in contact with the phenomena of the external world. During the second phase, the new information associated with a sensation is synthesized, arranged, and reconstructed and is when concepts, judgments, and conclusions are created. Mao emphasized that only when sensory observations have provided detailed and comprehensive information can they be the basis for forming correct concepts and theories (p. 11).

In relation to this awakening process of consciousness, Mao (1937/1966b) emphasized that the most important aspect is to be able to apply this understanding of the laws of the objective world to the processes in which people can actively change the world. Consciousness begins with practice, but the theoretical knowledge acquired through practice has to return again to practice (p. 14). The following quotation describes how the dialectical and materialistic theory of knowledge could be applied to practice, based on Mao (1937/1966b):

> Discover the truth through practice, and again through practice verify and develop the truth. Start from perceptual knowledge and actively develop it into rational knowledge; then start from rational knowledge and actively guide revolutionary practice to change both the subjective and the objective world. Practice, knowledge, again practice, and again knowledge. This form repeats itself in endless cycles, and with each cycle the content of practice and knowledge rises to a higher level. (p. 20)

Mao Zedong (1937/1966b) argued that during the process of knowledge development, when forming judgments and conclusions, people should use their prior sensory observations, with the help of the appropriate concepts. The actual function of consciousness is to discover the internal conflicts of the laws of objective things and phenomena for the purpose of achieving logical consciousness. This phase of rational consciousness must be researched through practice. Mao wrote that knowledge should be explored in all fields of practical life: production processes, class struggles, and scientific experiments. During this examination, people would become aware of their relation to nature, to other people, and to themselves (Mao, 1937/1966b, pp. 4–9, 11–18). Participation in production life is thus the process of self-actualization because, according to Marxist thinking, people actualize themselves best by expressing themselves at work and in production plants (Marx, 1867/1974, pp. 168, 435).

The immediate result of adopting the Marxist theory of knowledge is the synthesis of learning and work, school and life. In doing so, school teaching should be combined with productive work and scientific research. The following quotation, based on Mao's work *On Practice* (1937/1966b), illustrates how human knowledge depends on personal activity in production:

> Man's knowledge depends mainly on his activity in material production, through which he comes gradually to understand the phenomena, the properties, and the laws of nature, and the relations between himself and nature; and through his activity in production he also gradually comes to understand, in varying degrees, certain relations that exist between man and man. None of this knowledge can be acquired apart from activity in production. (pp. 1–2)

3.4.2   Aims and Values

After the Chinese Civil War ended in 1949, the main goal of the Communist Party was a classless society and the means to achieve it was revolutionary labor education. The aims of this form of education can be seen as an attempt to educate citizens to be well-rounded, politically and culturally conscious, and capable of both intellectual and manual work (Lu, 1958/1998, p. 855). In step with revolutionary ideas, the school should train citizens to be proficient and skilled, to internalize socialist ideology, and to work efficiently in collective production. Teaching should support and advance socialist production and be subjugated to politics. The organizational center of political life was to be the Communist Party, which would also lead education and teaching.

Based on an examination of revolutionary labor education, community-based learning in the late 1950s appeared to be school-centered, with particular emphasis on moral-political and intellectual aims. This placed a prime emphasis on moral-political and mental values, while also stressing traditional and cultural values. Mao (1957/1977) stated that the Chinese educational policy should provide students physical, moral, and intellectual education so they could become skilled workers with a socialist consciousness (p. 405). The idea behind this thinking was that a harmonious education requires the holistic integration of physical, moral-political, and intellectual activity and that such an education is best achieved through productive labor. The aim of education was to produce true builders of society who have internalized a collective sense of identity and a culture rooted in dialectical materialism. This was due to a firm belief that work has value in itself and that all social well-being can be created through human work. This view held that work is at the highest level of a value hierarchy.

Appreciation for work was intimately intertwined with moral-political values, which served to accentuate patriotism and loyalty toward a socialist system and the various virtues it represented. Work processes requiring intellectual effort also placed vital importance on mental values, which could be obtained while students were engaged in different types of work-study programs in schools. Traditional and cultural values were emphasized during work processes in order to help students develop mentally for the purpose of attaining a harmony in learning based on Confucian tradition. The intention of this was to maintain the country's political unity and cultural bases. Confucian values accepted the hierarchical arrangements and unequal power divisions of the prevailing society. The Chinese administration of the time adapted these traditional doctrines to its own needs although opposing Confucianism. A Confucian belief regarding general obedience to authorities was the basic virtue that allowed the use of traditional values to legitimate the system of administration. The highest degree of legitimation was represented by the Chinese ideological system, called the *symbolic universe*, which was manifested in the central role of socialist consciousness in the society. The following summarizes the aims of community-based learning in light of the revolutionary pedagogics introduced by Mao:

> At the beginning of the Great Leap Forward campaign (1958–1961), the Central Committee of the c.p.c. confirmed the three basic principles of education, which were to be closely intertwined and mutually supportive. Such education should (1) serve proletarian politics, (2) be combined with production and labor, and (3) be led by the Communist Party (Lu, 1958/1998, pp. 852, 855). During 1957 and 1958, Mao (1991/1998a) came to the conclusion that the aim of education should be a citizen who is

capable of both intellectual and manual labor. He stated that these two aspects should be united: the real Chinese should be both "red" (politically conscious) and an "expert" (skillfully competent) (p. 796). This form of community-based learning aimed to:
- enhance all-around development;
- improve the application of the subject matters learned at school to practice in the community;
- provide training in manual labor that also develops the physical body;
- erase the inequality between urban and rural areas, between manual and intellectual labor, and between workers;
- ease schools' economic difficulties and thus reduce educational expenses in society;
- increase productivity that benefits the whole socialist society; and
- teach the ideology of communism through local, productive work (Lu, 1958/1998, pp. 855–856; Ministry of Education of the C.P.G., 1998, pp. 800–801).

The Great Proletarian Cultural Revolution was a sociopolitical movement that took place in China from the mid-1960s to the mid-1970s. During this era, the society-centered pattern of community-based learning began to emphasize moral-political aims and their value dimensions. The goals of revolutionary education were guided by Mao's thoughts, as was life in general in the country at that time. Political ideology laid a foundation for all schooling and education, which served to accentuate moral-political values. The power-related value dimension also was central in the processes of leading educational work in the socialist revolutionary society. Values related to power emphasized the achievement or preservation of a dominant position in the social system. The main socialist values of the central administration of the time were striving to ensure that competing value considerations did not undermine the consensus in the country's values. The administration insisted that the basic values of socialism were to be inculcated to all Chinese people so that they could maintain them in order to improve society through constant revolution. The administrators oversaw all areas of life—politics, economics, natural resources, power, and truth—on an exclusive basis. It is understandable that this movement could significantly prevent China's society and economy from functioning normally. The following quotation expresses more clearly Mao's status during the Cultural Revolution (Decision of the Central Committee, 1966):

> In the Great Proletarian Cultural Revolution, it is imperative to hold aloft the great red banner of Mao Tse-tung's thought and put proletarian

politics in command. The movement for the creative study and application of Chairman Mao Tse-tung's works should be carried forward among the masses of the workers, peasants and soldiers, ... and Mao Tse-tung's thought should be taken as the guide to action in the Cultural Revolution. (p. 11)

In the context of the ongoing revolutionary process, rooted in dialectical materialism, community-based learning can be seen as focused on productive labor in teaching and education. This type of pedagogical practice appears to refer to the revolutionary approach of labor-related education, the center of which was ideological and political work in the prevailing proletarian revolution. The goals of this form of education were also included in the constitution of 1975, according to which education should (1) serve proletarian politics, (2) benefit workers, peasants, and soldiers, and (3) be combined with productive labor (China, 1975, Article 12). We could consider that during this era the focus was on political and ideological values in which the higher education and training offered to the peasant and working classes was especially to serve proletarian politics, with priority also placed on political and economic values. These values could arise from learning processes in which general school students participated in labor-related activities that combined manual labor with ideological campaigns in collective economic production. The following exemplifies the aims of labor-related education during the great revolutionary movement in the 1960s:

> The nature of sociopolitical thinking during the Great Proletarian Cultural Revolution represented an exceptionally radical orientation toward education and its practices. Mao (1967/1998b) insisted that the school should respond to the needs of a Chinese revolutionary society (p. 1383). Labor-related education should gradually remove the traditional dichotomy between rural and urban areas, between workers and peasants, and between manual and intellectual labor as part of preventing the restoration of capitalism, as documented in 1965 (see C.P.C. Central Committee, 1998, p. 1356). Such education was to make students become class-conscious citizens for the socialist society, in the process of which they could internalize the worker-peasant-soldier role. This led to a specific doctrine, according to which the real Chinese should be overridingly "red," a politically conscious member of the collective and people (see, e.g., Chen, 1981, p. 144). During this process, labor-related education aimed to:
> – teach by performing manual labor;
> – narrow the traditional dichotomies in the Chinese proletarian society;

- reduce educational expenses; and
- become familiar with fellow workers' mindset and communist ideology (see C.P.C. Central Committee, 1998, pp. 1356–1357).

3.4.3 Summing Up

The conceptual features of Maoist revolutionism can be interpreted from the perspective of community-based learning by applying Hlebowitsh's (2007) classification. Revolutionism sees the ideal student as being a class-conscious citizen who is a brave fighter in the class struggle, who is involved in ideological and political studies within the ongoing proletarian revolution, and is also becoming familiar with the productive labor activities offered by the local commune or separate production cooperatives. The ideal educational program is incorporated into productive labor, during the harmonious process of which the ideology and politics permeate the entire curriculum and school life. The student is oriented toward an ideal socialist society, the citizens of which live in the people's communes and work in agricultural and small-scale industrial production based on manual labor.

Some of Mao's ideas discussed above can be compared to the basic Deweyan ideas of progressivism, especially when analyzing the relationship between knowledge and experience. These two ideas, however, differ sharply with respect to their philosophical foundations. In Mao's view, the process of knowledge development is based on the dialectical and materialistic theory of knowledge. Mao (1937/1966b) argued that this process is, according to Marxist materialism, "the deepening movement of cognition, the movement by which man in society progresses from perceptual knowledge to logical knowledge in his complex, constantly recurring practice of production and class structure" (p. 6).

3.5 *Resistance to Educational Change*

This study shows that many countries also started to vigorously oppose the influence of international educational currents, even after their ideas had been in practice for several years. As indicated earlier in this chapter, progressive principles were applied in school experiments in China and the Soviet Union, and pedagogical progressivism became popular among some circles in China after John Dewey had lectured there between 1919 and 1921 (see Keenan, 1977).

Xu (1992) reported that Dewey's ideas on education were applied intensively in school experiments in various parts of revolutionary China. School programs emphasized learning, which was connected with activity and immediate experiences, and ultimately aimed at the social reform of the local area. In 1927, for example, Tao Xing-zhi established the Xiao Zhuang Normal School

IDEALS FOR COMMUNITY ENGAGEMENT FROM THE EAST AND WEST 41

in the countryside outside Nanjing for his education experiments. The school aimed to offer not only teacher training but also to reform the village community surrounding the school. Although the school experiment lasted only three years, it strengthened the dialogue concerning the status of progressive education in China (Xu, 1992, pp. 58–60). However, Xu further documented that, from the Guomindang (Nationalist Party of China) administration's standpoint, this progressive work-based inclination was seen to be increasingly connected to revolutionary factions and was considered a political threat. The administration decided that the progressive, communal school experiment had to be discontinued. The Chinese government at the time may have felt that the solution to the villages' economic and social problems required identifying the point at which the renewal originated from the national cultural values of China (Xu, 1992, pp. 116–117). The following quotation, based on Xu's research (1992), elucidates Tao Xing-zhi's school experiment in more detail:

> Xiao Zhuang Normal School started with thirteen students. In order to train them as teachers and educators, the school set up a central elementary school for the peasants' children to enable students to learn teaching in the real-life practice. As the Normal School expanded, it established four kindergartens for preschool education training, eight elementary and secondary schools for basic teacher training, evening schools for adult education, and a hospital, a carpenter workshop, and a tea house for vocational education. Besides teaching to teach in real school settings, the school also required students to immerse themselves in the rural life by having them work with the peasants, so as to transform their outlook and adapt them to the village life for village reconstruction.
>
> The school's involvement in educating village children and participating in village life, together with its vocational branches, soon claimed it an important role in the village. In order to help village's development, the school also taught peasants agricultural skills, organized self-defense leagues, proposed road building projects, and assisted in the village administrative decision-making. For instance, when the scarce water supply became a problem, the school suggested that the villagers hold a town meeting, and the students participated as an advisory committee. A solution was reached after a democratic discussion and vote. During the process both students and peasants learned problem solving by doing. (pp. 59–60)

Compared with the parallel processes that took place in the early Soviet Union, the reform-pedagogical school Blonsky introduced can be said to have eventually given way to the new Stalinist school in the 1930s. Even though the present study suggests that progressive and Marxist educational ideas have the same basis, if they are viewed as material counterparts to Hegel's absolute idealism, progressive pedagogical ideas can be seen as inevitably in contradiction with Marxist ideas, as implemented in revolutionary China and the early Soviet Union. There, they represented different views regarding the direction in which society should be developed, along with the underlying values and ideals. It is stated that "education is but one of the institutions in society, and the educational pendulum reflects broad social trends" (Ballantine & Hammack, 2009, p. 421). The following brief description of the breakdown of reformist educational practices during the early decades of the Soviet Union illustrates this in greater detail:

> While Blonsky was developing his own labor school in the Ukraine, amid great difficulties, experiments in an educational method that was the complete opposite of Blonsky's reform pedagogy were taking place. The creator of the new method was Anton Makarenko (1888–1939), who was director at the Maxim Gorky Colony for juvenile delinquent war orphans between 1920 and 1927. Makarenko chose a collective educational approach that was based on combining theoretical teaching with productive and practical labor in the Marxist spirit (see, e.g., Jackim, 2016, pp. 169–180). One of the central features of Makarenko's educational collective was strict discipline obtained through education, with the collectives organized according to a military model. The whole pedagogical collective consisted of both primary collectives as well as permanent or temporary labor and recreational collectives. Representative bodies were established to develop independent initiative and self-government and to strengthen the structure of the organization (Makarenko, 1949/1965, pp. 50–53, 88–89, 91, 97–98, 139–141). Makarenko (1949/1965) combined education with everyday life and activities: in addition to studying, children worked in different phases of agricultural and industrial production. For example, they obtained vocational skills by manufacturing cameras and electrical equipment in production plants (Makarenko, 1949/1965, pp. 128–129).

After Lenin's death, Joseph Stalin (1879–1953) gradually became the country's leader. The goal of the Soviet Union's First Five-Year Plan (1928–1933) was to increase production through the collectivization of agriculture and the systematic industrialization of the country (State Planning Commission of the U.S.S.R., 1933, pp. 4–5). This social and economic renewal also required school reform, the goal of which was to train specialists for the new society. Reform-pedagogical school experiments associated with progressive education were abandoned; Makarenko was to become the most central person in Soviet pedagogy.

A development similar to the one in the Soviet Union in the 1930s occurred in the People's Republic of China in the 1950s. As previously mentioned, Chinese education was reformed with the help of Soviet experts. The reconstruction of the entire economy was also based on Soviet-type economic planning, which was aimed at developing heavy industry.

However, during the Nikita Khrushchev era (1953–1964), the ideological conflict between the two countries intensified. Problems in Chinese productivity were warded off with the Great Leap Forward (1958–1961), the economic model of which differed from the Soviet one. The Chinese authorities attempted to create rapid industrialization and collectivization in the country by means of decentralized industry (see, e.g., Pantsov with Levine, 2012, pp. 453–454). This also meant reforming the educational system so that it would be based on China's own views. The authorities developed the work-study school, which was to be the main school in China, to engage students with productive labor and ideological political activities (see, e.g., Chen, 1981, pp. 68–70).

This type of development is an indication that the prevalent Soviet socialism at that time represented different value objectives from those the People's Republic of China was supporting in its social, economic, and political practice. This conflict continued to be tied in with different ways of understanding about what direction to develop the new socialist society.

The following section compares the views constituting the philosophical background for community-based learning in the United States, India, and China. The examination utilizes the different modes of social modernization that have prevailed in these countries.

4   Modernization Efforts prior to the Late 1970s

4.1   *Essentialism and American Educational Reform*
4.1.1   Philosophical Views

In the United States, a philosophical shift in education occurred in the late 1950s that was comparable to the Indian neocolonial approach later in the mid-1960s. The catalyst for this change was the threatening atmosphere that pervaded the country during the Cold War in the late 1940s. The educational system was necessary to strengthen the power of national defense, particularly against the potential supremacy of the Soviet Union. The social goal was now to train experts for an ideal American society following capitalist ideology. In accord with these changes, emphasis was placed on the idea that the philosophical background of community-based learning evidently relied on the principles of essentialist education, these being primarily consistent with the philosophical tradition of realism.

The basis of this educational trend, essentialism, lies deep in the history of the American school. The concept was introduced to the wider public in the late 1930s and early 1940s by William C. Bagley (1874–1946), a professor at Columbia University who protested against the freedom, individualism, and engagement in activities promoted in progressive education (Gutek, 2000, p. 66). Essentialism is an educational theory rooted in traditional philosophies, particularly realism, and its ontological, epistemological, and axiological postulates are largely in harmony with the tradition of realism. From the perspective of realism, reality is objective, independent of the observer's experience, because reality consists of the physical world. Consequently, knowledge is built through the rational observation and interpretation of natural laws, which means that values are also seen as absolutes based on natural laws (for realism as a systematic philosophy, see, e.g., Gutek, 1997, pp. 36–40).

The essentialist theory of education became the dominant philosophical approach during the 1950s, a period in which the United States experienced widespread fear of communism. As the critical educational debate was churning, it became clear that the leading politicians and authorities responsible for educational policies were ready to favor an essentialist educational philosophy, particularly after the Soviet Union launched a small satellite, *Sputnik*, into orbit around the earth in 1957. The momentous National Defense Education Act of 1958 (1958) had the goal of training experts in science and technology for a society dominated by capitalist ideology (Section 101). Teaching was expected to emphasize academic expertise instead of Rousseauean child-centered education and its reform-pedagogical ideals.

The demand to increase the number of experts in the natural sciences also resulted in the development of pedagogical approaches of community-based learning represented by various programs of outdoor and environmental education. These had originated in such reform-pedagogical movements as the camping education movement and the conservation movement. The course of development was promoted by the environmental awakening of the 1960s, which involved a new public awareness of environmental issues. The claim can be made that the supporters of essentialism now offered an opportunity to operate in a familiar philosophical context of education, even though the ontological and epistemological starting points of their approach differed completely from those of their predecessor, pedagogical progressivism. Unlike the representatives of progressive pedagogics, essentialists emphasized examining the natural laws of the physical world as well as the mastery of essential knowledge, rather than concentrating on the mode of learning (Armstrong, Henson, & Savage, 2009, pp. 268–269).

4.1.2 Aims and Values

Conservative social thinking strengthened in the United States in the late 1940s after the Second World War. This being the case, the popularity of the progressive reform-pedagogical movement also precipitously collapsed. Critical discussion of education took an unexpected turn during the Cold War period (1947–1989), a time when suddenly, in 1957, the Soviets successfully sent the first device into space. The event was interpreted in the United States as a major threat to national defense, and in order to raise the national defense level, it was necessary to raise the quality of scientific and technical knowledge among the citizenry. This required school reform, the goal of which was to produce competent experts for the new society following capitalist ideology and a full-fledged market economy. Many thought that experts who have special knowledge, skills, and training would be able to develop industries administered by the new technologically sophisticated society.

This major social change accelerated the development of the school-centered pattern of community-based learning so that the primary emphasis was on intellectual aims. The American essentialist school, influenced by realism, stressed the shared goal of these intellectual aims and the integration of motor, sociomoral, and intellectual education in accordance with the National Defense Education Act of 1958. Through these aims, the purpose was to train science and technology experts for the most developed capitalist society in the world. Education was harnessed to the international power struggle in an attempt to increase the country's political security and supremacy by accentuating intellectual aims, while, in fact, the intention was to promote theoretical values associated with truth, knowledge, and science.

Outdoor education can be seen as the earliest approach of the school-centered pattern in this era. The following describes the essence of the aims of outdoor education in the early years, when this mode of education was gradually becoming school-centered with greater emphasis on intellectual aims:

> The purpose of outdoor education was to provide teachers an approach to learning in which they were urged to utilize pedagogical resources in various outdoor settings. Sharp (1947) emphasized that outdoor education was to advance from school to society in continuously "widening circles," the activity reaching its peak in the school camp (p. 35). The subject

matter that could best be learned outside the classroom should indeed be learned outside of it (Sharp, 1947, pp. 34–35; Sharp, 1952, pp. 1, 3; Smith, 1956, p. 7). This form of outdoor education aimed to:
- integrate the contents of curricula;
- promote acquisition of knowledge, that is, to learn it faster, retain it longer, and understand it more deeply;
- arouse interest in learning;
- teach democratic ideology, that is, to respect one's fellow man and master cooperation skills; and
- offer immediate learning experiences in nature and the community (Sharp, 1943, pp. 363, 367; Sharp, 1946, p. 192; Sharp, 1947, pp. 33–34; Sharp, 1952, pp. 19–22).

The early 1950s and the mid-1960s were characterized by the standardization of outdoor education, which also included the uniformity of pedagogical aims (for a closer examination of the period, see Hammerman, Hammerman, & Hammerman, 2001, pp. 239–242). The tendency in this process was the holistic integration of outdoor education into the school curriculum by concretely extending the classroom to form an outdoor laboratory in the natural or cultural environment. The purpose of such an approach to outdoor education was to enrich the curriculum, reinforce teaching, and stimulate learning, thus widening its dimensionality. The theoretical values of education were also prioritized in the spirit of realism so that the accent was on developing problem-solving skills and utilizing all the senses through research-based learning. Instead, less stress was placed on the aims related to universal values, such as enhancing the ability of students to appreciate and understand the natural environment. However, the idealistic goal of education was to develop students' ability to act as constructive members of a democratic society. The following provides a detailed combination of qualities belonging to the aims of outdoor education in the 1960s:

> The Elementary and Secondary Education Act of 1965 (1965) had American teachers emphasize programs with out-of-school activities for the purpose of supplementing and enriching their instruction (Sections 301, 303). Fitzpatrick (1968) concluded that outdoor education was to utilize resources beyond the classroom to enhance and enrich teaching and learning (p. 78). Concerning this, Hug and Wilson (1965) wrote that outdoor education was based on exploratory and discovery learning, which was to proceed by means of problem solving, utilizing all of the senses in observation and perception (pp. 5–6, 8–10). Based on Fitzpatrick (1968, p. 49), outdoor education aimed to:

- enrich the curriculum;
- develop the individual's intellectual, physical, and mental abilities;
- stimulate learning;
- develop the knowledge, skills, and attitudes needed for the wise use of leisure time;
- promote awareness of nature and its relationship to humankind, that is, to appreciate and understand the natural environment as well as the relationship between humankind and nature;
- enhance the individual's abilities to play a more constructive role in society, that is, to develop civic-mindedness and promote democratic human relations and procedures; and
- offer direct learning experiences beyond the classroom.

In the United States in the 1950s and 1960s, the demand for an increase in the number of experts in the natural sciences intensified the development of community-based learning to an unforeseen extent when the U.S. Congress also expressed the desire to direct public school academic studies to out-of-school environments. This trend spread when the environmental movement was accompanied by a revived awareness of the decline in environmental equilibrium. This affected decision-making within educational policy to prioritize intellectual aims consistent with the prevailing ideas in society. The purpose of the Environmental Education Act (1970) was to develop curriculum that promoted an understanding of the principles of the natural and cultural environment. Thus, attempts were made to support activities designed to improve the environment and maintain an ecological balance during the society's rapidly changing science and technology (Sections 2–3). In the same year, a Department of Health, Education, and Welfare publication suggested that the aims of environmental education were to guide students in making sound ecological decisions and to anticipate their consequences, prepare value judgments, and act accordingly (Office of Education, 1970, pp. 10–11).

This kind of environmental policy appears to be focused on aims related to universal values. The intention was to enhance the will and ability of students and help them to understand values connected with the natural environment, ecological sustainability, and environmental protection. Stressing the universal values associated with nature also represented an aspiration for environmental ethics and values related to students' own ecological decisions and value judgments, and an awareness of their personal contributions. Values related to environmental literacy and decision-making were emphasized during active-learning projects that helped students build their ethical and mental abilities. These goal-directed activities were also used as a means to achieve the theoretical values of education that were prioritized so that the accent was on research processes concerning environmental issues and alternative solutions. The following exemplifies the characteristics of the aims of environmental education during the 1970s:

> Many outdoor education programs were intended to be environmental education programs. The purpose of such programs was to study in various sites close to nature, these being forests, woodlands, ponds, lakes, recreation areas, or wild land natural areas. Stapp (1969) proposed that the aim of environmental education was to produce a citizenry that is knowledgeable about the biophysical environment and its associated problems, aware of how to help solve these problems, and motivated to work toward their solution (p. 31). Hungerford, Peyton, and Wilke (1980) stated that the goal of environmental education was to aid students in becoming environmentally knowledgeable and skilled as well as dedicated citizens willing to work both individually and collectively toward achieving and/or maintaining a dynamic equilibrium between the quality of life and the environment (p. 43). This form of environmental education aimed to:
> – provide knowledge of ecological foundations;
> – develop the knowledge and skills needed to investigate environmental issues and evaluate alternative solutions for remediating these issues;
> – promote skills required in positive environmental action;
> – guide the development of a conceptual awareness connected with environmental issues and values; and
> – provide environmental education programs in school and in the environment outside the school (Childress, 1978, pp. 5–6; Hungerford et al., 1980, pp. 43–44).

4.1.3 Summing Up

If the conceptual features of essentialism are analyzed by applying Hlebowitsh's (2007) classification from the perspective of community-based learning, the conclusion can be made that the ideal student has a rational mind and concentrates on the basics of school subjects while examining natural and environmental phenomena using scientific methods. The ideal curriculum embodies programs of both outdoor education and environmental education, the experiential activity-based units of study of which are academic and subject-centered, with the contents being studied in a structured manner in and outside the school. The student is oriented toward an ideal democratic society that depends on the essential academic knowledge defined by experts in different fields, while operating in high-tech industrial production and service-based sectors.

Proponents of essentialism intended to emphasize teachers' central role in education. The whole learning process was to be centered on the teacher (see, e.g., Gutek, 2011, pp. 369–385). As a result, students were to take a passive role and, doing so, to be less involved in their learning. Essentialist education gained new strength in the late 1970s. Those years saw the neo-essentialist movement require that schools return to teaching essential academic content, such as mathematics, natural sciences, and social studies (see Webb, 2006).

4.2 Indian Modernization and Educational Reform
4.2.1 Philosophical Views

Over the course of time, the national philosophical traditions regarding the countries discussed here have been influenced by the international currents of ideas that have also been applied to educational practices. This has been particularly true when a country's political situation has been receptive to ideas from other countries. Such a philosophical turn in education took place in India as the education system was being urged to help accelerate the country's extensive modernization process, particularly since the third five-year period (1961–1966). Guided by Western specialists, the Indian government intensified national modernization with the help of an education system that would now apply work education based on materialistic values (Ministry of Education, 1966, pp. 210–216). The present study indicates that, in light of Indian social modernization, the philosophical background of community-based learning is being built on the ideas of neocolonial work education. This interpretation was ultimately consistent with the view of dialectical and historical materialism.

Particularly after the Russian Revolution, the socialist political movement found support in many of the Latin American and Asian countries that had been subjected to Western rule. The national leaders of colonies hoped for an escape from imperialistic policies through the social reform that was being applied in the Soviet Union. Among them, Jawaharlal Nehru (1889–1964), later the chair of the Congress Party, sought a solution for India's national future.

While residing in Europe in 1926 and 1927, Nehru familiarized himself with ideas that differed from the option British authorities offered. He was introduced not only to Western parliamentary democracy and British socialism but also to Marxism and its radical ideas. He visited the Soviet Union and, subsequently, China. Nehru believed that socialism could inevitably offer the means for solving India's post-independence poverty issues and a state of abasement, if a large majority of Indians wanted it (Gopal, 1975, pp. 210–213). However, socialism, which would reflect Marxism-Leninism, represented different underlying value objectives from those promoted in the social, economic, and political practices of the India that was then gaining independence. This contradiction was further intimately linked with diverse views regarding the direction in which society should develop.

In 1950, the independent Republic of India started to implement a domestic policy in accordance with Prime Minister Nehru's thinking. Referred to as nondogmatic socialism, this approach was based on ideas taken from Western parliamentary democracy as well as from socialism and secularism. Despite its uneven distribution of capital, the Indian economy was geared toward Western-style industrialization, with socialism as the goal. Starting with the second five-year period (1956–1961), modernization was seen as the goal of societal development. Many Indians shared the belief that this could be achieved through investment in sectors such as steel production, engineering, and the chemical industry. The model of economic development tied up with socialism also included protecting the Indian economy by impeding or limiting imports of foreign goods and services.

India had also chosen a rather eclectic approach to developing the country's educational and cultural life. In 1966, the authoritative Kothari Education Commission recommended that, in addition to the national tradition, one should also "draw upon liberalizing forces that have arisen in the Western nations and which have emphasized, among other things, the dignity of the individual, equality and social justice, e.g., the French Revolution, the concept of the welfare state, the philosophy of Marx and the rise of socialism" (Ministry of Education, 1966, p. 20). The purpose of vocationally productive education was now to emphasize a neocolonial approach, which was basically rooted in dialectical and historical materialism. The Kothari report presented exemplary Soviet programs of polytechnical work education as models that were adapted to the types of work-experience programs introduced as an integral part of Indian vocationally productive education (Ministry of Education, 1966, pp. 210–216). An increase in vocational orientation was set as a new goal for education, particularly in the upper secondary schools. Moreover, in addition to containing academic studies, school curricula at all levels were supplemented with programs of science- and technology-based work.

4.2.2   Aims and Values

India entered a new phase in the 1960s, giving precedence to education over aims connected with theoretical values. We can suggest in the spirit of the Kothari Commission report (1966) that the neocolonial school emphasized intellectual aims in an effort to integrate physical, sociomoral, and intellectual education within community-based learning (Ministry of Education, 1966). The purpose of such a preference was, consistent with dialectical and historical materialism, to train experts for a modern society of secularism and social equality. Specifically, procedural knowledge was rated highly among the aims of neocolonial work-experience education, that is, knowledge about how to do something, which was a prerequisite for applying modern technology and science to production processes. Even though social values were still promoted in teaching, the significance of science- and technology-related values was now given prominence in order to enable students to understand modern technology and its scientific principles. The following clarifies the features of the aims of work-experience education:

> The Education Commission, under the chairmanship of D. S. Kothari (1906–1993), demonstrated that achieving India's national goals depended on the social, economic, and cultural transformation of society. This, in turn, was connected with a restructuring of the educational system. The Commission report argued that a modern, developed, and technology-based society needed intellectually capable workers. For this reason, school curricula were to be supplemented with programs of work-experience education implemented both inside and outside the school. The productive processes of these programs were to combine industrialization with the application of science and technology (Ministry of Education, 1966, pp. 7–8). In relation to this, *The Curriculum for the Ten-Year School* (1975) aimed at reforming teaching using work-experience education, since the technological development of a modern society presupposed familiarization with new types of working skills and processes (National Council of Educational Research and Training [NCERT], 1975, p. 18). On the basis of these documents, work-experience education aimed to:
> - develop the knowledge, skills, and attitudes that are useful in the productive work of a modern society;
> - lead to an understanding of the need for and usefulness of modern labor-saving devices and tools and to understand the underlying scientific principles and the techniques involved in their use;
> - advance social and national integration, that is, to reduce the difference in the appreciation of intellectual and manual work with new technology, thus reducing class differences, particularly concerning the elite and the masses; and
> - offer programs of work-experience education inside and outside the school.

4.2.3 Summing Up

If Hlebowitsh's (2007) classification is used to analyze the specific conceptual features of neocolonialism presented in the Kothari report (1966) from the more general perspective of community-based learning, one could conclude that the ideal student is an intellectually capable and technologically literate individual who is being introduced to the changing activities and processes of vocationally productive work in society. The ideal curriculum embodies work-experience programs containing vocationally productive units of study based on the application of technology and science in and outside the school. The student is oriented toward an ideal democratic society that relies on secularism and social equality, the citizens of which work in scientifically and technologically advanced production.

Despite this determined school reform, nevertheless it soon became evident that many experts in education claimed that modest vocational work experience in production was insufficient to integrate the teaching and learning processes. For example, not even 10% of the primary and secondary schools offered their students work-experience activities. Gutek (2006) explained that in addition to the criticism directed at the schools, fierce resistance also arose at that time to new planning in economic policy. In this manner, the critics also wanted to avoid the problems typical of Western countries, such as environmental pollution, antisocial lifestyles, and social exclusion (p. 88).

4.3 Chinese Modernization and Its Educational Reforms

4.3.1 Philosophical Views

In the late 1970s, the People's Republic of China initiated a modernization process that was quite similar to that of India in the 1950s and 1960s. Such a major social shift was possible because China's political situation was open to economic reforms that were implemented in Singapore. This foreign success story is partly why the C.P.C. was ready to strengthen the fields of industry, agriculture, science and technology, and national defense (see Hua, 1977, pp. 73, 86–88). Five years later, industry was set as the material foundation for the modernization of the whole economy (Hu, 1982, p. 22; State Council, 1984, p. 72). This development was the beginning of an extensive process for changing the country's entire economic system. The central administration made a historic decision in 1984 to shift its highly centered, planned economic system to one that follows the principles of a market economy. Deng Xiaoping (1904–1997) was the principal leader of this major social reform in the People's Republic of China from 1978 to 1989, and again in 1992. The following provides an account of Deng's road as a committed supporter of revolutionary principles:

> Deng is the most influential politician in China when interpreting its modernization process from the late 1970s onward. Deng was born in Paifang, Guang'an County, Sichuan Province. In 1920, three years after the Russian Revolution, Deng traveled to France. While traveling and working there,

he took part in discussion groups and studied the basics of capitalism, imperialism, and the socialist practice in the new Soviet Union. He also participated in a meeting of young European communists, who declared their intention to unite with the Chinese Communist Youth League. After becoming a committed supporter of revolutionary principles while in France, Deng traveled to Russia in 1926 to study at Sun Yat-sen University in Moscow. He attended courses that dealt with revolutionary themes, including the works of Marx, Engels, and Lenin; the ideas of historical materialism; and the basis of the past political events of the Soviet Communist Party and the Chinese revolutionary movement. Deng returned to China in 1927 and joined the ongoing Chinese revolution. He played an integral part in the Communist Party's rise to power in China during the 1930s and 1940s (for Deng's biography above, see Vogel, 2011, pp. 15–26).

China also introduced quite significant administrative strategies, which required both an easing of central control and an expansion of market-based educational policy. This turn in social philosophy was realized when the government made the exceptional decision to integrate the educational system with national economic reforms at the beginning of the sixth five-year period (1981–1985) (*Principles for Future Economic Construction*, 1981/1991, pp. 237, 239).

In order to implement this enormous reform, some major educational documents were issued. Of these, the c.p.c. Central Committee allowed the local authorities in 1985 "the power for the administration of elementary education. ... They should encourage state-owned enterprises, public organizations and individuals to run schools and provide them with guidance" (*Decision of the C.P.C. Central Committee*, 1985/1991, p. 472). The intention was to accelerate the flow of development using local "economic and cultural resources" through required permissions from local people's authorities (p. 481). Furthermore, the State Council explicitly declared in another significant educational document that private citizens and organizations should establish schools (Department of Foreign Affairs of the State Education Commission of the P.R.C., 1994, p. 10). This document stated that school education was to be integrated with productive labor so that "each branch of society should actively provide sites for schools to carry out education through labor" (Department of Foreign Affairs of the State Education Commission of the P.R.C., 1994, p. 22). In these pedagogical settings "education through labor must be included in teaching plans, and gradually institutionalized and serialized" (Department of Foreign Affairs of the State Education Commission of the P.R.C., 1994, p. 22). The document argued that the most critical challenges are both the change in educational thinking and the reform of educational content and methods. As a basis of the 1994 document, the present study suggests that Chinese socialist modernization gives special importance to the view that the philosophical background of community-based learning strategies can be seen as resting upon the ideas of labor-related education, also referred to as postrevolutionary labor education. This analysis is in accord with the theory of dialectical materialism.

4.3.2 Aims and Values

China chose a way to change its educational future that is comparable to India and the United States. Starting post-Mao (from 1976 onward), the Chinese launched unparalleled social reforms and were willing to ensure a smooth transition from the previous social period and its conditions to the new one. The Chinese understood that they would have to quickly create an intellectual socialist workforce in order to build a modern socialist power. The period after the Cultural Revolution can be regarded as a socially transitional one and, as such, was known as the years of the Four Modernizations (1978–1982). Deng Xiaoping (1904–1997) was the leader of this major social reform in China.

The post-Mao era evidenced the society-centered pattern of community-based learning gradually becoming school-centered, with more emphasis placed on intellectual aims when specifically considering postrevolutionary education. Along these lines, the components of physical, moral-political, and intellectual education were intentionally integrated. This can be understood as referring to the postrevolutionary approach of labor-related education committed to the ideology of socialism. Such an approach can be seen as a method by which the postrevolutionary school could connect students' learning with modern production in real-life learning environments for the purpose of developing a socialist society with science and technology.

The Chinese experienced that by accentuating intellectual aims they could emphasize values related to science and technology, as they felt that without improving the bases of these scientific fields in the country it would be impossible for them to develop a modern agriculture, industry, or national defense. For this reason, the intention was to promote theoretical values associated with truth, knowledge, and science. This could be achieved through learning processes in which students were engaged in productive labor-related projects based on new technology. Special importance was also given to economic values instead of traditional and cultural values.

This rapid change in the national educational policy was manifested in 1978 in the third constitution of the People's Republic of China (P.R.C.). The constitution promulgated that the educational aims would no longer focus on worker-peasant-soldier class consciousness, but instead would more generally serve proletarian politics. The ultimate aim was the idea that a balanced education necessitates integrating physical, moral-political, and intellectual training. This form of education could best be obtained by means of productive labor in the context of the overall development of a socialist consciousness and culture (see China, 1978, Article 13). The following illustrates the nature of the aims of labor-related education in the late 1970s:

> The beginning of the Four Modernizations saw reforms initiated, policies opened up, and new educational programs developed. A true Chinese citizen was now to be a trained expert or a scholar who is committed to the proletarian ideology of socialism. The realization of the Four Modernizations required rapidly training a great number of people with skills and technical competence. This establishment of a proletarian intellectual workforce was to be crucial in China's future course of making itself a great modern socialist power (State Council, 1998a, p. 1579). Based on the educational programs presented by Fang Yi in 1977, this form of labor-related education aimed to:
> – accelerate a developing national economy based on new technology;
> – foster a national defense equipped with modern technology; and
> – significantly increase labor productivity (Fang, 1979, p. 40).

4.3.3 Summing Up

An examination of the conceptual features of postrevolutionism, using Hlebowitsh's (2007) classification from the perspective of Chinese community-based learning, suggests that postrevolutionism would see the ideal student as being a socialist and an expert, that is to say, a technologically literate, socialist intellectual who is a self-disciplined builder of an economic modernization. The ideal educational program serves a modern socialist society and embodies projects of productive labor and social practices, the units of study of which are academic and subject-centered in the school and the community. The student is oriented toward an ideal socialist society, the citizens of which work in the production processes that follow the principles of a socialist market economy.

Realization of the Four Modernization urgently required training and supporting a great number of both "red" and "expert" construction workers (State Council, 1998a, p. 1579). However, China met serious challenges during this early postrevolutionary era. The following quotation, based on Moise's (1986) work, describes various difficulties during that time:

> China went on a construction binge. Whole factories were purchased from abroad; others were built with local resources. Coordination was

poor; sometimes two factories were built where there were only enough raw materials, or only enough electric power, for one factory actually to function. Besides this, the range of projects being started simply ran beyond what the Chinese economy could pay for. By 1978 the frenzy for new projects reached a level that reminded some people of the Great Leap Forward. (p. 231)

5   New Philosophical Views and Ideals since the Late 1970s

5.1   *Revival of Conservatism in American Education*
5.1.1   Philosophical Views

The course of development in the United States was comparable to that in many European and Asian countries with regard to academic-oriented learning. This development is to be interpreted against the background provided by more comprehensive social phenomena. The Americans had earlier experienced a rapid remodernization of society by implementing education reform based on conservative functionalism. To achieve this goal, the teaching at a realism-oriented essentialist school would emphasize scientific investigation of the physical world as governed by natural laws. A teacher-directed teaching and learning process based on a subject-centered curriculum emphasized academic expertise, especially in the study of science and mathematics. The essentialist school developed into a center of structured learning connected with society in only a limited manner.

The supporters of neo-essentialism intended to improve on traditional essentialism. This new educational policy developed consistent with a neoliberal social doctrine and its global economic, political, and ecological issues, these including unemployment, inequality, exclusion, conflicts, and environmental problems. The United States started to develop community-based learning in conformity with a realism-inclined neo-essentialist educational theory. This also indicated vigorous efforts to standardize the experiential activity-based units of study within the ideal educational program as they were developed more toward the natural sciences, technology, and relevant applications. The new trend represented conservative neoliberal thinking in which the school's success, and thus the growth of human capital, was tightly linked with national economic productivity and growth.

Conservatism has seen a significant revival in the United States since 1980. Neo-essentialism is closely aligned with the neoconservative ideology. As the following quotation, based on Gutek (2009), demonstrates:

> Neo-Conservatives and Neo-Essentialists agree that schools should be academic institutions with a well-defined curriculum of basic skills and subjects and that they should cultivate traditional values of patriotism, hard work, effort, punctuality, respect for authority, and civility. They argue that schools and colleges should stress the required core based on Western civilization and traditional American values. ... In addition to the congruence of Neo-Essentialism and Neo-Conservatism on traditional educational principles, they also concur that schools have an important economic role in enhancing U.S. economic productivity in a highly competitive global economy. (p. 329)

The approach to essentialist or neo-essentialist education, consistent with realism, became the undeniable mainstream of community-based learning in the United States. Since the 1960s, the development had been nurtured by the era of environmental awakening, which engendered public awareness of the environment's ecological balance and its degeneration. At about the same time, concern increased about the withdrawal of American youth from the social and political life of their communities. Consequently, an ecological dimension was more strongly included in the intellectual aims of community-based learning from the 1970s onward, represented by environmental education and, respectively, a social dimension since the 1990s, manifested as service-learning.

The aims of both approaches had been linked to the promotion of theoretical values, particularly through improving students' rational problem-solving skills. The aims of community-based learning shifted in an increasingly academic direction through the values sustained by the neo-essentialist school, which relied on the philosophical tradition of realism. This policy emphasized national standardized objectives for learning as well as assessment criteria that made it possible to test the achievement of these objectives. A conservative consensus advocated this alternative, which provided the background for the need to enhance school accountability in order to increase economic productivity in a neoliberal society. The intention was to support individual achievement in society with such values of self-assertion as success, capability, and ambition considered important. Here, economic values were also given priority, as education was intentionally used as a tool to build a society with a competitive edge.

5.1.2 Aims and Values

Environmental education is a multidimensionally directed approach. It geared teaching toward an entirely new radical dimension, as the perspective of environmental awareness was integrated into community-based pedagogy. The aim was to promote student awareness of the environmental problems caused by economic growth and to hone skills in resolving these complex problems. This meant an overall effort to encourage attitudes of environmental responsibility in students by familiarizing them with the basics of ecology. The following expresses the nature of the aims of environmental education:

> Community-based learning remained school-centered during the last decade of the 20th century, when intellectual aims were still being emphasized in accord with the doctrines of a classical liberal society. The goal was thus to train experts for a science- and technology-dominated society. The acts of 1990 and 2000 on environmental education stated that environmental engineering could make possible the development of an advanced scientific and technical education, with the aim of creating effective capabilities in problem solving in the area of complex environmental issues (see National Environmental Education Act, 1990, Sections 5501–5504; John H. Chafee Environmental Education Act of 1999, 2000, Sections 2–5). Based on these documents, this form of education primarily aimed to:
> – develop the skills needed to solve environmental problems;
> – promote awareness of environmental problems and their origins, that is, to acquire an understanding of natural and cultural environments as well as the ability to comprehend the threats environmental problems pose on them; and
> – provide environmental education programs in the classroom and in the environment outside the classroom.

School-based service-learning can be seen as one of the most recent approaches of the school-centered pattern in the United States. This teaching and learning approach intended to integrate community service with academic study for the purpose of enriching learning, teaching civic responsibility, and strengthening communities (National Commission on Service-Learning, 2002, p. 15). The service-learning approach appears to be flexible in relation to other American approaches, as it could be connected to environmental or adventure education programs. These would include attempting to implement such processes as identifying the needs of community members surrounding the school and resolving their problems. Readiness to achieve change and self-direction were new value dimensions, and attaining them was to be a matter of developing students' metacognitive faculties, thus enhancing the resolution of community problems. The following exemplifies the essential features of the aims of school-based service-learning:

School-based service-learning emphasized intellectual aims that paralleled sociopolitical connections in contemporary American society. The federal authorities published several documents giving special importance to the academic studies of this education. Of these, the National and Community Service Act of 1990, amended in 1999, pointed out that service-learning aimed at meeting the needs of the community surrounding the school. A learning process based on active participation was to be integrated into the academic curriculum of the school (Section 101). The report of the National Commission on Service-Learning (2002) concluded that school-based service-learning was to contain community service combined with curriculum-based learning, including the appropriate academic content and standards. The learning process was to proceed through problem solving, utilizing critical, and reflective thinking in each phase of the process (pp. 15, 17). The Serve America Act (2009) endeavored to support high-quality service-learning projects that engage students in meeting community needs with demonstrable results, while enhancing students' academic and civic learning. It also aimed to renew the ethic of civic responsibility and the spirit of community (Sections 111, 1101). This form of school-based service-learning aimed to:

– develop the knowledge, skills, and attitudes necessary to define community needs and to meet and solve community problems;
– enrich learning;
– enhance metacognitive abilities, that is, develop skills pertaining to problem solving, thinking, and cooperating;
– strengthen students and their community, that is, teach students civic responsibility and thus guide them to assist their community as needed; and
– provide service-learning programs in the school and in the community outside the school (National Commission on Service-Learning, 2002, pp. 15–17).

5.1.3   Summing Up

The conceptual features of neo-essentialism can be examined from the perspective of community-based learning by applying Hlebowitsh's (2007) classification. Neo-essentialism interprets the ideal student as having a rational mind that concentrates on the basics of school subjects, while examining natural and environmental phenomena through scientific methods. The ideal subject-matter curriculum embodies programs of both environmental education and school-based service-learning, the experiential and standardized activity-based units of study of which are academic and subject-centered, and their contents are studied in a structured manner in and outside of school. This also directs students toward scientific and technological practices in conjunction with national and international evaluations. The school is expected to have an important role in enhancing economic productivity in a highly competitive global economy. The student is oriented toward an ideal democratic society that depends on essential academic knowledge defined by experts in different fields in the midst of social, economic, political, and environmental instability.

Educational policies based on a businesslike operational culture have also faced opposition. Many academics argued that the No Child Left Behind Act of 2001 (2002) had American teachers emphasizing national standardized school achievement tests and determining performance levels in them (see Section 1001). The following quotation, based on Darling-Hammond's (2007) article, crystalizes this criticism in more detail:

> Critics claim that the law's focus on complicated tallies of multiple-choice-test scores has dumbed down the curriculum, fostered a "drill and kill" approach to teaching, mistakenly labeled successful schools as failing, driven teachers and middle-class students out of public schools and harmed special education students and English-language learners through inappropriate assessments and efforts to push out low-scoring students in order to boost scores. ... At base, the law has misdefined the problem. It assumes that what schools need is more carrots and sticks rather than fundamental changes. (para. 6)

As previously indicated, pedagogical progressivism became popular in some Chinese circles after Dewey lectured there between 1919 and 1921. Similarly, this chapter also discussed how some countries started to oppose the influence of international educational ideas, although they had been in practice for several years. The following discusses these kinds of philosophical turns in two places, China and India.

5.2   Borrowing Educational Ideas in China
5.2.1   Philosophical Views

During the 1980s, China witnessed a growing interest in a socialist modernization process. At that time, China, as a socialist country, was ready to apply ideologies based on classical liberalism and a free-market economy to its social philosophy. This time was also characterized by an effort to harness the educational system to serve the society, the goal of which was to increase economic prosperity by means of a socialist market economy. Despite many challenges, there was a clear desire to support the teaching of technology-oriented subjects connected with industry and economics for the purpose of ensuring a professional workforce. In the same manner, the Chinese sought to increase the number of out-of-school and labor-related activities for students attending schools that provided a general education. In this way, an effort was made to accelerate the developmental path created by the modernization of society. The Chinese socialist administration decided to advance its national modernization with the help of a market economy system and a school system adjusted to it.

The examination of this process, in the context of a socialist market economy, suggests that these different views of the trends in societal development are deeply contradictory, as they are associated with different life-sustaining value objectives and views of human nature held in them. These are related to the fundamental cognitive orientations of world view and outlook on life.

The ultimate change appeared when the Education, Science, Culture, and Public Health Committee officially launched the outline of curriculum reform for basic education in 2001 for the entire general education system, referred to as the *Jichu jiaoyu kecheng gaige gangyao of 2001*. It included a compulsory course on Integrated Practical Activity with such modules as Research Study, Community Service and Social Practice, Labor and Technical Education, and Information Technology Education. The reform aimed at strengthening the connections between curriculum content and life outside the school by focusing on students' own learning experiences. The instruction could take place in real-life learning environments, such as production units, museums, and natural areas, for the purpose of gaining out-of-school experiences. The learning process was to proceed by collecting and processing information, grasping new knowledge, and analyzing and solving problems while communicating and cooperating with each other (Ministry of Education of the P.R.C., 2003, pp. 907–908).

This curriculum reform holds a syncretistic and eclectic view when observed in relation to the orientation of a socialist world view based on the theory of dialectical materialism. This can be interpreted as meaning that these Chinese educational views and ideas may have been borrowed from Deweyan pedagogical methods and the philosophical meanings associated with them. The progressive learner-centered teaching and learning process is based on both an experiential curriculum and an experimental education. It aims at mastery of cooperative learning and working, information acquisition and processing, and problem solving. The Chinese curriculum reform of 2001 could be an attempt to legitimize the adaptation of progressive views to new social needs using the idiom "walking on the old road in new shoes," the practical implementation of which is to use different types of activity and socio-pedagogical teaching methods. As Guo (2012) stated, although the curriculum of 2001 introduced Western pedagogical methods, communist ideologies still remain a dominating feature of Chinese education and philosophy (p. 88).

5.2.2   Aims and Values

In China, the early 1980s witnessed a pedagogical turn in educational policy that was comparable to what had taken place earlier in the United States and India. Since that time, the school-centered pattern of community-based learning can be seen as placing particular emphasis on intellectual aims, especially when considering postrevolutionary labor education, which allowed economic and materialistic values to become prominent. The new industrial policies greatly advanced the significance of science- and technology-related values. The most far-reaching value dimension was related to power, which was intertwined with the desire to achieve a dominant role within the world economic system. This was evident when the Twelfth Party Congress further reinforced the advancement of socialist modernization by making industrial development a priority in 1982 (Hu, 1982, p. 22). Such a shift was due to a firm belief in the need for national economic change, which resulted in requiring the education system to accelerate the country's modernization process. Zhao (1983/1998) contended that the development of education, science, and technology is the key issue when carrying out cultural and economic modernization. In order to accelerate this process, he suggested that all levels of administration must make intellectual development an important priority (p. 2098).

The C.P.C. Central Committee argued in 1985 that massive socialist modernization in China requires workers who are well educated, technically skilled, and professionally competent. Similarly, China needs personnel who are equipped with current knowledge of science, technology, and economic management. All citizens should also be imbued with a pioneering spirit (*Decision of the C.P.C. Central Committee*, 1985/1991, pp. 465–466). The intention was to support modernization in society by prioritizing economic and theoretical values. Such values of self-actualization as effectiveness, capability, and competence were regarded as crucial. The critical purpose of education was to serve the values of the Chinese modernization process, as the following quotation from the education law illustrates: "Education must serve the socialist modernization drive and must be combined with productive labour in order to foster builders and successors for the socialist cause" (State Education Commission of the P.R.C., 1995, Article 5).

The turn of the 21st century saw fundamental educational changes in China. Of these, the C.P.C. Central Committee and the State Council decided in 1999 to focus educational reform on quality education. The official report stated that particular importance should be given to guiding young people in community service and community building. All aspects of society should provide the necessary conditions for schools to carry out productive labor, scientific and technological activities, and other social activities (C.P.C. Central Committee, 2003, p. 287). In 2001, the State Council established important guidelines for basic education reform and development (State Council, 2003). These guidelines emphasized that schools should strengthen cooperation with their communities and make full use of community resources (p. 889).

On the basis of the documents discussed above, postrevolutionary education, following the theory of dialectical materialism, can be observed as attempting to stress the shared goals of intellectual aims and holistic integration of physical, moral-political, and intellectual education. Through these aims, the intention was to provide experts for the world's most advanced socialist society. The intellectual aims of community-based learning were seen to be increasingly connected to promoting economic, theoretical, technological, and power-related values. Even so, the most interesting fact is that, guided by these values, the Education, Science, Culture, and Public Health Committee later in 2001 issued major curriculum reform for basic education. This reform aimed to prioritize the aforementioned complex set of values in order to enhance the modernization of Chinese society. The epoch-making curriculum, *Jichu jiaoyu kecheng gaige gangyao of 2001*, showed that the values needed in a society were to arise from learning situations in which students improved their information-gathering and problem-solving skills while involved in various labor-related technology projects offered inside and outside the school (Ministry of Education of the P.R.C., 2003, pp. 907–908).

This allows for the analysis that within the context of approaching postrevolutionary labor education, the reform of community-based learning at the time constituted the postrevolutionary method of labor and technical education. The intention was to introduce students to labor-related out-of-school activities so they could study in real-life learning environments, such as local production units. The overall social goal was to make China the most modern technology-based socialist society. The following describes the nature of the aims of labor and technical education:

> China moved to a new era of education in the early 1980s. This was important for the purpose of accelerating the country's modernization in accord with the ideas of socialist ideology. The preparation of intellectually capable workers for a modern society characterized by socialism was set as a joint social and educational goal. Such views on the role of education required the postrevolutionary school to train socialist-minded experts, intellectuals who have the latitude to develop socialist

modernization. The *Education Law of the People's Republic of China* (1995) specified that this should be implemented through an all-inclusive development process that encompasses moral, intellectual, and physical aspects (State Education Commission of the P.R.C., 1995, Article 5). Based on the *Jichu jiaoyu kecheng gaige gangyao of 2001*, labor and technical education aims to:
- enhance the awareness of exploration and innovation;
- foster students' sense of social responsibility;
- promote students' awareness and ability to use information technology;
- utilize various learning environments inside and outside the school;
- improve the close relationship between the school and society; and
- strengthen the ideology of collectivism and socialism (Ministry of Education of the P.R.C., 2003, pp. 907–908).

In 2017, the Education, Science, Culture, and Public Health Committee issued the curriculum outline for comprehensive practical activities in primary and secondary schools. This document attempted to integrate production with instruction by applying scientific principles to work processes, particularly in the community's physical and social environments. Similarly, it held the view that the holistic integration of teaching, production, and social practice could provide students with an in-depth understanding of the basic values of socialism (Ministry of Education of the P.R.C., 2017). The following details the features of the aims of integrated practical activities:

> In the late 2010s, the social function of education in China intended to increase the productivity of the national economy, accelerate the developmental path of the modernization of science and technology, advance social and national integration, and maintain social, moral, and political values. Furthermore, many documents on the state of education attempted to reform the aims and practices of education, especially in the direction of active-learning pedagogics such as integrated practical activities. This pedagogical approach was to place primary emphasis on educational aims arising from students' learning activities that are based on applying knowledge to real-life situations. The multidisciplinary, integrated modules Research Study, Social Service, Information Technology, Labor and Technical Activities, and Career Experience formed a framework for teaching and learning (Ministry of Education of the P.R.C., 2017). Based on this document, integrated practical activities could aim to:
> - enhance learning in the use of information technology, that is, to guide students to design and produce digital works;

- encourage innovative ideas concerning accurate explanations for the prevailing problems in the community with the intention of solving these problems;
- develop self-reliance, love of life, and the willingness to actively participate in school and community life; and
- promote a national spirit and cultivate harmonious feelings for the C.P.C.

To consider the outcomes of modernization in China, we can take the view that many people tend to emphasize more economic values in situations where materialism and prosperity become more important than previously. The Chinese interpretation of neoliberalism is characterized by the values of economic modernization, as encapsulated by the idiom "some get rich first, so others can get rich later," which openly ignores the inequality that would result from this policy. Political ideology is a powerful basis for education and, by its very nature, it emphasizes moral-political values in the process of developing a socialist society. The following quotation, based on a speech given by General Secretary Xi Jinping (1953–) (Xi, 2017), illustrates that the C.P.C. is the central body defining educational policy and its values:

> We will draw on core socialist values to guide education, efforts to raise cultural-ethical standards, and the creation, production, and distribution of cultural and intellectual products, and see that all areas of social development are imbued with these values and that they become part of people's thinking and behavior. ... We should fully implement the Party's education policy, foster virtue through education, enhance our students' well-rounded development, promote fairness in education, and nurture a new generation of capable young people who have a good and all-around moral, intellectual, physical, and aesthetical grounding and are well-prepared to join the socialist cause. (pp. 37, 40)

5.2.3 Summing Up

If Hlebowitsh's (2007) classification is used to analyze the specific conceptual features of the postrevolutionism presented in the *Jichu jiaoyu kecheng gaige gangyao of 2001* from the more general perspective of community-based learning, one could conclude that the ideal student is an intellectually capable and technologically literate socialist-minded expert who is being introduced to labor-related, out-of-school activities in the community. The ideal curriculum embodies different forms of community service and labor- and technology-related programs, the units of study of which are based on the application of experiential, active-learning pedagogics in and outside the school. The student is oriented toward an ideal socialist society, the citizens of which work in scientifically and technologically advanced production, thus following the principles of a socialist market economy.

Typical of this social development in China was a domestic policy with economic growth as its goal. Economic and technological reforms were guided by doctrines borrowed from Western countries. Such a reorganization of the economy also required fundamental educational changes. The reforms of 2001 reflected neoliberal educational policies and practices (Tan, 2016, p. 46; Tan & Reyes, 2016, p. 19). Based on her study, Tan (2016) wrote that many Chinese educators refused to acknowledge the new subjective and relativist concepts of knowledge and, instead, they experienced that knowledge exists in the objective world and as external reality. Moreover, educators did not stand behind the alternative evaluation procedures presented in the new curriculum, as they thought that these were not accurate enough compared to assessments based on standardized tests (Tan, 2016, pp. 84, 86).

5.3   Resistance to Educational Change in India

5.3.1   Philosophical Views

India chose an entirely different approach to developing its education system, compared to the Western-minded principles in China outlined above. The neocolonial educational policies and Westernization strategy can be said to have gradually come into conflict in India. Gutek (2006) wrote that a group of Indian educators criticized their country's educational policy, which was based on a modernization theory, because it was considered to represent a neocolonial Westernization strategy. The critics maintained that education and society could be modernized by discovering ways based on traditional Indian cultural values instead of materialistic ones (p. 88). In essence, such a dissimilarity in values and ideals in India at the time could be associated with conceptual systems pertaining to the human experience. These are more broadly linked to the values that guide societal and individual life as well as to beliefs related to the world.

In 1977, Western-minded, neocolonial educational policy in India eventually became inconsistent as the Congress Party's long period in power came to an end and domestic policy taking a more fundamentalist direction. A desire arose to utilize Indian traditional cultural values to find solutions to reform education and society. That same year, the Patel Review Committee published a plan that approached the issue from the standpoint of the Gandhian philosophy of basic education, but with a new, unexpected connection. The Patel report implied that the philosophical background of community-based learning rests on separate, even contradictory, views. The report's conclusions could lead readers to the view that socially useful productive work is based on the ideas of postcolonial work education—ideas that respect the Gandhian philosophy of basic education but that are closely linked to the philosophical views of rationalism (Ministry of Education & Social Welfare, 1977, p. 6). From the perspective of rationalism, knowledge is primarily based on reason instead of experience, whereas the basic ideas of Gandhi's *satyagraha* maintain the importance of harmony between thought and deed. This kind of syncretistic view relied on the idea of promoting economic and technological reforms by breaking away from the colonial tradition and integrating the practices of work education with the national cultural tradition, and its work and customs.

5.3.2 Aims and Values

Since the late 1970s, the intellectual aims of community-based learning in India, the United States, and China became increasingly connected to promoting theoretical values, as shown by the prevailing school-centered patterns of such education. At the time, India again aspired to detach itself from the tradition of a colonial educational philosophy and develop its own national educational thought. In the postcolonial school, in accordance with the Patel Committee report, the government attempted to integrate work with instruction by applying scientific principles to work processes, particularly in the community's physical and social environments (Ministry of Education & Social Welfare, 1977). The familiar neo-traditional education was, arguably, now being developed intentionally in a more academic direction in the spirit of rationalism, while being more effectively embedded in the instruction of natural sciences and other academic subjects. The ultimate contributor to this syncretistic view was the political decision that India needed economic and technological reform if it was to overcome the problems of underdevelopment.

This postcolonial pedagogical approach to socially useful productive work emphasized theoretical values associated with intellectual aims, while trying to develop students' ability to understand the needs of a technology-based society, as well as their problem-solving skills, at various stages of the learning process. Socially desirable values, attitudes, and beliefs were put forward, particularly in social service and community work programs. However, it was most noteworthy that, guided by theoretical values, teachers tried to resolve the problems of the community surrounding the school, as well as those of its members, in order to narrow the gap between education and work, school and community, or between well-off and underprivileged community members. Simultaneously, fostering in students virtues arising from rationalism and an empirical, scientific attitude was seen to be desirable. The following provides detailed characteristics of the aims of socially useful productive work:

> In the late 1970s, many people in India believed that the small number of vocationally productive work experiences for students was incapable of integrating the teaching and learning process. The Patel Committee approached the problem from the standpoint of the Gandhian philosophy of basic education. The Committee report emphasized the social usefulness of productive work offered by schools providing general education. It supported the view that socially useful productive work aimed at understanding the needs of a progressive, technology-based society. The learning process was to proceed by means of problem solving that, at different stages, made use of observation, inquiry, experimentation, and practice (Ministry of Education & Social Welfare, 1977, pp. 11, 13). The following points, as referred to in the 1977 report, illustrate that socially useful productive work may have aimed to:
> - guide the planning, analysis, and detailed preparation of every phase of work;
> - help understand the scientific principles and processes connected with various forms and settings of work in different physical and social environments;
> - lead to the use of modern tools, materials, and techniques;
> - promote equal opportunities for work and learning, that is, to narrow the gap between education and work, to eliminate the separation between school and the rest of the community, and to build a connection between affluent and disadvantaged members of the community; and
> - offer economic and social programs inside and outside the classroom (pp. 11–13).

In the early 2000s and later, postcolonial education was also relevant to Indian education, which had a Hindu nationalist orientation and sought ways to adapt to both neoliberal social change and associated globalization efforts. In essence, the development was linked to the view that economic growth was possible through multinational enterprises and the technological innovations these possessed. Emphasizing economic values allowed for an enhancement in the usefulness of education and an increase in national prosperity. These values were related to the ideas of postcolonial educational aims, the grounds of which primarily supported the needs of a technology-based society.

At the same time, however, official reports continued to emphasize Gandhian educational aims and their value dimensions. Of these, the Committee for

Evolution of the New Education Policy promulgated a report in 2016 arguing that value education must be an integral part of the Indian education system. It stated that the essential purpose of value education is to promote equity, social justice, tolerance, and national integration into society. The core values for a well-established education system are truth (*satya*), righteous conduct (*dharma*), peace (*shanti*), love (*prem*), and nonviolence (*ahimsa*). Teachers, parents, and community leaders should have a crucial role in educating children and young people to respect these values. This should enable students to become responsible citizens of India in a globalized world (Ministry of Human Resource Development, 2016, pp. 169–170). The following clarifies the existing aims of work-experience education and socially useful productive work:

> Indian work-related, community-based learning remained school-centered at the turn of the second millennium, and later, when intellectual aims continued to be emphasized in step with the ideology of social modernization. Using work experiences and socially useful productive work, educational authorities attempted to train experts for a technologically developing industrial society (see, e.g., NCERT, 1986, 1988, 2000, 2005, 2009). Based on existing national curriculum documents, this form of education aimed to:
> - develop the knowledge, skills, and attitudes that are connected to productive work in a modern society;
> - help understand the facts, concepts, terms, and scientific principles linked with different forms and conditions of work;
> - promote abilities needed for productive efficiency, that is, to acquire the skills of recognition, selection, planning, and development required to master both innovative methods and materials, as well as the skills of observation, dexterity, and participation needed for work practice;
> - lead to an understanding of the use of tools and equipment in production and service processes, as well as to comprehend one's own role in productive situations; and
> - offer work education programs inside and outside the school (NCERT, 1986, p. 18; NCERT, 1988, pp. 28–29; NCERT, 2000, pp. 69–71, 95; Central Board of Secondary Education, 2004, pp. 5–6).

5.3.3 Summing Up

The conceptual features of postcolonialism presented in the Patel report (1977) can be examined from the perspective of community-based learning, again applying Hlebowitsh's (2007) classification. Doing so shows that, according to a postcolonial view, the ideal student is an observing, investigating, and experimenting problem-solver being introduced to the activities of vocationally productive work necessary in the community and participating in social service. The ideal curriculum embodies programs of socially useful productive work, with the vocationally productive units of study based on the application of scientific and technological principles and processes in and outside the school. The student is oriented toward an ideal democratic society that aims at secularism and social equality, the citizens of which work in scientifically and technologically advanced production.

This kind of postcolonial work education was also associated with education consistent with Hindu nationalist ideology at the beginning of the 21st century. Then, India attempted to adapt to neoliberal social change and related globalization aspirations. This economic and technological reform was guided by a neoliberal social doctrine that was realized as part of the World Bank's adjustment program (Kumar, 2004, pp. 116, 125). International neoliberal thinking continued to be seamlessly associated with globalization efforts.

Such an international economic order also required educational reforms that would allow it to maximally exploit the neoliberal economy. Efforts were taken to harness the school system to serve the needs of both international competition and increasing economic prosperity in society. Educators were expected to help students cope with the new challenges, threats, and opportunities resulting from this type of globalization process (Boers, 2007, pp. 109–110; Kamat, 2004, pp. 281–282). The new direction gave support to conservative thinking, similar to the United States outlined previously. This meant that the measurable success of the school and human capital growth were both linked to economic productivity and growth.

The following final section summarizes the philosophical background of community-based learning in the United States, India, and China. The different types of philosophical views, as well as their pedagogical and social implications, are compared from the perspective of social change. Moreover, the section briefly reflects on the aims and values of community-based learning in these countries. The essential types and degrees of emphasis placed on educational aims are initially compared in light of the factors in society from the perspective of social trends. Finally, the discussion compares the educational aims and associated value dimensions within a social context.

6   Conclusion

6.1   *Changing Philosophical Views*

This study has shown that educational ideas transfer from one country to another, thus leading to new forms of education. Reformist educational ideas that developed into international systems of thought have been integrated into national educational ideas in the United States, India, and China. However, some of these views eventually became mutually contradictory due to their different value objectives and related conceptions of what it is to be a human. This contradiction has been simultaneously linked to a broader social change connected to variation in the mutual patterns of emphasis and influence between the social, economic, and political factors in society. Even views that have similar philosophical starting points, such as progressive and Marxist educational ideas, can become contradictory when they cross national borders. These phenomena are summarized in this section from the perspective of social changes in these countries.

In the United States, the national philosophical tradition of community-based learning can be understood as being founded on the ideas of progressive education. These ideas rely on the epistemological tradition of pragmatism and a naturalistic system of concepts pertaining to the people expressed by functionalism. In India, the philosophical tradition of community-based learning is related to the ideas of neo-traditional education. These rely on a tradition that insists on truth, as included in the philosophy of *satyagraha* and its Indian cultural historical context. In sharp contrast, the Chinese philosophical tradition of community-based learning is rooted in the ideas of revolutionary education, ideas that rely on the radical social theory of dialectical materialism.

The traditions in question suggest that the ideal educational program in the United States is based on experience gained through problem-centered and goal-directed activities, whereas in India it is based on craft-related work that is connected to traditional production, and in China it is based on productive labor that is supplied by the local commune or production cooperatives. In these approaches, learning is closely integrated into life in the surrounding community. Work is performed in the early industrial production of an ideal American society, in the preindustrial handicraft and agricultural production of an ideal Indian society, or in the agricultural and small-scale industrial production offered by the people's communes of an ideal Chinese society.

Over time, international reform-pedagogical ideas, such as Rousseauean child-centered education or Marxist polytechnical education, have also been adapted to the national philosophical traditions in the countries under study. In India, the intention in the 1960s was to accelerate the extensive modernization process through education. Consequently, there was a tendency to emphasize that the philosophical background of community-based learning rests on the ideas of neocolonial education, this being primarily founded on the theory of dialectical and historical materialism. According to this tradition, the ideal educational program encompasses vocationally productive units of study that are based on applying technology and science within and outside the school in order to work in advanced industrial production in an ideal society.

These three countries have experienced resistance to the application of international educational ideas over the course of time. In the United States, Rousseauean child-centered education and its reform-pedagogical values and ideals were criticized in the 1940s and 1950s at the beginning of the Cold War. As a consequence, a trend appeared promoting the mindset that the philosophical background of community-based learning can be seen as resting upon the ideas of essentialist education, the roots of which are primarily in the philosophical tradition of realism. According to this tradition, the experiential activity-based units of study in the ideal educational program are academic and subject-centered. These units are studied in a structured manner, both in and outside the school, in order to respond to the high-technology demands imposed by an ideal society.

A similar kind of development to that described earlier in the United States took place in the People's Republic of China in the 1950s. Soviet-type economic planning based on centralized industry was criticized and abandoned, and the Chinese took measures to decentralize industry for the purpose of creating rapid industrialization and collectivization in the country. As an integral part of this trend, the administration began to stress the philosophical view that community-based learning was to be built on the ideas of revolutionary education. Such an educational understanding was in keeping with the theory of dialectical materialism. The units of study in an ideal work-study school embodied labor-related programs and ideological campaigns in and outside the school. Agriculture and small-scale industry played an important role in employment creation, resource utilization, and income generation in an ideal society. This implied that the then prevalent Soviet socialism represented different value objectives from those China promoted in its social, economic, and political practice during that time. This social and educational reform was also guided by an independent view of the kind of future that China should have as a socialist country.

In India, a gradual shift in a more conservative direction has been noticed, with materialistic values being replaced by the modernization of education and society by means of traditional Indian cultural values. Thus, the end of the 1970s saw proponents of social modernization beginning to emphasize a philosophical view of community-based learning built on the ideas of postcolonial education. These reflect the Gandhian philosophy of basic education, while also being linked as closely as possible to the philosophical tradition of rationalism. The ideal educational program is implemented in traditional contexts, as scientific principles and processes are applied to the vocationally productive units of study in and outside the school. This is how work can also be carried out in advanced industrial production in an ideal society. Such a trend was linked to an Indian modernization process that was in accord with Hindu nationalist educational ideology.

From the 1980s, the economic and technological reform that China and India attempted to implement was connected to the reorganization of the world economy being undertaken as a component of the World Bank's structural adjustment program. China reformed its planned economic system in the mid-1980s by shifting to the principles of a market economy. Then it introduced significant administrative strategies that required both easing central control and implementing a market-based educational policy. Eventually, it integrated the school system with national economic reforms. In contrast to the Chinese, India reformed its economic policies, the consequence of which was that, since the early 1990s, the new liberal economic policy has dominated its entire social development. The goal was now a classical liberal society with an open economy, which naturally required abandoning a centrally controlled economy (see Prasad, 2008, pp. 4–5). This is partly why educational systems in the three countries have become harnessed to international competition and the pursuit of economic wealth, particularly since the turn of the present century. Educational policies based on a business-focused operational culture have also faced opposition in these countries (see, e.g., Darling-Hammond, 2007, para. 6; Feng, 2006, pp. 138–141; Liu, Cui, & Lu, 2013, pp. 193–195; NCERT, 2005, pp. 9–10, 125).

The new educational policies developed in the context of a neoliberal social doctrine that intertwined global economic, political, and ecological issues. The United States started to develop community-based learning in keeping with a realism-inclined, neo-essentialist educational theory. This also implied the acceptance of robust efforts to standardize the experiential activity-based units of study within the ideal educational program, while these were directed toward more scientific and technological practices to allow for national and international evaluation and comparison.

China, in contrast, began to develop its community-based learning by adopting the view of progressive-minded, postrevolutionary education. This suggested that the ideal curriculum program embodies units of study based on experiential, active-learning pedagogics within and outside the school. In this manner, the present analysis sees the philosophical background of community-based learning as founded on the ideas that reflect both the Western and Chinese philosophies of education. The intention was to educate capable workers for neoliberal industrial production in a socialist society, applying the principles of a market economy. Such views indicate the acceptance of a syncretistic doctrine when seen from the tradition of the dialectical and materialistic theory of knowledge, and the fundamental cognitive orientations of world view and outlook on life, both of which are based on the theory of dialectical materialism.

6.2 *Interplay between Education and Society*

The present chapter shows that the aims of community-based learning have reflected the social thinking of the time in the three countries discussed. Changes can be observed in these aims over time due to variation in the mutual patterns of emphasis and influence between the social, economic, and political factors in society. In terms of the society-centered pattern of community-based learning in the United States, it can be said that the progressive schools, in particular, attempted to stress motor and sociomoral aims within the views of an early industrial society in the 1920s and 1930s, if the focus is on the integration of the components of motor, sociomoral, and intellectual education. The late 1950s saw that the essentialist and neo-essentialist schools started to follow the school-centered pattern of such education and to stress the intellectual aims specific to an advanced science and technology society.

Reciprocally, with regard to the society-centered pattern of community-based learning in India, it is possible to conclude that the neo-traditional schools emphasized the physical and sociomoral aims within the views of a preindustrial agrarian society in the 1940s and 1950s, specifically in terms of integrating physical, sociomoral, and intellectual education. Again, in the mid-1960s, when India was striving for an advanced state of modernization, the neocolonial and postcolonial schools began to stress intellectual aims, consistent with the school-centered pattern of such education.

Compared to the United States and India, in relation to the society-centered pattern of community-based learning in China, we could consider that in the late 1950s the revolutionary schools gave special importance to the moral-political and intellectual aims within the ideas of a revolutionary society, and overridingly to the moral-political aims from the mid-1960s to the mid-1970s, when specifically examining the integration of physical, moral-political, and intellectual education. Since the early 1980s, the postrevolutionary schools have emphasized intellectual aims, following the school-centered pattern of community-based learning appropriate for creating the most modern, technology-based socialist society.

6.3 *The Central Aims within Their Changing Social Context*

This study shows that the aims of community-based learning in the United States, India, and China reflected the social thinking of the time. Based on the analysis of experiential education in the United States, of vocationally productive education in India, and of productive labor education in China, it could be claimed that the essence of these three is integrated with goal-directed subcomponents, whose mutual patterns of emphasis demonstrate changes following social trends.

The present study sees that variation in the mutual patterns of emphasis regarding the subcomponents of the aims is linked to broader social change in these countries, this being further connected with variation in the patterns of emphasis and influence with regard to the social, economic, and political factors in society (cf. Mallinson, 1980, p. 272). In this dialectical process, goal-directed activities within the school institution also affect each of the factors in society, which, in turn, affect each other and the goals of the school institution. The study suggests that development in the countries in question proceeded toward emphasizing school-centered intellectual aims, when community-based learning allows experts to be trained for an advanced society in which mental work is performed in modern production. Simultaneously, this study documented signs of individualism superseding communality, as well as of interdependence superseding self-sufficiency and self-reliance.

6.4   Changing Aims and Values

According to this study, variation in the patterns of emphasis in the subcomponents constituting the aims of community-based learning is connected to the way in which the patterns of emphasis and influence reflecting the social, economic, and political factors of a society are given prominence over the course of time in the three countries studied. Furthermore, this dialectical process has been linked to changes in the different types and degrees of emphasis placed on the central dimensions of social values in these countries. The following briefly analyzes the aims of community-based learning from the viewpoint of these dimensions by applying the theory presented by Schwartz (1992, p. 45) on the universal structure of values.

This study indicates that an examination of American, Indian, and Chinese educational policies reveals the basic features of community-based learning to have become differentiated according to their types and degrees of emphasis under the influence of different social trends. The society-centered pattern gave particular importance to the significance of socioethical and universal values, characterized by community-centeredness, practicality, and the ideal transformation of reality when analyzing community-based learning. These types of value dimensions gained acceptance in the United States in the 1920s and 1930s and in India in the 1940s and 1950s.

After the founding of the People's Republic of China in 1949, basic values held in China remained stable until the late 1970s. The society-centered pattern of community-based learning placed priority on moral-political and mental values in the late 1950s. At that time, work was at the highest level of a value hierarchy. Appreciation for work was intimately intertwined with moral-political values that served to accentuate patriotism and loyalty toward a socialist system and the various virtues it represented. From the mid-1960s to the mid-1970s, the society-centered pattern of such education placed special emphasis on political and ideological values connected to the power-related value dimension.

Reciprocally, consistent with the school-centered pattern of such education, the United States and India made progress in stressing science- and technology-related values. The tendency included an increasingly individualistic and theoretical value orientation and a more realistic adaptation to reality. In both countries, such a shift resulted from a firm belief in the need for national economic and political change. During the Cold War in the 1950s and 1960s, the United States relied on values connected with power and security in accord with the school-centered pattern, resulting in education being harnessed to international competition and the struggle for power. Following such a pattern, and guided by its theoretical values, in the 1960s and 1970s India sought technological reform to overcome problems of underdevelopment. Later, at the beginning of the 21st century, both countries were willing to adapt to neoliberal social change and associated efforts to impose globalization in step with this pattern. Emphasizing economic values in such education, the two countries attempted to increase the utility of both education and national prosperity by giving prominence to individual self-directiveness and maximal efficiency in accordance with the new economic policy.

Starting in the early 1980s, the process of modernization brought enormous changes to the Chinese economy and society. New industrial policies extensively increased the significance of science- and technology-related values in agreement with the school-centered pattern when examining community-based learning. The intention was to support modernization in society by prioritizing economic and theoretical values. Such values of self-actualization as effectiveness, capability, and competence were regarded as crucial. The most far-reaching value included was the power-related value dimension, the intention of which was to achieve a dominant role within a world economic system. In the late 2010s, political ideology was still a strong foundation for education. The tendency included an increasingly moral-political value orientation in the process of building a socialist society. Herdin and Aschauer (2013) noted that although the country's economy was expanding, "it seems that Western values have at most penetrated only the outer cultural surface in China" (p. 20).

Contemporary societies are facing social, economic, and environmental challenges. Global education reform is searching for new models in twenty-first-century pedagogy to meet these problems. The OECD Learning Framework 2030 (2018) presented a set of pedagogical aims and underlying values that can be applied to community-based learning. The following quotation from this document provides a detailed example of value-oriented aims:

> Education has a vital role to play in developing the knowledge, skills, attitudes and values that enable people to contribute to and benefit from an inclusive and sustainable future. Learning to form clear and purposeful goals, work with others with different perspectives, find untapped opportunities and identify multiple solutions to big problems will be essential in the coming years. Education needs to aim to do more than prepare young people for the world of work; it needs to equip students with the skills they need to become active, responsible and engaged citizens. ...
>
> Educators must not only recognise learners' individuality, but also acknowledge the wider set of relationships—with their teachers, peers, families and communities—that influence their learning. A concept underlying the learning framework is "co-agency"—the interactive, mutually supportive relationships that help learners to progress towards their valued goals. In this context, everyone should be considered a learner, not only students but also teachers, school managers, parents and communities. (p. 4)

References

Allport, G. W., Vernon, P. E., & Lindzey, G. (1970). *Study of values* (3rd ed.). Boston, MA: Houghton Mifflin.

Armstrong, D. G., Henson, K. T., & Savage, T. V. (2009). *Teaching today: An introduction to education* (8th ed.). Upper Saddle River, NJ: Pearson.

Ballantine, J. H., & Hammack, F. M. (2009). *The sociology of education: A systematic analysis* (6th ed.). Upper Saddle River, NJ: Pearson.

Berry, T. (1960). Dewey's influence in China. In J. Blewett (Ed.), *John Dewey: His thought and influence* (pp. 199–232). New York, NY: Fordham University Press.

Betti, E. (1962). *Die Hermeneutik als allgemeine Methodik der Geisteswissenschaften* [Hermeneutics as a general method for the humanities]. Tübingen, Germany: Mohr.

Blonskij, P. P. (1973). *Die Arbeitsschule* [Labor school]. Paderborn, Germany: Ferdinand Schöningh. (Original work in Russian published 1919 as *Trudovaya shkola*)

Boers, D. (2007). *History of American education*. New York, NY: Peter Lang.

Botkin, J. W., Elmandjra, M., & Malitza, M. (1979). *No limits to learning: Bridging the human gap. A report to the Club of Rome.* Oxford, U.K.: Pergamon Press.

Brickman, W. (1960). John Dewey in Russia. *Educational Theory, 10*(1), 83–86.

Brookfield, S. (1990). *Adult learners: Adult education and the community.* Milton Keynes, U.K.: Open University Press.

Central Board of Secondary Education. (2004). *Work education in schools.* Delhi, India: Ministry of Human Resource Development, Government of India.

Chen, J. (1990). *Confucius as a teacher: Philosophy of Confucius with special reference to its educational implications.* Beijing, P.R.C.: Foreign Languages Press.

Chen, T. H. (1981). *Chinese education since 1949: Academic and revolutionary models.* New York, NY: Pergamon Press.

Childress, R. B. (1978). Public school environmental education curricula: A national profile. *The Journal of Environmental Education, 9*(3), 2–11.

China. (1975). *Constitution of the People's Republic of China, adopted on January 17, 1975 by the Fourth National People's Congress of the People's Republic of China at its first session.* Beijing, P.R.C.: Foreign Languages Press.

China. (1978). *Constitution of the People's Republic of China, adopted on March 5, 1978 by the Fifth National People's Congress of the People's Republic of China at its first session.* Beijing, P.R.C.: Foreign Languages Press.

Clapp, E. R. (1939). *Community schools in action.* New York, NY: Viking Press.

Collinson, D., Plant, K., & Wilkinson, R. (2000). *Fifty Eastern thinkers.* London, U.K.: Routledge.

C.P.C. Central Committee. (1998). Zhong gong zhong yang guan yu ban nong ban du jiao yu gong zuo de zhi shi [Instructions by the C.P.C. Central Committee on educational work related to partial farming and partial studying]. In D. He (Ed.), *Zhong hua ren min gong he guo zhong yao jiao yu wen xian: 1949–1975* [The important educational documents of the People's Republic of China: 1949–1975] (Vol. 1, pp. 1356–1359). Haikou, P.R.C.: Hainan Publishing.

C.P.C. Central Committee. (2003). Zhong gong zhong yang guo wu yuan guan yu shen hua jiao yu gai ge quan mian tui jin su zhi jiao yu de jue ding [Decisions of the C.P.C. Central Committee and the State Council on deepening education reform and fully advancing quality education]. In D. He (Ed.), *Zhong hua ren min gong he guo zhong yao jiao yu wen xian: 1998–2002* [The important educational documents of the People's Republic of China: 1998–2002] (Vol. 4, pp. 286–290). Haikou, P.R.C.: Hainan Publishing.

Cremin, L. A. (1968). *The transformation of the school: Progressivism in American education, 1876–1957.* New York, NY: Knopf.

Cremin, L. A. (1988). *American education: The metropolitan experience 1876–1980.* New York, NY: Harper & Row.

Cuban, L. (1992). Curriculum stability and change. In P. W. Jackson (Ed.), *Handbook of research on curriculum* (pp. 216–247). New York, NY: Macmillan.

Danilchenko, M. G. (1993). Pavel Petrovich Blonsky (1884–1941). *Prospects: Quarterly Review of Comparative Education, 23*(1–2), 113–124.

Danner, H. (1979). *Methoden geisteswissenschaftlicher Pädagogik: Einführung in Hermeneutik, Phänomenologie und Dialektik* [Methods of humanistic pedagogy: Introduction to hermeneutics, phenomenology, and dialectic]. München, Germany: Reinhardt.

Darling, J., & Nordenbo, S. E. (2005). Progressivism. In N. Blake, P. Smeyers, R. Smith, & P. Standish (Eds.), *The Blackwell guide to the philosophy of education* (pp. 288–308). Malden, MA: Blackwell.

Darling-Hammond, L. (2007, May 21). Evaluating "no child left behind": The problems and promises of Bush's education policy. *The Nation.* Retrieved from https://www.thenation.com/article/evaluating-no-child-left-behind/

Datta, D. M. (1953). *The philosophy of Mahatma Gandhi.* Madison, WI: University of Wisconsin Press.

Decision of the Central Committee of the Chinese Communist Party concerning the Great Proletarian Cultural Revolution. (1966, August 12). *Peking Review, 9*(33), pp. 6–11.

Decision of the C.P.C. Central Committee on the reform of the educational structure. (1991). In *Major documents of the People's Republic of China: December 1978–November 1989* (pp. 465–484). Beijing, P.R.C.: Foreign Languages Press. (Original work published 1985 in *Xin hua*)

Department of Foreign Affairs of the State Education Commission of the P.R.C. (1994). *Suggestion of the State Council on the implementation of the outline for reform and development of education in China.* Beijing, P.R.C.: Author.

Dewey, J. (1929). *Impressions of Soviet Russia and the revolutionary world: Mexico – China – Turkey.* New York, NY: New Republic.

Dewey, J. (1933). *How we think: A restatement of the relation of reflective thinking to the educative process* (Rev. ed.). Boston, MA: Heath.

Dewey, J. (1940). My pedagogic creed. In J. Dewey & J. Ratner (Eds.), *Education today* (pp. 3–17). New York, NY: Putnam. (Original work published in 1897)

Dewey, J. (1950a). *The child and the curriculum.* Chicago, IL: University of Chicago Press. (Original work published in 1902)

Dewey, J. (1950b). *Democracy and education: An introduction to the philosophy of education.* New York, NY: Macmillan. (Original work published in 1916)

Dewey, J. (1951). *Experience and education.* New York, NY: Macmillan. (Original work published in 1938)

Dewey, J. (1952). Introduction. In E. R. Clapp (Ed.), *The use of resources in education* (pp. vii–xi). New York, NY: Harper.

Dewey, J. (1953). *The school and society.* Chicago, IL: University of Chicago Press. (Original work published in 1899)

Dewey, J. (1960). From absolutism to experimentalism. In R. J. Bernstein (Ed.), *On experience, nature, and freedom* (pp. 3–18). Indianapolis, IN: Bobbs-Merrill. (Original work published 1930 in *Contemporary American philosophy*, Vol. 2)

Dewey, J. (1970). Matthew Arnold and Robert Browning. In J. Ratner (Ed.), *Characters and events: Popular essays in social and political philosophy by John Dewey* (Vol. 1, pp. 3–17). New York, NY: Octagon Books. (Original work published 1891 as "Poetry and philosophy" in *The Andover Review*)

Dewey, J., & Dewey, E. (1915). *Schools of to-morrow*. London, U.K.: Dent.

Dewey, J. M. (Ed.). (1971). Biography of John Dewey. In P. A. Schilpp (Ed.), *The philosophy of John Dewey* (2nd ed., pp. 3–45). La Salle, IL: Open Court. (Original work published in 1939)

Doniger, W. (2010). *The Hindus: An alternative history*. Oxford, U.K.: Oxford University Press.

Durkheim, E. (1956). *Education and sociology* (S. D. Fox, Trans.). Glencoe, IL: Free Press. (Original work in French published 1922 as *Éducation et sociologie*)

Durkheim, E. (1977). *The evolution of educational thought: Lectures on the formation and development of secondary education in France* (P. Collins, Trans.). London, U.K.: Routledge & Kegan Paul. (Original work in French published 1938 as *L'evolution pédagogique en France*)

Education Department. (1961). *Report of the Syllabus Committee for Post Basic Education*. Ahmedabad, India: Government of Gujarat.

Elementary and Secondary Education Act of 1965, 20 U.S.C. § 301, 303. (1965).

Engels, F. (1926). Friedrich Engels' preface to the third German edition. In K. Marx (Ed.), *The eighteenth Brumaire of Louis Bonaparte* (E. Paul & C. Paul, Trans., pp. 21–22). London, U.K.: Allen & Unwin. (Original work in German published 1852 as *Der achtzehnte Brumaire des Louis Bonaparte*)

Environmental Education Act, 20 U.S.C. § 2–3. (1970).

Fang, Y. (1979). A report on the state of science and education delivered by comrade Fang Yi at the Seventh Enlarged Meeting of the Standing Committee of the Fourth National Committee of the Chinese People's Political Consultative Conference. *Chinese Education*, 12(1–2), 33–47.

Feng, D. (2006). China's recent curriculum reform: Progress and problems. *Planning and Changing*, 37(1–2), 131–144.

Fischer, L. (1986). *The life of Mahatma Gandhi*. London, U.K.: Grafton Books. (Original work published in 1951)

Fitzpatrick, C. N. (1968). *Philosophy and goals for outdoor education* (Doctoral dissertation). Colorado State College, Greeley, CO. Retrieved from ProQuest Dissertations and Theses database. (UMI No. 69-2839)

Freire, P. (1970). *Pedagogy of the oppressed*. New York, NY: Continuum.

Fullan, M. G. (1993). *Change forces: Probing the depths of educational reform*. London, U.K.: Falmer Press.

Gandhi, M. K. (1947). *India of my dreams* (K. Prabhu, Ed.). Bombay, India: Hind Kitabs.

Gandhi, M. K. (1948a). Discipline for the realization of truth. In N. K. Bose (Ed.), *Selections from Gandhi* (pp. 13–19). Ahmedabad, India: Navajivan.

Gandhi, M. K. (1948b). Fundamental beliefs and ideas. In N. K. Bose, *Selections from Gandhi* (pp. 20–47). Ahmedabad, India: Navajivan.

Gandhi, M. K. (1948c). Industrial organization: Old and new. In N. K. Bose (Ed.), *Selections from Gandhi* (pp. 64–74). Ahmedabad, India: Navajivan.

Gandhi, M. K. (1948d). On education. In N. K. Bose, *Selections from Gandhi* (pp. 251–267). Ahmedabad, India: Navajivan.

Gandhi, M. K. (1950). Questions before educational conference. In *Educational reconstruction: A collection of Gandhiji's articles on the Wardha scheme along with a summary of the proceedings of the All India National Educational Conference held at Wardha, 1937* (5th ed., pp. 29–32). Sevagram, India: Hindustani Talimi Sangh. (Original work published 1937 in *Harijan*)

Gandhi, M. K. (1958). *Sarvodaya: The welfare of all* (B. Kumarappa, Ed.). Ahmedabad, India: Navajivan.

Gandhi, M. K. (1959). *An autobiography or the story of my experiments with truth* (2nd ed., M. Desai, Trans.). Ahmedabad, India: Navajivan. (Original work in Gujarati published 1927)

Gandhi, M. K. (1961). *Satyagraha in South Africa* (2nd ed., V. G. Desai, Trans.). Ahmedabad, India: Navajivan. (Original work in Gujarati published 1928)

Gandhi, M. K. (1962a). *Basic education* (B. Kumarappa, Ed.). Ahmedabad, India: Navajivan. (Original work published in 1951)

Gandhi, M. K. (1962b). *True education*. Ahmedabad, India: Navajivan.

Gandhi, M. K. (1963). *Towards new education* (B. Kumarappa, Ed.). Ahmedabad, India: Navajivan. (Original work published in 1953)

Gandhi, M. K. (1991). Tolstoy on non-retaliation. In R. Iyer (Ed.), *The essential writings of Mahatma Gandhi* (pp. 73–75). Delhi, India: Oxford University Press. (Original work in Gujarati published 1909 in *Indian Opinion*)

Garrison, J., & Neiman, A. (2005). Pragmatism and education. In N. Blake, P. Smeyers, R. Smith, & P. Standish (Eds.), *The Blackwell guide to the philosophy of education* (pp. 21–37). Malden, MA: Blackwell.

Gibson, H. W. (1939). *Camp management: A manual of organized camping* (Rev. ed.). New York, NY: Greenberg.

Gopal, S. (1975). *Jawaharlal Nehru: A biography, 1889–1947* (Vol. 1). London, U.K.: Jonathan Cape.

Grasso, J., Corrin, J., & Kort, M. (2004). *Modernization and revolution in China: From the Opium Wars to world power* (3rd ed.). Armonk, NY: Sharpe.

Guo, L. (2012). New curriculum reform in China and its impact on teachers. *Canadian and International Education, 41*(2), 87–104.

Gutek, G. L. (1997). *Philosophical and ideological perspectives on education* (2nd ed.). Boston, MA: Allyn & Bacon.

Gutek, G. L. (2000). *American education 1945–2000: A history and commentary*. Prospect Heights, IL: Waveland Press.

Gutek, G. L. (2006). *American education in a global society: International and comparative perspectives* (2nd ed.). Long Grove, IL: Waveland Press.

Gutek, G. L. (2009). *New perspectives on philosophy and education*. Columbus, OH: Pearson.

Gutek, G. L. (2011). *Historical and philosophical foundations of education: A biographical introduction* (5th ed.). Boston, MA: Pearson.

Hammerman, D. R., Hammerman, W. M., & Hammerman, E. L. (2001). *Teaching in the outdoors* (5th ed.). Danville, IL: Interstate.

Hawkins, J. N. (2007). The intractable dominant educational paradigm. In P. D. Hershock, M. Mason, & J. N. Hawkins (Eds.), *Changing education: Leadership, innovation and development in a globalizing Asia Pacific* (pp. 137–162). Hong Kong, P.R.C.: Comparative Education Research Centre, University of Hong Kong.

Herdin, T., & Aschauer, W. (2013). Values changes in transforming China. *An International Journal of Pure Communication Inquiry, 1*(2), 1–22.

Hickman, L. A. (1996). Dewey, John (1859–1952). In J. J. Chambliss (Ed.), *Philosophy of education: An encyclopedia* (pp. 146–153). New York, NY: Garland.

Hlebowitsh, P. (2007). *Foundations of American education*. Dubuque, IA: Kendall Hunt.

Holmes, L. E. (1991). *The Kremlin and the schoolhouse: Reforming education in Soviet Russia, 1917–1931*. Bloomington, IN: Indiana University Press.

Hopkins, D. (2013). Exploding the myths of school reform. *School Leadership & Management, 33*(4), 304–321.

Hu, Y. (1982). Create a new situation in all fields of socialist modernization: Report to the Twelfth National Congress of Communist Party of China. In *The Twelfth National Congress of the C.P.C.* (pp. 7–85). Beijing, P.R.C.: Foreign Languages Press.

Hua, K. (1977). Political report to the Eleventh National Congress of the Communist Party of China. In *The Eleventh National Congress of the Communist Party of China* (pp. 1–111). Beijing, P.R.C.: Foreign Languages Press.

Hug, J. W., & Wilson, P. J. (1965). *Curriculum enrichment outdoors*. Evanston, IL: Harper & Row.

Hungerford, H., Peyton, R. B., & Wilke, R. J. (1980). Goals for curriculum development in environmental education. *The Journal of Environmental Education, 11*(3), 42–47.

Illich, I. (1970). *Deschooling society*. London, U.K.: Boyars.

Jackim, O. (2016). Anton Semyonovich Makarenko: A few Western myths debunked. In J. M. Paraskeva (Ed.), *The curriculum: Whose internalization?* (pp. 169–180). New York, NY: Peter Lang.

James, W. (1891). *The principles of psychology* (Vol. 2). London, U.K.: Macmillan.

James, W. (1963). Pragmatism. In *Pragmatism and other essays* (pp. 1–132). New York, NY: Washington Square Press. (Original work published 1907 as *Pragmatism: A new name for some old ways of thinking*)

James, W. (1983). Talks to teachers on psychology and to students on some of life's ideals. In F. H. Burkhardt, F. Bowers, & I. K. Skrupskelis (Eds.), *The works of William James* (pp. 1–167). Cambridge, MA: Harvard University Press. (Original work published 1899 as *Talks to students on some of life's ideals*)

John H. Chafee Environmental Education Act of 1999, 20 U.S.C. § 2–5. (2000).

Kamat, S. (2004). Postcolonial aporias, or what does fundamentalism have to do with globalization? The contradictory consequences of education reform in India. *Comparative Education, 40*(2), 267–287.

Keenan, B. (1977). *The Dewey experiment in China: Educational reform and political power in the early Republic.* Cambridge, MA: Council on East Asian Studies, Harvard University.

Kilpatrick, W. H. (1922). *The project method: The use of the purposeful act in the educative process* (Teachers College Bulletin, Tenth Series, No. 3). New York, NY: Teachers College, Columbia University.

Kilpatrick, W. H. (1940). *Group education for a democracy.* New York, NY: Association Press.

Kilpatrick, W. H. (1949). *Modern education: Its proper work.* New York, NY: Hinds, Hayden, & Eldredge.

Kimonen, E. (2015). *Education and society in comparative context: The essence of outdoor-oriented education in the USA and India.* Rotterdam, The Netherlands: Sense Publishers.

Knight, N. (2015). Introduction: Soviet Marxism and the development of Mao Zedong's philosophical thought. In N. Knight (Ed.), *Mao Zedong on dialectical materialism: Writings on philosophy, 1937* (pp. 3–83). London, U.K.: Routledge.

Krupskaya, N. K. (1957a). The difference between professional and polytechnical education. In N. K. Krupskaya (Ed.), *On education: Selected articles and speeches* (G. P. Ivanov-Mumjiev, Trans., pp. 188–191). Moscow, U.S.S.R.: Foreign Languages Publishing. (Original work in Russian published 1930 in *O Nashih Detjah*)

Krupskaya, N. K. (1957b). The young pioneer movement as a pedagogical problem. In N. K. Krupskaya (Ed.), *On education: Selected articles and speeches* (G. P. Ivanov-Mumjiev, Trans., pp. 118–122). Moscow, U.S.S.R.: Foreign Languages Publishing. (Original work in Russian published 1927 in *Uchitelskaya Gazeta*)

Krupskaja, N. K. (1965). Yhteiskunnallinen kasvatus [Social education]. In N. Krupskaja (Ed.), *Kasvatuksesta: Valittuja kirjoituksia ja puheita* [On education: Selected articles and speeches] (O. Kukkonen, Trans., pp. 145–154). Moskova, U.S.S.R.: Edistys. (Original work in Russian published 1922 in *Na Putyakh k Novoi Shkole*) [in Finnish]

Kumar, K. (2004). Educational quality and the new economic regime. In A. Vaugier-Chatterjee (Ed.), *Education and democracy in India* (pp. 113–127). New Delhi, India: Manohar.

Kumar, K. (2005). *Political agenda of education: A study of colonialist and nationalist ideas* (2nd ed.). New Delhi, India: Sage.

Lenin, V. I. (2012). The tasks of the youth leagues: Speech delivered at the Third All-Russia Congress of the Russian Young Communist League. In *V. I. Lenin: Collected works* (J. Katzer, Ed., Vol. 31, pp. 283–298). Moscow, U.S.S.R.: Progress. (Original work in Russian published 1920 in *Pravda*)

Lenin, V. I. (2013). On polytechnical education: Notes on theses by Nadezhda Konstantinovna. In *V. I. Lenin: Collected works* (A. Rothsein, Trans., Y. Sdobnikov, Ed., Vol. 36, pp. 532–534). Moscow, U.S.S.R.: Progress. (Original work in Russian published 1929 in *Na Putyakh k Novoi Shkole*)

Liu, J. (2006). *An introduction to Chinese philosophy: From ancient philosophy to Chinese Buddhism*. Malden, MA: Blackwell.

Liu, S., Cui, R., & Lu, G. (2013). The challenges of basic education curriculum change in rural primary schools in West China. In E. Kimonen & R. Nevalainen (Eds.), *Transforming teachers' work globally: In search of a better way for schools and their teachers* (pp. 175–198). Rotterdam, The Netherlands: Sense Publishers.

Löfstedt, J.-I. (1980). *Chinese educational policy: Changes and contradictions 1949–79*. Stockholm, Sweden: Almqvist & Wiksell.

Lu, D. (1998). Jiao yu bi xu yu sheng chan lao dong xiang jie he [Education must be combined with production and labor]. In D. He (Ed.), *Zhong hua ren min gong he guo zhong yao jiao yu wen xian: 1949–1975* [The important educational documents of the People's Republic of China: 1949–1975] (Vol. 1, pp. 852–857). Haikou, P.R.C.: Hainan Publishing. (Original work published 1958 in *Hong qi*)

Makarenko, A. (1965). *Problems of Soviet school education* (O. Shartse, Trans.). Moscow, U.S.S.R.: Progress. (Original work in Russian published 1949 as *Problemy shkolnogo sovetskogo vospitaniya*)

Mallinson, V. (1980). *An introduction to the study of comparative education* (4th ed.). London, U.K.: Heinemann.

Mao, T. (1965). The role of the Chinese Communist Party in the National War. In *Selected works of Mao Tse-tung* (Vol. 2, pp. 195–211). Oxford, U.K.: Pergamon Press. (Original work in Chinese published 1938)

Mao, T. (1966a). On contradiction. In *Mao Tse-tung: Four essays on philosophy* (pp. 23–78). Beijing, P.R.C.: Foreign Languages Press. (Original work in Chinese published 1937)

Mao, T. (1966b). On practice: On the relation between knowledge and practice, between knowing and doing. In *Mao Tse-tung: Four essays on philosophy* (pp. 1–22). Beijing, P.R.C.: Foreign Languages Press. (Original work in Chinese published 1937)

Mao, T. (1975). A talk to the editorial staff of Shansi-Suiyuan Daily. In *Selected works of Mao Tse-tung* (Vol. 4, pp. 241–245). Oxford, U.K.: Pergamon Press. (Original work in Chinese published 1948)

Mao, T. (1977). On the ten major relationships. In *Selected works of Mao Tse-tung* (Vol. 5, pp. 284–307). Oxford, U.K.: Pergamon Press. (Original work in Chinese published 1956)

Mao, Z. (1977). On the correct handling of contradictions among the people. In *Selected works of Mao Tse-tung* (Vol. 5, pp. 384–421). Oxford, U.K.: Pergamon Press. (Original work published 1957 in *Ren min ri bao*)

Mao, Z. (1998a). Gong zuo fang fa (cao an) (jie lu) [The work method (draft) (extract)]. In D. He (Ed.), *Zhong hua ren min gong he guo zhong yao jiao yu wen xian: 1949–1975* [The important educational documents of the People's Republic of China: 1949–1975] (Vol. 1, pp. 796–797). Haikou, P.R.C.: Hainan Publishing. (Original work published in 1991)

Mao, Z. (1998b). Zai hang zhou hui yi shang de jiang hua [Speech at the Hangzhou meeting]. In D. He (Ed.), *Zhong hua ren min gong he guo zhong yao jiao yu wen xian: 1949–1975* [The important educational documents of the People's Republic of China: 1949–1975] (Vol. 1, p. 1383). Haikou, P.R.C.: Hainan Publishing. (Original work published in 1967)

Marx, K. (1968). Instruktionen für die Delegierten des Provisorischen Zentralrats zu den einzelnen Fragen [Instructions for the Delegates of the Provisional General Council concerning the specific questions]. In K. Marx & F. Engels (Eds.), *Werke* (Vol. 16, pp. 190–199). Berlin, Germany: Dietz. (Original work in German published 1866 in *Der Vorbote*)

Marx, K. (1974). *Pääoma: Kansantaloustieteen arvostelua. Pääoman tuotantoprosessi* [Capital: A critique of political economy. The process of production of capital] (O. V. Louhivuori, T. Lehén, & M. Ryömä, Trans., Vol. 1). Moskova, U.S.S.R.: Edistys. (Original work in German published 1867 as *Das Kapital: Kritik der politischen Oekonomie. Der Produktionsprocess des Kapitals*) [in Finnish]

Marx, K. (1978). Taloudellis-filosofiset käsikirjoitukset 1844 [Economic and philosophic manuscripts of 1844] (A. Tiusanen, Trans.). In K. Marx & F. Engels (Eds.), *Valitut teokset* (Vol. 1, pp. 171–311). Moskova, U.S.S.R.: Edistys. (Original work in German published 1927 as *Marx–Engels Gesamtausgabe*) [in Finnish]

Mayhew, K. C., & Edwards, A. C. (1966). *The Dewey school: The Laboratory School of the University of Chicago 1896–1903*. New York, NY: Atherton Press. (Original work published in 1936)

Mchitarjan, I. (2000). John Dewey and the development of education in Russia before 1930: Report on a forgotten reception. *Studies in Philosophy and Education, 19*(1–2), 109–131.

Ministry of Education. (1956). *Syllabus for basic schools*. Delhi, India: Government of India.

Ministry of Education. (1966). *Report of the Education Commission 1964–66: Education and national development* (5th ed.). Delhi, India: Government of India.

Ministry of Education and Scientific Research. (1958). *Handbook for teachers of basic schools*. Delhi, India: Government of India.

Ministry of Education of the C.P.G. (1998). Jia qiang si xiang jiao yu, lao dong jiao yu, ti chang qun zhong ban xue, qin jian ban xue [Strengthen ideological education, work education, and recommend the masses run schools and, furthermore, do it economically]. In D. He (Ed.), *Zhong hua ren min gong he guo zhong yao jiao yu wen xian: 1949–1975* [The important educational documents of the People's Republic of China: 1949–1975] (Vol. 1, pp. 799–802). Haikou, P.R.C.: Hainan Publishing.

Ministry of Education of the P.R.C. (2003). Ji chu jiao yu ke cheng gai ge gang yao (shi xing) [Outline of the curriculum reform for basic education (trial)]. In D. He (Ed.), *Zhong hua ren min gong he guo zhong yao jiao yu wen xian: 1998–2002* [The important educational documents of the People's Republic of China: 1998–2002] (Vol. 4, pp. 907–909). Haikou, P.R.C.: Hainan Publishing. (Original work published 2001 in *Ren min jiao yu*)

Ministry of Education of the P.R.C. (2017). Jiao yu bu guan yu yin fa "zhong xiao xue zong he shi jian huo dong ke cheng zhi dao gang yao" de tong zhi [Notice of the Ministry of Education on printing and distributing the outline of the curriculum for comprehensive practical activities in primary and secondary schools]. Retrieved from http://www.moe.gov.cn/srcsite/A26/s8001/201710/t20171017_316616.html

Ministry of Education & Social Welfare. (1977). *Report of the Review Committee on the curriculum for the ten-year school: Including syllabus frames*. New Delhi, India: Government of India.

Ministry of Human Resource Development. (2016). *National policy on education 2016: Report of the Committee for Evolution of the New Education Policy*. New Delhi, India: Government of India.

Moise, E. E. (1986). *Modern China: A history*. London, U.K.: Longman.

National and Community Service Act of 1990 (as amended through P.L. 106–170), 20 U.S.C. § 101. (1999).

National Commission on Service-Learning. (2002). *Learning in deed: The power of service-learning for American schools*. The report from the National Commission on Service-Learning. Newton, MA: Education Development Center.

National Council of Educational Research and Training. (1975). *The curriculum for the ten-year school: A framework*. New Delhi, India: Author.

National Council of Educational Research and Training. (1986). *National curriculum for primary and secondary education: A framework*. New Delhi, India: Author.

National Council of Educational Research and Training. (1988). *National curriculum for elementary and secondary education: A framework*. New Delhi, India: Author.

National Council of Educational Research and Training. (2000). *National curriculum framework for school education*. New Delhi, India: Author.

National Council of Educational Research and Training. (2005). *National curriculum framework 2005*. New Delhi, India: Author.

National Council of Educational Research and Training. (2009). *National curriculum framework 2005: Abridged*. New Delhi, India: Author.

National Defense Education Act of 1958, 20 U.S.C. § 101. (1958).

National Environmental Education Act, 20 U.S.C. § 5501–5504. (1990).

No Child Left Behind Act of 2001, 20 U.S.C. § 1001. (2002).

OECD Learning Framework 2030. (2018). *The future of education and skills: Education 2030. The future we want*. Paris, France: OECD.

Office of Education. (1970). *Environmental education: Education that cannot wait*. Washington, D.C.: U.S. Department of Health, Education, and Welfare.

Olsson, O. (1926). *Demokratiens skolväsen: Iakttagelser i amerikanska skolor* [The school system of democracy: Observations in American schools]. Stockholm, Sweden: Norstedt & Söner.

Pantsov, A. V., with Levine, S. I. (2012). *Mao: The real story*. New York, NY: Simon & Schuster.

Parker, F. W. (1894). *Talks on pedagogics: An outline of the theory of concentration*. New York, NY: Kellogg.

Parkhurst, H. (1930). *Education on the Dalton Plan*. London, U.K.: Bell.

Pearson, W. W. (1917). *Shantiniketan: The Bolpur school of Rabindranath Tagore*. London, U.K.: Macmillan.

Peirce, C. S. (1960a). The fixation of belief. In C. Hartshorne & P. Weiss (Eds.), *Collected papers of Charles Sanders Peirce: Pragmatism and pragmaticism* (Vol. 5, pp. 223–247). Cambridge, MA: Harvard University Press. (Original work published 1877 in *Popular Science Monthly*)

Peirce, C. S. (1960b). How to make our ideas clear. In C. Hartshorne & P. Weiss (Eds.), *Collected papers of Charles Sanders Peirce: Pragmatism and pragmaticism* (Vol. 5, pp. 248–271). Cambridge, MA: Harvard University Press. (Original work published 1878 in *Popular Science Monthly*)

Peirce, C. S. (1960c). Questions concerning certain faculties claimed for man. In C. Hartshorne & P. Weiss (Eds.), *Collected papers of Charles Sanders Peirce: Pragmatism and pragmaticism* (Vol. 5, pp. 135–155). Cambridge, MA: Harvard University Press. (Original work published 1868 in *Journal of Speculative Philosophy*)

Peirce, C. S. (1965). Phenomenology. In C. Hartshorne & P. Weiss (Eds.), *Collected papers of Charles Sanders Peirce: Principles of philosophy* (Vol. 1, pp. 139–308). Cambridge, MA: Harvard University Press. (Original work published in 1931)

Phillips, D. (2004). Toward a theory of policy attraction in education. In G. Steiner-Khamsi (Ed.), *The global politics of educational borrowing and lending* (pp. 54–67). New York, NY: Teachers College Press.

Prasad, C. S. (2008). *Economic survey of India: 1947–48 to 2008–09*. New Delhi, India: New Century.

Prast, H. A., & Viegut, D. J. (2015). *Community-based learning: Awakening the mission of public schools*. Thousand Oaks, CA: Corwin Press.

Price, R. F. (2005). *Education in modern China*. London, U.K.: Routledge. (Original work published in 1970)

Principles for future economic construction. (1991). In *Major documents of the People's Republic of China: December 1978–November 1989* (pp. 207–245). Beijing, P.R.C.: Foreign Languages Press. (Original work published 1981 in *Beijing Review*)

Quotations from Chairman Mao Tse-tung. (1964). Beijing, P.R.C.: Foreign Languages Press.

Raju, P. T. (1992). *The philosophical traditions of India*. Delhi, India: Motilal Banarsidass.

Ravitch, D. (1983). *The troubled crusade: American education, 1945–1980*. New York, NY: Basic Books.

Rizvi, F. (2007). Rethinking educational aims in an era of globalization. In P. D. Hershock, M. Mason, & J. N. Hawkins (Eds.), *Changing education: Leadership, innovation and development in a globalizing Asia Pacific* (pp. 63–91). Hong Kong, P.R.C.: Comparative Education Research Centre, University of Hong Kong.

Schwartz, S. H. (1992). Universals in the content and structure of values: Theoretical advances and empirical tests in 20 countries. In M. P. Zanna (Ed.), *Advances in experimental social psychology* (Vol. 25, pp. 1–65). San Diego, CA: Academic Press.

Serve America Act, 20 U.S.C. § 111, 1101. (2009).

Sharp, L. B. (1935). The public school camp. *The Camping Magazine, 7*(3), 25–29.

Sharp, L. B. (1941). Growth of the modern camping movement. *The Commonhealth, 28*(1), 4–6.

Sharp, L. B. (1943). Outside the classroom. *The Educational Forum, 7*(4), 361–368.

Sharp, L. B. (1946). Basic planning for camping and outdoor education. In *The American school and university: Yearbook* (pp. 192–198). New York, NY: Buttenheim.

Sharp, L. B. (1947). Camping and outdoor education. *The Bulletin of the National Association of Secondary-School Principals, 31*(146), 32–38.

Sharp, L. B. (1952). What is outdoor education? *The School Executive, 71*, 19–22.

Sharp, L. B., & Osborne, E. G. (1940). Schools and camping: A review of recent developments. *Progressive Education, 17*(4), 236–241.

Shulman, L. S. (2004). *The wisdom of practice: Essays on teaching, learning, and learning to teach* (S. M. Wilson, Ed.). San Francisco, CA: Jossey-Bass.

Skatkin, M. S., & Tsov'janov, G. S. (1994). Nadezhda Konstantinovna Krupskaya (1869–1939). *Prospects: Thinkers on Education, 3*(89–90), 49–60.

Smith, J. W. (1956). *Outdoor education*. Washington, DC: American Association for Health, Physical Education, and Recreation.

Snyder, J., Bolin, F., & Zumwalt, K. (1992). Curriculum implementation. In P. W. Jackson (Ed.), *Handbook of research on curriculum* (pp. 402–435). New York, NY: Macmillan.

Spencer, H. (1861). *Education: Intellectual, moral, and physical*. London, U.K.: Williams and Norgate.

Spranger, E. (1966). *Types of men: The psychology and ethics of personality* (P. J. W. Pigors, Trans.). New York, NY: Johnson Reprint. (Original work in German published 1914 as *Lebensformen*)

Stapp, W. B. (1969). The concept of environmental education. *The Journal of Environmental Education, 1*(1), 30–31.

State Council. (1984). *The Sixth Five-Year Plan of the People's Republic of China for economic and social development 1981–1985*. Beijing, P.R.C.: Foreign Languages Press.

State Council. (1998a). Guo wu yuan pi zhuan jiao yu bu guan yu yi jiu qi qi nian gao deng xue xiao zhao sheng gong zuo de yi jian [The State Council's communication of the opinions of the Ministry of Education of the Central People's Government on student enrollment in higher education institutions in 1977]. In D. He (Ed.), *Zhong hua ren min gong he guo zhong yao jiao yu wen xian: 1976–1990* [The important educational documents of the People's Republic of China: 1976–1990] (Vol. 2, pp. 1579–1582). Haikou, P.R.C.: Hainan Publishing.

State Council. (1998b). Zheng wu yuan guan yu gai ge xue zhi de jue ding [State Council's decision about reforming the school system]. In D. He (Ed.), *Zhong hua ren min gong he guo zhong yao jiao yu wen xian: 1949–1975* [The important educational documents of the People's Republic of China: 1949–1975] (Vol. 1, pp. 105–107). Haikou, P.R.C.: Hainan Publishing.

State Council. (2003). Guo wu yuan guan yu ji chu jiao yu gai ge yu fa zhan de jue ding [The State Council's decision on basic education reform and development]. In D. He (Ed.), *Zhong hua ren min gong he guo zhong yao jiao yu wen xian: 1998–2002* [The important educational documents of the People's Republic of China: 1998–2002] (Vol. 4, pp. 887–891). Haikou, P.R.C.: Hainan Publishing. (Original work published in *Guo wu yuan wen jian*)

State Education Commission of the P.R.C. (1995). *Education law of the People's Republic of China*. (1995). Beijing, P.R.C.: Author.

State Planning Commission of the U.S.S.R. (1933). *Summary of the fulfilment of the First Five-Year Plan for the development of the national economy of the U.S.S.R.* Report of the State Planning Commission of the Council of People's Commissars of the Union of Soviet Socialist Republics. Moscow, U.S.S.R.: Author.

Steiner-Khamsi, G. (2016). New directions in policy borrowing research. *Asia Pacific Education Review, 17*(3), 381–390.

Tagore, R. (1921). *Personality: Lectures delivered in America*. London, U.K.: Macmillan.

Tagore, R. (1961). *Towards universal man*. London, U.K.: Asia Publishing.

Tähtinen, U. (1964). *Non-violence as an ethical principle: With special reference to the views of Mahatma Gandhi* (Annales Universitatis Turkuensis, Series B, No. 92). Turku, Finland: University of Turku.

Tähtinen, U. (1970). *Mitä Gandhi todella sanoi* [What Gandhi really said]. Porvoo, Finland: WSOY. [in Finnish]

Tähtinen, U. (1979). *The core of Gandhi's philosophy*. New Delhi, India: Abhinav.

Tähtinen, U. (1982). *Non-violent theories of punishment: Indian and Western* (Annales Academiae Scientiarum Fennicae, Series B, No. 219). Helsinki, Finland: Academia Scientiarum Fennica.

Tähtinen, U. (1986). Mahatma Gandhin väkivallaton vastarinta [The nonviolent resistance of Mahatma Gandhi]. *Katsaus, 14*(4), 26–28. [in Finnish]

Tan, C. (2016). *Educational policy borrowing in China: Looking west or looking east?* London, U.K.: Routledge.

Tan, C., & Reyes, V. (2016). Neo-liberal education policy in China: Issues and challenges in curriculum reform. In S. Guo & Y. Guo (Eds.), *Spotlight on China: Changes in education under China's market economy* (pp. 19–33). Rotterdam, The Netherlands: Sense Publishers.

Tolstoy, L. (1969). From count Leo Tolstoy. In S. Narayan (Ed.), *The selected works of Mahatma Gandhi: Selected letters* (Vol. 5, pp. 21–26). Ahmedabad, India: Navajivan. (Original letter written in 1910)

Urban, W. J., & Wagoner Jr., J. L. (2009). *American education: A history* (4th ed.). New York, NY: Routledge.

Vinal, W. G. (1936). The school camp line-up for nature education. *The Clearing House, 10*(8), 462–466.

Vogel, E. F. (2011). *Deng Xiaoping and the transformation of China*. Cambridge, MA: Belknap of Harvard University Press.

Waks, L. J. (2007). The concept of fundamental educational change. *Educational Theory, 57*(3), 277–295.

Webb, L. D. (2006). *The history of American education: A great American experiment*. Upper Saddle River, NJ: Pearson.

Xi, J. (2017). *Secure a decisive victory in building a moderately prosperous society in all respects and strive for the great success of socialism with Chinese characteristics for a new era*. Retrieved from http://www.xinhuanet.com/english/download/Xi_Jinping's_report_at_19th_CPC_National_Congress.pdf

Xu, D. (1992). *A comparison of the educational ideas and practices of John Dewey and Mao Zedong in China: Is school society or society school?* San Francisco, CA: Mellen Research University Press.

Yao, X. (2013). The way of harmony in the four books. *Journal of Chinese Philosophy, 40*(2), 252–268.

Zajda, J. I. (1980). *Education in the U.S.S.R.*. Oxford, U.K.: Pergamon Press.

Zakir Husain Committee. (1938). *Basic national education: Report of the Zakir Husain Committee and the detailed syllabus with a foreword by Mahatma Gandhi* (3rd ed.). Segaon, India: Hindustani Talimi Sangh.

Zhang, D. (2002). *Key concepts in Chinese philosophy* (E. Ryden, Trans. & Ed.). New Haven, CT: Yale University Press, & Beijing, P.R.C.: Foreign Languages Press.

Zhao, Z. (1998). Zheng fu gong zuo bao gao (jie lu) [Government work report (extract) in 1983]. In D. He (Ed.), *Zhong hua ren min gong he guo zhong yao jiao yu wen xian: 1976–1990* [The important educational documents of the People's Republic of China: 1976–1990] (Vol. 2, pp. 2098–2100). Haikou, P.R.C.: Hainan Publishing. (Original work published in 1983)

PART 2

*The Research and Evolution of
Community-Based Learning*

∴

CHAPTER 2

Community-Based Learning: An Exploration from Philanthropy to Praxis

Thomas L. Alsbury, Suzan Kobashigawa and Mary Ewart

Abstract

This chapter explores the historical context that shaped the current purpose and design of community-based learning in the United States. A review and analysis of the literature reveals the diverging evolution of pluralistic program purposes and the interweaving of philanthropic service, pragmatic vocational skills development, and social justice activism. Historically, this program was intended to provide a countercultural experience for students to shape their understanding of social and cultural privilege. Today, the most common program design incorporates work-based learning and service-learning constructs that primarily focus on volunteerism and skills development. The chapter discusses current emerging trends that return these programs to their historical roots in social justice engagement. Recent classroom and community applications, including second language, newcomer, and place-bound programs, focus on cultural and social capital issues and encourage community activism. The chapter concludes with remarks on how the lack of consistency and the dichotomy of program purposes in community-based learning have persisted from its inception to the current day and contribute to the lack of widespread adoption and program clarity. Recommendations for scaling up the use of this reform include establishing a balanced purpose that encompasses both social justice and skill development, which promises to allow more widespread adoption and provide broader funding sources.

Keywords

community-based learning – service-learning – work-based learning – social justice – reflectivity – place-based learning – newcomer programs

1 **Introduction**

Community-based learning in its various forms has become more popular in recent years in U.S. public schools. This chapter reviews the philanthropic beginnings of this educational reform movement and its transition into a popular experiential requirement for high school graduation. It discusses the broad and sometimes disparate definitions, purposes, and designs of community-based learning, from service-learning to social activism. We explore community-based learning programs focused specifically on linguistically diverse student groups and urban settings. The chapter discusses the influence of community-based learning programs on improved language acquisition, enhanced cultural intelligence, and community orientation for students new to the United States.

While gains in social and cultural capital, work ethic, and community service are possible outcomes, the benefits of this learning approach vary widely among students, based on the level of their participation, the quality of the program design, and the extent to which the school and staff support students participating in the program. The chapter concludes with a discussion regarding the dual purposes plaguing community-based learning throughout its history and recommends a balanced program purpose, which might allow this type of learning to expand more broadly into schools and positively support the educational needs of all students.

1.1 *History of Community-Based Learning*

The beginnings of community-based learning in the United States, many contend, started in 1889 when Jane Addams (1860–1935) established Hull House in Chicago. Hull House was fashioned after Toynbee Hall in London as an experiment to embed a community of university students to "live as neighbours of the poor, and, without ... claiming to have come as teachers, ... might form the friendships which are the channels of all true service" (Barnett & Barnett, 1909, p. 259). Addams' organizational philosophy was to provide education using a vehicle of service to society through authentic engagement with the community. She indicated that "the settlement is an effort to live among all sorts and conditions of men and insist that a life is not lived as it should be unless it comes in contact with all kinds of people" (Addams, 1895, p. 97). In the early 20th century, John Dewey (1915) expanded upon this idea by encouraging the inclusion of community-based learning within public K–12 schools. Dewey (1915/2008) believed service was an expression of, and extrinsically linked to, fostering democratic society. As such, he designed his experimental school so students could practice community-based learning.

In fact, the recommendation for schools to incorporate real-world problem solving through community-based learning has been a central element in reform movements since the beginning of the 20th century (Dewey, 1902, 1938; Lipka et al., 1998). Resnick (1987) noted that the difference in current versus past curriculum is that all students, not just a few, must master real-world problem solving. He said that "it is a new challenge to develop educational programs that assume that all individuals, not just an elite, can become competent thinkers" (p. 7).

Since these early efforts to infuse community-based learning into the curriculum within experimental schools, little progress has been made in implementing this educational experience into most U.S. K–12 public schools, despite the fact that national and state curriculum performance standards in the 1990s emphasized the need for students to engage in critical thinking and inquiry in the context of real-world problem solving (American Association for the Advancement of Science, 1993; National Council of Teachers of English/International Reading Association, 1996; National Council of Teachers of Mathematics, 1989, 1995, 2000; National Research Council, 1995).

Despite its early beginnings and the curricular push for real-world experiences, the broad use of community-based learning in K–12 public schools was thwarted by a number of competing reform efforts starting in the early 1980s. The back-to-the-basics reform movement shifted the curricular focus to emphasize standardized learning objectives. In addition, there was a strong push in the United States for schools to better prepare students to perform well on national or state tests. The advent of the No Child Left Behind Act of 2001 (NCLB) further de-emphasized community-based learning approaches. The act's focus on math and literacy achievement on high-stakes accountability tests forced most schools to dramatically reduce their course offerings in career and technical education (Fletcher, 2006), further limiting opportunities for this type of learning. In addition to the NCLB refocusing school reforms away from community-based learning, legal challenges in the late 1990s (Hyman, 1999) confronted many urban school systems that were requiring high school students to complete community-based learning projects or service work before graduation (e.g., Chicago Public Schools, 2006; Detroit Public Schools, 2001; District of Columbia Public Schools, 2007; Los Angeles Unified School District, 2004; Seattle Public Schools, 2009).

Despite this, two specific examples of community-based learning—work-based learning and service-learning—have emerged as a significant and growing component of most K–12 school systems in the United States throughout the past three decades. However, involving students in community-based learning experiences has been limited to two primary approaches. In the first approach, students are encouraged or required to engage in community service in order to "do good for others" and thereby foster a sense of community belonging, care, and responsibility (Wade, 1997). This form of volunteerism is typically an extracurricular activity not connected with academic learning or the formal curriculum. In the second approach, schools require these experiences as an integral element of a student's learning experiences (Kendall, 1990; Kunin, 1997). These two approaches to community-based learning have shown some resilience despite the recent push narrowing the curricular focus to math and literacy and mandating high-stakes accountability testing for all students. This resilience may be credited to the dominance of constructivist teaching approaches that became popularized in teacher preparation programs in the early 1980s. The constructivist teaching approach was partially based on Dewey's notions of the school as "a genuine form of active community life" and "education through experience" (Dewey, 1915/2008, p. 10).

Rare examples of comprehensive integration of community-based learning school-wide can be seen in such entrepreneurial designs as Matt Candler's 4.0 School movement (Lopez, 2015). Candler developed what he called the "rooted school," which incorporates community-based school projects. He said that the "Rooted School aims to bridge the gap between what's being taught in high schools and what skills are needed for the jobs being created in … high-growth, high-wage industries" (Lopez, 2015, para. 11). While the practice of isolated community-based learning projects as a graduation requirement was relatively widespread in the early 21st century, examples of more systemic school-wide reforms were confined to communities experiencing some unique crisis. For example, these reforms were allowed in New Orleans because of the temporary dissolution of the public school system after the community was devastated by hurricane Katrina. In the wake of the crisis, community officials chose to reopen schools as innovative charter schools. Other than in locally isolated exceptions, the use of community-based learning systemically in schools has not been practiced to date.

1.2 *Definitions*

The National and Community Service Trust Act of 1993 (National and Community Service Trust Act, 1993, Section 103) and the Council of Chief State School Officers (1993) offer a variety of definitions for community-based and service-learning. The Alliance for Service-Learning in Education Reform (ASLER, 1993) definition encapsulates most other meanings. ASLER defines community-based learning as "a method by which young people learn and develop through active participation in thoughtfully organized service experiences" (p. 2). ASLER further describes effective community-based learning as experiences:

- meeting actual community needs;
- coordinated in collaboration with the school and community;
- integrated into each young person's academic curriculum;
- providing structured time for a young person to think, talk, and write about what he or she did and saw during the actual service activity;
- providing young persons with opportunities to use newly acquired academic skills and knowledge in real-life situations in their own communities;
- enhancing lessons taught in school by extending student learning beyond the classroom; and
- helping to foster the development of a sense of caring for others (p. 2).

Community-based learning has been defined in a myriad of ways and is frequently used interchangeably with terms like *service-learning, work-based learning,* and *community service,* to name a few. However, the meanings of each can be unique, so it is important to clarify definitions when reviewing various community-based learning programs. Each type of community-based learning program or activity is designed based on a unique purpose and composition. It is notable that among the community-based programs mentioned earlier, "community-based learning" was envisioned and practiced first. The term "service-learning" was coined much later by Ramsey and Sigmon around 1967 (Sigmon, 1990; Southern Regional Education Board, 1973).

In general, community-based learning, service-learning, and other related programs can be defined as a community activity in which school-age students engage in an embedded experience tied to the school curriculum. Service-learning is unique because it refers to service work hours that (a) are not directly linked to the school curriculum, (b) do not require the student to produce a product, (c) do not facilitate formal student reflection, and (d) are evaluated only on completion of the assigned service task. However, confusion arises because service-learning has sometimes been designed to include all of the features normally ascribed to community-based learning (Seitsinger, 2005). For example, university community-based learning programs range from simple volunteerism providing labor to nonprofit organizations, to apprenticeships and work-study programs meant primarily to benefit the student. In addition, some university departments or courses adopt community-based learning as a form of civic engagement. This variation in the definition and use of terms can create challenges when discussing and researching programs.

In contrast to volunteerism or community-service work, students engaged in community-based learning (a) are required to participate by their school, (b) are involved in learning activities coordinated and planned by school officials, (c) receive clear expectations regarding requirements for an academic product from the community experience, and (d) experience formal evaluations of their community-based learning experience. Involvement in this type of learning is believed to help students better understand their course content and enhance their studies.

A less widespread definition for community-based learning is the focus on social justice. Some define and design this type of learning to promote cultural and racial understanding or to foster a commitment to social activism (Fleisher, 1994; Lee, Menkart, & Okazawa-Rey, 1998; Lewis, 1991). Wade (2000) suggested that "children will not fulfill the social studies' mission of informed and active citizenship through book learning alone" (p. 6) and indicated that community-based learning should be about social change, not just filling a gap in services. As previously noted, two major approaches to community-based learning have been broadly practiced in the U.S. over the past few decades: work-based learning and service-learning.

1.2.1 Work-Based Learning

The first form of community-based learning includes career exploration programs commonly employed in secondary schools (e.g., Experience-Based Career Education, Cooperative Education, Tech Prep, School-to-Work, Job Shadowing, and Youth Apprenticeship). Proponents contend that this form of community-based learning can inform students' career and academic paths (Bailey, Hughes, & Moore, 2004; Cotterell, 1996; Hamilton & Hamilton, 1997, 2000). Studies confirm that participation in work-based learning provides students with opportunities for career options, workplace skills, and the knowledge needed to navigate and achieve their occupational goals (Csikszentmihalyi & Schneider, 2000; Röhrle & Sommer, 1994; Zeldin & Charner, 1996).

One popular form of work-based learning to emerge in high schools is called the Senior Project. Senior Projects, as the name implies, is typically a community-based learning project required of high school seniors as their final culminating activity to earn their diploma. Senior Projects involve student participation in a community-service project, concluding with a reflective paper or other product describing their experiences.

1.2.2 Service-Learning

The second form of community-based learning includes service activities ranging from cleaning up trash or assisting the elderly with yard care (McLellan & Youniss, 2003) to long-term mentor-student relationships in service organizations, which is tied to the academic curriculum and requires student reflection on the personal and social impact of their service (Stafford, Boyd, & Lindner, 2003). Studies conclude that required service-learning for high school students promotes personal growth and civic responsibility (Marks & Kuss, 2001; McLellan & Youniss, 2003; Skinner & Chapman, 1999). For example, Marks and

Kuss (2001) found that participation in service-learning helps high school students feel more connected to their community, improves self-worth, and creates a more positive disposition toward community citizenship.

Senior Projects and work-based and service-based learning swept the United States in the 1990s and remain a popular element in comprehensive high school reform (Jones & Hill, 2003; Marks & Kuss, 2001; RMC Research Corporation, 2007; Schmidt, Shumow, & Kackar, 2007; Skinner & Chapman, 1999). A required community-based learning project or service-learning has also enjoyed limited inclusion in some middle schools (Seitsinger, 2005) in the form of vocational coursework or as an optional project-based assignment to fulfill a general citizenship requirement. However, apart from the Senior Project and work-based and service-based learning projects, community-based learning is limited to single teachers who voluntarily incorporate projects or community experiences into their courses. Even then, these assignments are often optional for students.

1.2.3 Purposes of Community-Based Learning

In addition to the variation in definition, the purpose and design of community-based learning can vary widely. In most of these learning experiences, students apply what they learned in academic classrooms into genuine settings. These opportunities engage students in higher order thinking skills of application, analysis, and synthesis of the knowledge (Eyler & Giles, 1999; McIlrath & Mac Labhrainn, 2007; Sigmon & Pelletier, 1996; Zlotkowski, 1999). However, some define the purpose of community-based learning as experiences intended to enhance students' personal development. Eyler, Giles, Stenson, and Gray (2001) discovered that this type of learning increased the students' understanding of individual differences, their self-awareness and self-confidence, and their commitment to service. Astin, Vogelgesang, Ikeda, and Yee (2000) found that community-based learning could be designed to influence career choice and plans to participate in community service in later life. Similar studies confirm positive outcomes and recommend the use of community-based learning in educational settings (Eyler, 2000; Gray et al., 1999; McKenna & Rizzo, 1999). Common desired outcomes for community-based learning include motivating reluctant learners, instilling the value of hard work, and teaching students that volunteering or helping others is an important part of being a good citizen.

Another purpose of community-based learning, popular since the inception of the educational approach, focuses on social justice. Many assert that community-based learning should be purposed to provide students with a greater understanding of what it means to be a fully engaged democratic citizen (see, e.g., Battistoni, 1997; Battistoni, Longo, & Jayanandhan, 2009; Cone, 2003; Cone, Kiesa, & Longo, 2006; Schamber & Mahoney, 2008). Murphy and Rash (2008) noted that through this type of learning "students begin to realize that both social problems and correctives have a communal side that cannot be ignored" (p. 68).

However, the design of community-based learning projects can be counterproductive in addressing and combating social injustice, and some argue it can even reinforce privilege and inequality. For example, students who approach a community-service project as providing assistance to those in need may reinforce the belief that a group is vulnerable or powerless (Camacho, 2004; Eby, 1998; Mitchell, 2008; Peterson, 2009). If the students' learning experience is prioritized above the needs of the community members, students and school officials may end up treating community partners as "subjects for experience and practice" (Eby, 1998, p. 3). Similarly, if the design of the community-based learning project reinforces differences (e.g., class, race, educational level) between the students and the community, power dynamics can reinforce presumed privilege and hierarchy rather than community unity, which might have been the original intent.

In order to avoid reinforcing separation and value inequity between the students and the community, community-based learning definition and design must address class-based issues (Cone, 2003; Weah, Simmons, & Hall, 2000). One suggestion for combating this concern is to repurpose community-based learning projects from the "doing" of service to a valuable learning opportunity. In this way, community members who host students are providing value-added experiences and, in a very real sense, are the ones providing service to the students and the school.

Another way to ensure equity in community-based learning is to define the experience as a form of "reciprocal service," a foundational concept within the design of what has been called "asset-based" community-based learning. Garoutte and McCarthy-Gilmore (2014) defined an asset-based approach to these learning projects as experiences

– designed with the assumption that all communities are asset rich;
– challenging the assumption that some communities are inherently reliant on outside assistance;
– focusing on relationship development between the student and the community; and
– presuming the internal capacity for the community to resolve its own issues (p. 50).

In this form of community-based learning, "community development is constructed on solutions originating from the people and organizations within community itself. In focusing on solutions driven by community members, the top-down approach orchestrated by outside organizations is reconfigured" (Garoutte & McCarthy-Gilmore, 2014, p. 50). Wade (2000) noted that teachers should "encourage students to examine the root causes underneath community needs and take action to address those causes" (p. 9). Ideas include teaching students that service is "not about meeting someone's immediate needs but working toward an ideal society" (p. 8). Other activities include encouraging students, even in early elementary grades, to write letters to public officials, send out press releases, conduct surveys, circulate petitions, and value "collective action" over individual achievement.

1.2.4 Reflective Instructional Methodology

In all the iterative purposes of community-based learning used in school settings, reflection as an instructional approach within community-based learning is a predominant requirement that has grown in importance over time. This trend follows the Deweyan concept that we do not learn from our experiences, we learn from processing our experiences. Rodgers (2002) summarized Dewey's ideals for a meaningful reflective experience:

- Reflection is a meaning-making process that moves a learner from one experience into the next with deeper understanding of its relationship with and connections to other experiences and ideas. It is the thread that makes continuity of learning possible and ensures the progress of the individual and, ultimately, society. It is a means to essentially moral ends.
- Reflection is a systematic, rigorous, and disciplined way of thinking, with its roots in scientific inquiry.
- Reflection needs to happen in community, in interaction with others.
- Reflection requires attitudes that value the personal and intellectual growth of oneself and others (p. 845).

When designing and implementing community-based learning projects, providing opportunity and evaluating for reflection are key to practical, purposeful, and memorable learning experiences for students. The process of reflection connects the students' experiences to both the learning objectives of the course and broader social issues relevant to the community.

The form of reflection is related to the purpose of the particular community-based learning project. For example, "critical reflection" intends to press students to look for the deeper meaning behind their community-service project. Critical reflection is intended to prompt students to question current community conditions and disparities among various demographic groups within their community and to understand their role in the larger social society. The purpose of community-based learning determines its placement and consequent evaluation along the continuum, from simply providing free service to the community (volunteerism) to social activism.

1.3 Connections to Learning Theory

The various purposes and intended outcomes of community-based learning experiences can be effectively framed with Bronfenbrenner's Ecological Systems Theory (Bronfenbrenner, 2005b). Bronfenbrenner (2005a) developed an ecological systems theory that, when applied to student participants in community-based learning, would suggest that student development arises through interactions between students and their social environment. Indeed, Bronfenbrenner suggested that these interactions between students and the surrounding society would provide a set of instructions and cues to students that would affect how they view their own role and position in the existing society, as well as possibly influencing that society. Bronfenbrenner (2005a) described the interactions between individuals and the society as a "progressive, mutual accommodation" (p. 107) where society influences individuals and individuals can shape the society. Bronfenbrenner's theoretical model illustrates a series of nested and hierarchical systems within the society, from those direct and personal interactions between individuals and their family and friends to the broader society, where indirect interactions influence the individual's understanding of societal norms. In Bronfenbrenner's (1977) model, individuals are immediately influenced and influence the *microsystem*, which includes individuals' direct interactions with the surrounding people and culture (pp. 514–515). Bronfenbrenner (2005a) described the *microsystem* as a "pattern of activities, roles and interpersonal relations experienced by the developing person" in a given setting and focused particularly on the interactions with "other persons with distinctive characteristics of temperament, personality and systems of belief" (p. 148).

In applying community-based learning to Bronfenbrenner's theory, students are offered a directed experience with other individuals in their community who they may or may not have interacted with on their own. In applying the theory, the purpose and design of the community experience could dramatically change the students' interactions with other individuals in their local community and thus change their perspective on society. Specifically, the type of community-based learning previously categorized as *work-based learning* tends to be an experience (a) selected by the student, and (b) designed to provide the student with personal work experience and career development. As such, this learning opportunity would tend to be limited to interactions with people, beliefs, and experiences familiar to and in agreement with the student's previously held views of society. Students would likely select an experience in a workplace they envision as a future place of employment and possibly within an academic preparation they hope to pursue in college. This community learning experience would be less liable to place the student in a space that differed greatly from their own previous experiences with societal norms, increase interactions with individual socio-economically different from the student, nor call for the student to experience social injustice or act to change their own or others societal views. Conversely, service-based learning is an experience typically (a) selected based upon community needs rather than student preferences, and (b) designed to provide students with the opportunity to experience social injustice and challenge societal ideology and values. Some service-based learning projects emphasize student activism focused on student efforts to not only experience and learn from but to actively change their society. This highlights the importance of the intended purpose and design of community-based learning programs and the pluralistic outcomes of the learning experience on student participants and on society.

2   Applications of Community-Based Learning

As covered previously, community-based learning is a broad concept and, as such, has many different applications in various K–12 public schools. Public schools throughout the United States apply the fundamentals of community-based learning in diverse ways in their educational settings through work-based, service, and community-integration applications.

2.1   *Work-Based Learning*

Based on new U.S. legislation related to college and career readiness (see Every Student Succeeds Act [ESSA], 2015), work-based learning has become a recent focus across many states. An application of community-based learning, work-based learning focuses on different applications. The Washington State Office of the Superintendent of Public Instruction (2012) stated that "work-based learning activities provide extended learning experiences that connect acquired knowledge and skills to a student's future" (p. 2). In Iowa, learning experiences that qualify include classroom speakers, interviews and career fairs, field trips and business/industry tours, job shadowing, service-learning, internships, cooperative work experiences, and apprenticeships (Iowa Department of Education, 2017). One long-standing example of a state-funded and state-administered work-based learning program is the State of California's Regional Occupational Centers and Programs (ROCP), which, according to Frey (2014), has provided career courses for California high school students for over 40 years. Originally founded in 1967, California built regional centers and programs to offer courses in order to meet the local labor market demand (EdSource, 2005). This translated into programs in forensic science, manufacturing, engineering, automotive technology, software engineering, graphic design, health care, veterinary medicine, firefighting, emergency medical response, and many more (EdSource, 2005). According to the California Department of Education (2017), at its maximum, ROCP had 74 sites providing programs focused on ensuring opportunities and services for students in school-to-career and school-to-vocational college transition, as well as apprenticeships and job placement.

Many programs were designed to allow students to continue to attend the traditional high school while engaging in the work-based learning experience. Often, this means students enrolled in ROCP classes attend high school in the morning and take traditional courses with their peers. After lunch, the students typically attend class at a site related to their area of study (EdSource, 2005, p. 3). An EdSource report (2005) described a student's typical day as follows:

> Students interested in becoming carpenters might enroll in a Construction Technology program to learn about power tools, project planning and layout, blueprint reading, and other areas. They build model houses—some the size of a dollhouse—as well as the larger one the size of a child's playhouse. Building the structures helps them master practical skills, such as hammering while standing on a house's roof. Students use math skills extensively, including trigonometry when they calculate measurements and scale projects up or down. (p. 3)

While the 2010 creation and adoption of the Common Core State Standards in California increased focus on career and technical education, the state also experienced a recession in 2009 and, with that, changes in the way it funds education. Legislation in 2009 made funding for ROCP flexible and, in 2013, the Local Control Funding Formula repealed the 2009 flexibility and abolished the ROCP grant (California Department of Education, 2017). Though this did not eliminate these centers and programs, it raised concerns that, as dedicated funds were lost, programs would close, and they would be difficult to reopen even if funds returned (Frey, 2014).

2.2   *Service-Learning*

The other facet of community-based learning, service-learning, is typically realized through an explicit, short-term project where students work in the community or volunteer for a charity in order to learn the value of helping people and become more empathetic and compassionate. Frequently, students are required to log a certain number of volunteer hours to fulfill a graduation requirement. This approach is sometimes included in work-based learning, illustrating the complexity and overlap between different applications of community-based learning experiences.

Service-learning is something schools can do independently or through the support of organizations founded to support this work. Youth Service America is one of these organizations. Youth Service America (2017) states that its "mission is to help all young people find their voice, take action, and make an impact on vital community issues" (para. 1). The organization achieves this mission by leading its own campaigns to activate youth nationally, funding grants to support educators and other youth groups, training those interested in service-learning, and recognizing the work being done currently by youth throughout the country (Youth Service America, 2017). Examples of explicit service-learning projects include volunteering at a food bank or shelter, organizing a blood drive, hosting a winter clothing and blanket drive for local clothing banks, or training seniors to use technology.

2.3   *Community Integration*

Various examples of community-based learning programs can be designated as a work-based or service-learning experience based upon their community-integration design. Two specific and notable types of community integration exist for immigrants or first-generation students: newcomer programs for recently arrived English-language learners and place-based learning, specifically in a Hawaiian context. In both types, community is critical to the students' growth and learning. Students are encouraged to engage with the community, become familiar with services and resources, and apply classroom learning. A key difference between the two, however, is that with the newcomer programs, community is a resource for students (Short & Boyson, 2012; WIDA Consortium, 2015), but it does not play a significant role in the formulation and shaping of curriculum, policies, or professional development. In place-based learning, community partners are an integral part of the school and drive the curriculum and programming (Smith, 2002; Smith & Sobel, 2010). Both newcomer programs and place-based learning need the community as a resource to meet student needs and to fulfill learning in a robust and dynamic way, and both are highlighted to illustrate the variety of community-based learning in the United States.

2.3.1   Newcomer Programs

Short and Boyson (2012) defined a newcomer student as someone who is "new to the English language, the United States, and our school system, and is within one year of arrival. ... Other defining characteristics include interrupted formal schooling, little to no native language literacy, age, and grade level" (p. 11). Newcomer students' challenges exponentially increased when compared to English-language learners who were born in the United States or who arrived at a fairly young age. Newcomer programs fulfill different student needs, which are unnecessary or irrelevant to their English-language-learning peers. While different programs and approaches to help transition newcomers to the K–12 education system exist, newcomer programs are vital because of the way they meet the students' most basic and immediate needs and help them to acclimate to the school and the surrounding community.

Newcomer students can be as young as preschool or kindergarten (3–5 years of age). While it is challenging for younger students to integrate into the K–12 school system, the curriculum content focuses on both language development and academic content. However, for older students, curriculum shifts primarily to academic content and assumes that students have the language foundation (including literacy) to continue learning. Because of this shift, newcomer programs tend to focus on middle school to high school students who have more obstacles in their schooling path. Newcomer students at this age have additional characteristics that hinder their learning, which can include limited or interrupted formal education (due to poverty, war, persecution), posttraumatic stress disorder, zero-to-limited English proficiency or literacy skills in their native language, as well as family responsibilities (caring for siblings, the home, and/or contributing to family income) that younger English-language learners or age-level, English-speaking peers may not experience (Short & Boyson, 2012; WIDA Consortium, 2015). Roxas (2011) noted that it can be particularly difficult for students who encounter peers from ethnic or religious groups that may have been their adversaries in their home country.

A hallmark of newcomer schools is how they integrate the community into their programs, especially since students (and their families) are new to the schooling process and likely their community. Some newcomer programs establish community partnerships that enable students to access services as well as engage in learning in innovative ways (Short & Boyson, 2012; WIDA Consortium, 2015). These partnerships are especially critical for newcomer students, who can use this community "anchor" to ground them in their local environment. Newcomer students have the chance to gain membership into the community instead of feeling like the perennial stranger, even after months or years in one community. Short and Boyson (2012) noted that community partners may be "libraries, local museums, county health departments, transit authorities, youth and family services, and sports clubs" (p. 27). Community partners can also include organizations focused on the arts (theater, painting, drawing, ceramics, music, etc.), technology (including robotics), and life skills (cooking, bike repair) (Short & Boyson, 2012; Seattle World School, 2018; WIDA Consortium, 2015).

An example of community-based learning with newcomer students is seen in Roxas' (2011) article "Creating Communities: Working With Refugee Students in Classrooms," where he follows teacher Patricia Engler, who integrates community learning and engagement with her newcomer refugee students. Core to Engler's approach to learning is community building in the classroom and in the local community. For one activity, Engler's students work on establishing relationships and understandings with each other, community members included. She brings in staff from a local arts organization to help students create a mural that represents them and their families. In the relaxed atmosphere of painting, chatting with each other and being supported by community members, the students naturally create relationships and connections, gain new awareness of people in their local environment, and come away with an improved capacity to engage (Roxas, 2011, p. 1).

During the school year, Engler connects her students with the local community, strengthening the connection as community members come into the classroom and give students the opportunity to see the different roles and functions they play. Engler reflected that

> my children exhibit posttraumatic stress symptoms. ... Therefore, to get my students the help that they need and in a nontraditional Western way, I have to be resourceful. ... I do need the community's help; I can't do it all myself. (Roxas, 2011, p. 5)

The community is needed not solely for the students' sake but for the teacher who struggles to meet all the students' needs, which, when met, will make the education journey smoother and more successful. But students are not the only recipients of this partnership—the community also benefits. Students and their families become involved members, enriching the local environment. Newcomer students who engage in their community can then pay it forward to newer students coming to the United States and, while not mentioned specifically in the newcomer literature, the community members themselves, in some way, must be impacted. This type of partnership in newcomer programs is similar to what local schools have with their community partners, and it may indicate the type of relationship that schools have, where community members' presence, resources, and expertise are respected but are overshadowed by school priorities, which include achieving higher test scores and maintaining state standards. As a result, community partners' expertise and resources are supplemental, not intrinsic, to a school's curriculum, let alone its values and ethos.

2.3.2 Place-Based Programs

While newcomer programs utilize community-based learning to orient students to the United States, the community partners are supplementary to the curriculum. However, place-based programs, another form of community-based learning, incorporate a more holistic view of community and use the local environment as a foundational piece for all aspects of the school. The Rural School and Community Trust, a national nonprofit organization addressing the crucial relationship between good schools and thriving communities, defines place-based education as

> learning that is rooted in what is local—the unique history, environment, culture, economy, literature, and art of a particular place. The community provides the context for learning, student work focuses on community needs and interests, and community members serve as resources and partners in every aspect of teaching and learning. (Colchado et al., 2003, para. 4)

In placed-based education, the community in which a school resides provides the context, content, experts, laboratory, and experiences for students to learn. Moreover, place-based learning is fluid and adapts to the students' local environment (Smith, 2002). "A hallmark of placed-based learning is that the curriculum adapts to the unique characteristics of particular communities ... and uses the natural and cultural history of the community as the foundation for the curriculum" (Place-Based Learning and Community Engagement in School, n.d., para. 3). While students learn geography, mathematics, biology, etc., the learning is influenced in the local community, and the local environment and stakeholders (including students, teachers, parents, and community members) mold the subject matter, activities, and projects that are uniquely local.

In Hawaii, place-based education has found a home in Native Hawaiian communities and schools, and with students. Native Hawaiian culture is deeply rooted in the environment, where the land, water, animals, and plants have divine origin or connection (Beckwith, 1982; Daws, 1974), and where genealogy is tied to the land (Kana'iaupuni & Malone, 2006). It is no surprise then that place-based education would be a natural fit for Native Hawaiian culture and students.

For decades, the achievement gap for Native Hawaiian students has been both long-standing and significant (Singh, Amor, & Zhang, 2014; Yamauchi & Purcell, 2009). Moreover, they must also overcome the "negative statistics associated with Native Hawaiian children: high rates of poverty, substance abuse, juvenile deviance and criminal activity, teenage pregnancies, poor educational outcomes, domestic abuse, depression, and suicide" (Kana'iaupuni, Ledward, & Jensen, 2010, p. 3). The traditional educational system has not closed the achievement or social gap but instead serves as a reminder to Native Hawaiian students that their identity and cultural values are dissonant with schools and the larger mainstream culture (Kana'iaupuni et al., 2010). A different way of schooling, though, can reshape student cultural identity, which can increase "self-confidence, self-esteem, and resiliency among both children and adults" (Kana'iaupuni et al., 2010, p. 3). Culture-based education can work toward this transformation of cultural identity, with place-based education as one way to do this: "Typical of this approach, these innovative schools implement project-based and place-based teaching and learning for children, integrating culture, community and the natural environment" (Kana'iaupuni et al., 2010, p. 3). Place-based education in Hawaii has reintroduced Native Hawaiian students to the local community and to the land that connects them to their culture and their identity. But more than the connection, place-based education inspires students to interact, engage, learn, and become agents of change in their community.

Yamauchi and Purcell (2009) summarized the five common characteristics of place-based education, originally articulated by Smith (2002):

> First, place-based education incorporates aspects of the particular places in which students live. Second, placed-based education applies a constructive approach to education whereby students create knowledge instead of just being passive recipients of it. Third, students' questions and concerns are central to the learning process. Fourth, teachers become colearners with their students. ... Finally, school and community are not separated, as community members become active in education and students are likewise active in their communities. (Yamauchi & Purcell, 2009, p. 171)

These characteristics serve as the foundation for place-based schools and, in particular, one school on western Oahu, in the state of Hawaii. Yamauchi & Purcell (2009) situated their research in a school and area that "were disturbed by the high dropout rate and low achievement among youth in their area, the majority of whom were of Native Hawaiian ancestry" (Yamauchi & Purcell, 2009, p. 170). The research specifically focused on the community members' roles and involvement in this particular school. The researchers identified seven ways in which community partnerships functioned at this particular place-based school: funding, program development, supervision and organization of service-learning, teacher development, curriculum development, cultural consultation, and political support. In each of these areas, the community played a distinctive and critical role in the function of the school, at some points preventing its closure (Yamauchi & Purcell, 2009).

In each of the ways previously noted, the community partners and members played vital roles that impacted the program's administration, operation, curricular content, and professional development. With regard to funding, community partners supported the program financially, especially when student numbers grew and transportation was limited. Transportation was critical for the program, as students needed to get to their service-learning activities, including an archaeological site and a local stream where they helped to conduct tests. Community partners contributed funds so students could get to their service-learning projects (Yamauchi & Purcell, 2009).

Community partners also helped to shape the program by participating in meetings to "discuss program goals, outcomes, and future direction" (Yamauchi & Purcell, 2009, p. 177). The community was not only respected for its expertise and resources but were also co-collaborators in the education process. The community also supervised the service-learning experience by providing sites and/or supervising students. Students could learn about (a) the health profession through participating at a clinic; (b) archaeological excavating from professionals who taught them about digs, from mapping to disseminating the findings; (c) plant reforestation by working with a botanist; and (d) testing a water stream system and testifying before the Board of Water Supply (Yamauchi & Purcell, 2009).

Community partners were also professionals who provided expertise on teacher and curriculum development, as well as consultation on Hawaiian culture, values, and content. The partners would initiate the drive for consistent integration of Hawaiian culture into the program, questioning whether the program sufficiently incorporated Hawaiian culture into its core. Community partners were also the ones who advocated for the program and teachers, at times contributing funds to maintain teaching staff or speaking to administrators about the rationale and value of the program (Yamauchi & Purcell, 2009).

Without the community partners, the program at the school would surely have folded, but it survived because it was deeply embedded in the community. And while students in the program could continue their studies, they weren't the only beneficiaries of the program. The community partnerships benefited as well. Community partners could tap into the school for volunteers to help carry out projects, which made a difference in their cause. Through the service-learning experience, students could learn more about the profession and consider it for their career. Moreover, participation in the school program provided positive exposure for community partners (Yamauchi & Purcell, 2009).

The researchers also note the hurdles they observed, including "lack of support from the school system ... teacher burnout ... [and] interpersonal conflicts" (Yamauchi & Purcell, 2009, pp. 182–184), which serve as reminders to purposefully work toward proactive measures for long-term sustainability. All members of a place-based program should advocate on behalf of their program, work to find ways to eliminate teacher burnout, and work toward better communication to avoid interpersonal conflicts. While these challenges are present in this program, they are not exclusive to place-based programs but are present in most educational programs with limited funds and high expectations for learning.

Many believe it's important that communities integrate both types of community-based learning programs. Newcomer programs serve students who have recently arrived in the United States, who need more time to become familiar with the school system, school culture, American culture, and their local community. The newcomer programs are generally more conventional in nature, where community partners are sought as resources for student needs. With place-based programs, community partnerships serve a much more critical role in schools, as they shape curriculum and learning, provide service-learning for students, and offer teaching experts in the field and the subject matter. Community partners also become advocates, funders, mentors, and recruiters. Both types of programs show the continuum of community-based learning within the school system and the investment that teachers, schools, and, especially, communities make in this endeavor.

Some studies have argued against mandatory service-learning, noting no significant differences in benefits to students between mandatory or voluntary service-learning. Jones and Hill (2003) and Marks and Jones (2004) reported that students viewed their mandatory service-learning as an unwanted burden that poisoned their interest in future volunteerism. Another problem is that students in urban schools already experience the realities of social inequity, so it is unlikely that mandatory service-learning would provide the dissonance needed to initiate different concepts of social justice within their communities (Furman & Shields, 2003; Saltmarsh, 2005). Finally, not all communities are diverse enough to provide the kind of service-learning opportunities that would lead to reflections about social equity. Some community placements may even perpetuate social biases (Anyon, 1980).

3   Conclusion

Early in the history of K–12 public schools in the United States, Cooley (1912) argued for schools to "be in the closest possible relation to the occupations" (p. 154). An early battle over the balance between purely academic studies and the need for students to engage in vocational experiences and be trained in real-world work in the public schools was eventually settled by a 1918 report of the Commission on the Reorganization of Secondary Education. This report, *Cardinal Principles of Secondary Education*, served as the blueprint for the American comprehensive high school (Commission on the Reorganization of Secondary Education, 1918). Among other things, this report led to the development of vocational and academic studies existing under the same roof.

Dewey (1915) was one of the main opponents to Cooley's call for a dual education system where students would spend their time first in an academic school and then later in community-based vocational placement. The irony is that Dewey also spoke to the importance of community-based learning elements in the comprehensive school (Dewey, 1902). Significant to the topic of community-based learning, the comprehensive school concept that Dewey espoused effectively removed the opportunity for a formal community-based experience from school systems for several decades. In fact, it was not until the federal vocational program grants of the 1990s and the work-based learning and service-learning senior projects of the 2000s that community-based learning would be formalized in schools.

Challenges to the wholesale incorporation of community-based learning include the push for teachers to focus on documenting student performance on basic academic objectives and high-stakes accountability testing, as exemplified by the U.S. government's No Child Left Behind Act of 2001. These educational movements led to reduced courses in the arts, music, vocational skills, and community-based learning. Even with the recent increased popularity in community-based learning projects, complications have arisen over the many and various definitions and purposes for these projects. Community-based learning programs have been developed to address a pluralistic and sometimes polarizing diversity of purposes and outcomes for student participants. For some, community-based learning is intended to provide students with an ethic of hard work, while others believe the experiences should focus on teaching students to recognize and take action to improve social justice.

As Bronfenbrenner's Ecological Systems Theory (2005) predicted, the community learning experience can influence or be influenced by students. Program purpose and design can allow students to experience injustice and take action in their local community microsystem or, conversely, can reinforce preexisting societal norms and encourage students to determine how they fit into society. This dichotomy of intended purposes for community-based learning is reminiscent of the early debate between Dewey and David Snedden (Dewey, 1915; Snedden, 1915). Snedden (1915) asserted that the purpose of community-based experiences was vocational education resulting in "a greater productive capacity" (p. 42). Conversely, Dewey and Dewey (1915) argued the following:

> Unless the mass of workers are to be blind cogs and pinions in the apparatus they employ, they must have some understanding of the physical and social facts behind and ahead of the material and appliances with which they are dealing. (p. 246)

Dewey (1915) believed that separate vocational and academic experiences was undemocratic, noting, "I am utterly opposed to giving the power of social predestination, by means of narrow trade-training, to any group of fallible men no matter how well-intentioned they may be" (p. 42).

While Dewey and Snedden were debating the policy of separate versus combined academic and vocational educational training, the principle dichotomy within their disagreement closely mirrors the current discourse regarding the purposes of schooling in general and community-based learning in particular. Braundy (2004) noted that "Dewey built his ideas on the concept that in a democracy, everyone is important and responsible to and for what is done in the name of progress" (para. 12). It seems that the debate over the purpose and design of community-based learning continues. In fact, Apple (1988) argued that the current push to formalize the inclusion of vocational education like community-based learning and to equalize its status in schools and the inevitable academization of the reform, could cause it to "actually lose its existing possibilities for social criticism and for integrating head, hand, and heart together" (p. 322).

Perhaps a balanced approach to community-based learning is the most effective resolution to the debate. Surely both work-based and social-based purposes could be simultaneously achieved given the appropriate design of the community-based learning experience. Indeed, this approach would take better advantage of the interdependent dynamic described in Bronfenbrenner's Ecological Systems Theory (2005), wherein individuals both influence and are influenced by societal interactions. However, considerable expertise is necessary for schools and teachers planning community-based learning to effectively provide the training and incentive for students to learn from the experience, reflect upon the cultural experiences gained, and value community assets (Eyler & Giles, 1999). Teachers need to facilitate students' critical thinking and problem-solving skills. In order to promote the expanded use of community-based learning, teacher preparation programs should incorporate instruction on the use of community-based learning as an effective and standards-based instructional approach.

Community-based learning is an important addition to any systemic school reform effort and could improve the excellence and cultural responsiveness needed in the American curriculum to realize increased equity (Every Student Succeeds Act, 2015, sections 1005, 4601; Task Force on Education of Young Adolescents, 1989). When community-based learning is effectively implemented, students have the opportunity to gain subject area knowledge, practice applying this knowledge in authentic settings, experience issues of social justice in their community, and reflect on their own personal responsibility for bettering their community and nation.

References

Addams, J. (1895). Hull House as a type of college settlement. In *Annual State Conference of Charities and Corrections, Milwaukee, WI, November 19–24, 1894, under the auspices of the Wisconsin State Board of Control of Charitable, Reformatory, and Penal Institutions* (pp. 97–115). Madison, WI: Democrat.

Alliance for Service Learning in Education Reform. (1993). Standards of quality for school-based service-learning. *Equity & Excellence in Education, 26*(2), 71–73. doi:10.1080/1066568930260216 Chester, VT: Author.

American Association for the Advancement of Science. (1993). *Project 2061: Benchmarks for science literacy.* Washington, DC: Author.

Anyon, J. (1980). Social class and the hidden curriculum of work. *Journal of Education, 161*(1), 67–92.

Apple, M. W. (1988). Work, power, and curriculum reform: A response to Theodore Lewis's vocational education as general education. *Curriculum Inquiry, 28*(3), 310–331.

Astin, A. W., Vogelgesang, L. J., Ikeda, E. K., & Yee, J. A. (2000). *How service learning affects students.* Los Angeles, CA: Higher Education Research Institute.

Bailey, T. R., Hughes, K. L., & Moore, D. T. (2004). *Working knowledge: Work-based learning and education reform.* New York, NY: Routledge Falmer.

Barnett, S. A., & Barnett, D. H. (1909). *Toward social reform.* New York, NY: Macmillan.

Battistoni, R. M. (1997). Service learning and democratic citizenship. *Theory into Practice, 36*(3), 150–156.

Battistoni, R. M., Longo, N. V., & Jayanandhan, S. R. (2009). Acting locally in a flat world: Global citizenship and the democratic practice of service-learning. *Journal of Higher Education Outreach and Engagement, 13*(2), 89–107.

Beckwith, M. (1982). *Hawaiian mythology.* Honolulu, HI: University of Hawaii Press.

Braundy, M. (2004). Dewey's technological literacy: Past, present, and future. *Journal of Industrial Teacher Education, 41*(2). Retrieved from https://scholar.lib.vt.edu/ejournals/JITE/v41n2/braundy.html

Bronfenbrenner, U. (1977). Toward an experimental psychology of human development. *American Psychologist, 32*(7), 513–531.

Bronfenbrenner, U. (2005a). Ecological systems theory. In U. Bronfenbrenner (Ed.), *Making human beings human: Bioecological perspectives on human development* (pp. 106–173). Thousand Oaks, CA: Sage.

Bronfenbrenner, U. (Ed.). (2005b). *Making human beings human: Bioecological perspectives on human development.* Thousand Oaks, CA: Sage.

California Department of Education. (2017, May 8). *Regional Occupational Centers and Programs: Frequently Asked Questions (FAQs) on the Regional Occupational Centers and Programs Grant and the flexibility provisions in Senate Bill 4 of the 2009–10 Third Extraordinary Session (SBX3.4).* Retrieved from https://www.cde.ca.gov/re/cc/ccssfaqs.asp

Camacho, M. M. (2004). Power and privilege: Community service learning in Tijuana. *Michigan Journal of Community Service Learning, 10*(3), 31–42.

Chicago Public Schools. (2006). *Student resources: Service learning.* Retrieved from https://cps.edu/ServiceLearning/Pages/ServiceLearning.aspx

Colchado, J., Hobbs, V., Hynes, M., King, J., Newell, M., Parker, S., & Wilson, S. (2003, July 1). *Engaged institutions: Impacting vulnerable youth through place-based learning* (The Rural School and Community Trust). Retrieved from http://www.ruraledu.org/articles.php?id=2081

Commission on the Reorganization of Secondary Education. (1918). *Cardinal principles of secondary education* (Bulletin No. 35). Washington, DC: Bureau of Education, Department of the Interior.

Cone, R. E. (2003). Service-learning and civic education: Challenging assumptions. *Peer Review, 5*(3), 12–15.

Cone, R. E., Kiesa, A., & Longo, N. V. (2006). *Raise your voice: A student guide to making positive social change.* Boston, MA: Campus Compact.

Cooley, E. G. (1912). Principles that should underlie legislation for vocational education. In W. T. Bowden (Ed.), *Proceedings of the sixth annual meeting of the National Society for the Promotion of Industrial Education* (Bulletin No. 16, pp. 146–154). Peoria, IL: Manual Arts Press.

Cotterell, J. (1996). *Social networks and social influence.* New York, NY: Routledge.

Csikszentmihalyi, M., & Schneider, B. (2000). *Becoming an adult: How teenagers prepare for the world of work.* New York, NY: Basic Books.

Daws, G. (1974). *Shoal of time: A history of the Hawaiian Islands.* Honolulu, HI: University of Hawaii Press.

Detroit Public Schools. (2001). *Graduation requirements.* Retrieved from http://www.detroit.k12.mi.us/admin/curriculum/graduationrequirements

Dewey, J. (1902). *The child and the curriculum.* Chicago, IL: University of Chicago Press.

Dewey, J. (1915, May 15). Education vs. trade-training—Dr. Dewey's reply. *The New Republic, 3*(28), 42–43.

Dewey, J. (1938). *Education and experience.* New York, NY: Colliers.

Dewey, J. (2008). *Democracy and education.* Palm Springs, CA: Watchmaker. (Original work published in 1915)

Dewey, J., & Dewey, E. (1915). *Schools of to-morrow.* London, U.K.: Dent.

District of Columbia Public Schools. (2007). *District of Columbia Board of Education: Notice of final rulemaking.* Retrieved from https://dcps.dc.gov/sites/default/files/dc/sites/dcps/page_content/attachments/FINAL%20DCPS%20Graduation%20Requirements%20Policy.pdf

Eby, J. W. (1998). *Why service-learning is bad.* Retrieved from https://www1.villanova.edu/content/dam/villanova/artsci/servicelearning/WhyServiceLearningIsBad.pdf

EdSource. (2005, June). *The evolution of career and technical education in California.* Retrieved from https://edsource.org/wp-content/publications/CareerTech05.pdf

Every Student Succeeds Act, 20 U.S.C. § 1005, 4601. (2015).

Eyler, J. (2000). What do we most need to know about the impact of service learning on student learning? *Michigan Journal of Community Service Learning, 7,* 11–17.

Eyler, J., & Giles, D. E. (1999). *Where's the learning in service-learning?* San Francisco, CA: Jossey-Bass.

Eyler, J., Giles Jr., D. E., Stenson, C. M., & Gray, C. J. (2001). *At a glance: What we know about the effects of service learning on college students, faculty, institutions, and communities, 1993–2000.* Washington, DC: Corporation for National and Community Service.

Fleisher, P. (1994). *Changing our world: A handbook for young advocates.* Tucson, AZ: Zephyr.

Fletcher Jr., E. C. (2006). No curriculum left behind: The effects of the no child left behind legislation on career and technical education. *Career and Technical Education Research, 31*(3), 157–174.

Frey, S. (2014, January 26). *New report fuels fears of decline of regional occupational programs.* Retrieved from https://edsource.org/2014/new-report-fuels-fears-of-decline-of-regional-occupational-programs/56617

Furman, G. C., & Shields, C. M. (2003, April). *How can educational leaders promote and support social justice and democratic community in schools?* Paper presented at annual meeting of the American Educational Research Association, Chicago, IL.

Garoutte, L., & McCarthy-Gilmore, K. (2014). Preparing students for community-based learning using an asset-based approach. *Journal of the Scholarship of Teaching and Learning, 14*(5), 48–61.

Gray, M. J., Ondaatje, E. H., Fricker, R., Geschwind, S., & Goldman, C. A., Kaganoff, T., ... Klein, S. P. (1999). *Combining service and learning in higher education: Evaluation of the Learn and Serve America, higher education program.* Santa Monica, CA: Rand Education.

Hamilton, M. A., & Hamilton, S. F. (1997). *Learning well at work: Choices for quality.* Washington, DC: National School-to-Work Office.

Hamilton, S. F., & Hamilton, M. A. (2000). Research, intervention, and social change: Improving adolescents' career opportunities. In L. J. Crockett & R. K. Silbereisen (Eds.), *Negotiating adolescence in times of social change* (pp. 267–282). Cambridge, U.K.: Cambridge University Press.

Hyman, R. T. (1999). *Mandatory community service in high school: The legal dimension.* Dayton, OH: Education Law Association.

Iowa Department of Education. (2017). *Iowa work-based learning guide.* Retrieved from https://www.educateiowa.gov/sites/files/ed/documents/Iowa%20Work-based%20 learning%20guide%20final.pdf

Jones, S. R., & Hill, K. E. (2003). Understanding patterns of commitment: Student motivation for community service involvement. *Journal of Higher Education, 74*(5), 516–539.

Kanaʻiaupuni, S. M., Ledward, B., & Jensen, U. (2010, September). *Culture-based education and its relationship to student outcome.* Kamehameha Schools Research and Evaluation Division. Retrieved from http://www.ksbe.edu/_assets/spi/pdfs/CBE_relationship_to_student_outcomes.pdf

Kanaʻiaupuni, S. M., & Malone, N. (2006). This land is my land: The role of place in native Hawaiian identity. *Multidisciplinary Research on Hawaiian Well-Being, 3*(1), 281–307.

Kendall, J. C. (Ed.). (1990). *Combining service and learning: A resource book for community and public service* (Vol. 1). Raleigh, NC: National Society for Internships and Experiential Education.

Kunin, M. M. (1997). Service-learning and improved academic achievement: The national scene. In J. Schine & K. J. Rehage (Eds.), *Ninety-sixth yearbook of the National Society for the Study of Education: Service Learning* (Pt. 1, pp. 149–160). Chicago, IL: University of Chicago.

Lee, E., Menkart, D., & Okazawa-Rey, M. (Eds.). (1998). *Beyond heroes and holidays: A practical guide to K–12 anti-racist, multicultural education and staff development.* Baltimore, MD: McArdle.

Lewis, B. A. (1991). *The kid's guide to social action: How to solve the social problems you choose—and turn creative thinking into positive action.* Minneapolis, MN: Free Spirit.

Lipka, R. P., Lounsbury, J. H., Toepfer Jr., C. F., Vars, G. F., Alessi Jr., S. P., & Kridel, C. (1998). *The eight-year study revisited: Lesson from the past for the present.* Columbus, OH: National Middle School Association.

Lopez, A. (2015, March 27). Entrepreneurs are changing the future of education by starting new schools in New Orleans. *Forbes.* Retrieved from https://www.forbes.com/sites/adrianalopez/2015/03/27/entrepreneurs-are-changing-the-future-of-education-by-starting-new-schools-in-new-orleans/#3aab8c157229

Los Angeles Unified School District. (2004). *Service-learning guidebook.* Retrieved from https://1.cdn.edl.io/O4YG2OwLdP6R4UavEUmBThovZbaYNcN7gwY3WBRvU-zlBsj52.pdf

Marks, H. M., & Jones, S. R. (2004). Community service in the transition. *The Journal of Higher Education, 75*(3), 307–339.

Marks, H. M., & Kuss, P. (2001). Socialization for citizenship through community service: Disparities in participation among U.S. high school students. *Sociological Focus, 34*(4), 377–398.

McIlrath, L., & Mac Labhrainn, I. (2007). *Higher education and civic engagement: International perspectives.* London, U.K.: Ashgate.

McKenna, M. W., & Rizzo, E. (Eds.). (1999). Outside the classroom: Student perceptions of the benefits of service learning. *Journal of Prevention and Intervention in the Community, 18*(1–2), 111–123.

McLellan, J. A., & Youniss, J. (2003). Two systems of youth service: Determinants of voluntary and required youth community service. *Journal of Youth and Adolescence, 21*(1), 47–58.

Mitchell, T. D. (2008). Traditional vs. critical service-learning: Engaging the literature to differentiate two models. *Michigan Journal of Community Service Learning, 14*(2), 50–65.

Murphy, J. W., & Rash, D. (2008). Service-learning, contact theory, and building black communities. *The Negro Educational Review, 59*(1–2), 63–78.

National and Community Service Trust Act of 1993, 20 U.S.C. § 103. (1993).

National Council of Teachers of English/International Reading Association. (1996). *Standards for the English language arts.* Urbana, IL: Author.

National Council of Teachers of Mathematics. (1989). *Curriculum and evaluation standards for school mathematics.* Reston, VA: Author.

National Council of Teachers of Mathematics. (1995). *Assessment standards for teaching mathematics.* Reston, VA: Author.

National Council of Teachers of Mathematics. (2000). *Principles and standards for school mathematics.* Reston, VA: Author.

National Research Council. (1995). *National science education standards*. Washington, DC: National Academy.

No Child Left Behind Act of 2001, 20 U.S.C. § 1116. (2001).

Peterson, T. H. (2009). Engaged scholarship: Reflections and research on the pedagogy of social change. *Teaching in Higher Education, 14*(5), 541–552. doi:10.1080/13562510903186741

Place-Based Learning and Community Engagement in School. (n.d.). *Research base*. Honolulu, HI: Author. Retrieved from https://www.placeshawaii.org/research

Resnick, L. B. (1987). *Education and learning to think*. Washington, DC: National Academy Press.

RMC Research Corporation. (2007, May). *Policy, K–12 service-learning*. Washington, DC: Corporation for National and Community Service. Retrieved from https://gsn.nylc.org/clearinghouse

Rodgers, C. (2002). Defining reflection: Another look at John Dewey and reflective thinking. *The Teachers College Record, 104*(4), 842–866.

Röhrle, B., & Sommer, G. (1994). Social support and social competencies: Some theoretical and empirical contributions to their relationship. In F. Nestman & K. Hurrelmann (Eds.), *Social networks and social support in childhood and adolescence* (pp. 113–129). New York, NY: Walter de Gruyter.

Roxas, K. (2011). Creating communities: Working with refugee students in classrooms. *Democracy & Education, 19*(2), 1–8.

Saltmarsh, J. (2005). The civic promise of service learning. *Liberal Education, 91*(2), 50–55.

Schamber, J. F., & Mahoney, S. L. (2008). The development of political awareness and social justice citizenship through community-based learning in a first-year general education seminar. *The Journal of General Education, 57*(2), 75–99. doi:10.1353/jge.0.0016

Schmidt, J. A., Shumow, L., & Kackar, H. (2007). Adolescents' participation in service activities and its impact on academic, behavioral, and civic outcomes. *Journal of Youth and Adolescence, 36*(2), 127–140.

Seattle Public Schools. (2009). *High school graduation requirements*. Retrieved from https://www.seattleschools.org/academics/college_career_readiness/graduation_requirements

Seattle World School. (2018). *Extended learning program*. Retrieved from http://sws.seattleschools.org/

Seitsinger, A. M. (2005). Service-learning and standards-based instruction in middle schools. *The Journal of Educational Research, 99*(1), 19–30.

Short, D., & Boyson, B. (2012). *Helping newcomer students succeed in secondary schools and beyond*. Washington, DC: Center for Applied Linguistics.

Sigmon, R. L. (1990). Service-learning: Three principles. In J. C. Kendall & Associates (Eds.), *Combining service and learning: A resource book for community and public service* (Vol. 1, pp. 37–56). Raleigh, NC: National Society for Internships and Experiential Education.

Sigmon, R. L., & Pelletier, S. G. (Eds.). (1996). *Journey to service-learning: Experiences from independent liberal arts colleges and universities*. Washington, DC: Council of Independent Colleges.

Singh, M., Amor, H. B. H., & Zhang, S. (2014, April). *Native Hawaiian students' achievement gap in reading: A longitudinal study from Hawaii*. Paper presented at the annual meeting of the American Educational Research Association, Philadelphia, PA.

Skinner, R., & Chapman, C. (1999). *Service-learning and community service in K–12 public schools*. National Center for Education Statistics, Office of Educational Research and Improvement, U.S. Department of Education. Retrieved from https://nces.ed.gov/pubs99/1999043.pdf

Smith, G. A. (2002). Place-based education: Learning to be where we are. *Phi Delta Kappan, 83*(8), 584–594.

Smith, G. A., & Sobel, D. (2010). *Place- and community-based education in schools*. New York, NY: Routledge.

Snedden, D. (1915, May 15). Vocational education. *The New Republic, 3*(28), 40–42.

Southern Regional Education Board. (1973). *Service-learning in the South: Higher education and public service 1967–1972*. Atlanta, GA: Author.

Stafford, J., Boyd, B., & Lindner, J. R. (2003). Community service versus service-learning: Which is best for 4-H? *Journal of Extension, 41*(6). Retrieved from https://www.joe.org/joe/2003december/a1.php

Task Force on Education of Young Adolescents. (1989). *Turning points: Preparing American youth for the 21st century*. New York, NY: Carnegie Council on Adolescent Development.

Wade, R. C. (Ed.). (1997). *Community service-learning: A guide to including service in the public school curriculum*. New York, NY: State University of New York Press.

Wade, R. C. (2000). Beyond charity: Service learning for social justice. *Social Studies and the Young Learner, 12*(4), 6–9.

Washington State Office of the Superintendent of Public Instruction. (March 2012). *Worksite learning manual*. Retrieved from https://www.puyallup.k12.wa.us/UserFiles/Servers/Server_141067/File/Instruction%20&%20Learning/CTE/Work-Based%20Learning/WorksiteLearningManual.pdf

Weah, W., Simmons, V. C., & Hall, M. (2000). Service-learning and multicultural/multiethnic perspectives: From diversity to equity. *Phi Delta Kappan, 81*(9), 673–675.

WIDA Consortium. (2015). SLIFE: Students with limited or interrupted formal education. *WIDA Focus On*. Wisconsin Center for Education, University of Wisconsin–Madison. Retrieved from https://broadyesl.files.wordpress.com/2015/05/wida_focus_on_slife-final.pdf

Yamauchi, L. A., & Purcell, A. K. (2009). Community involvement in a place-based program for Hawaiian high school students. *Journal of Education for Students Placed at Risk, 14*(2), 170–188.

Youth Service America. (2017). *About YSA*. Retrieved from https://ysa.org/about/

Zeldin, S., & Charner, I. (1996). *School-to-work through the lens of youth development.* Washington, DC: Academy for Educational Development, National Institute for Work and Learning.

Zlotkowski, E. (1999). Pedagogy and engagement. In R. G. Bringle, R. Games, & E. A. Malloy (Eds.), *Colleges and universities as citizens* (pp. 96–120). Boston, MA: Allyn & Bacon.

CHAPTER 3

Community-Based Learning and Student Outcomes: What Research Reveals

Thomas L. Alsbury, Suzan Kobashigawa and Mary Ewart

Abstract

This chapter provides an overview of research findings on the effectiveness of using community-based learning. Through a literature review, emerging themes include the benefits of community-based learning, with a focus on substantive outcomes, including improvements in cultural capital, social advocacy, and inequitable privilege as well as in students' understanding, empathy, and activism for diverse communities. Additional pragmatic outcomes include an increase in student work ethic, a desire to engage in volunteerism, and improved vocational skills development. In addition, students who engaged in community-based learning appear to experience better school attendance, more academic motivation, fewer at-risk behaviors, and greater classroom achievement. Research found that the outcomes, primarily in student social and cultural competency and sensitivity, were most dominant and consistent across studies. However, findings varied based on program purpose and design as well as the level of relationship development between school and community mentors and student participants. Classroom applications in English language learner courses and student-centered instructional practice are reviewed. The chapter concludes with the contention that program quality varies dramatically within and among schools, primarily due to the differing quality of the relationship between adult supervisors and mentors and their students and the design and intent of the program.

Keywords

community-based learning – cultural capital – social advocacy – work skills development – student achievement – English language learners – mentoring

1 Introduction

Community-based learning as a school-based reform introduces the potential, proponents contend, to transform student learning and perceptions about their own community and society in general. The enthusiasm surrounding the expansion of these programs among universities in the United States has led to the creation of national organizations like the National Service-Learning Clearinghouse, Campus Compact, the International Partnership for Service-Learning, and Learn and Serve America, as well as many university-based Centers for Service and Learning (e.g., the Center for Service and Learning at Indiana University-Purdue University). Indeed, there are even academic journals, like the *Michigan Journal of Community Service Learning*, an international journal that specifically publishes service-learning scholarship, or *Metropolitan Universities*, a journal of the Coalition of Urban and Metropolitan Universities, which has members from more than 80 universities and whose mission is to connect teaching and research with community service. Furthermore, universities such as Duke, Cornell, Rutgers, Pennsylvania State, Princeton, the University of Pennsylvania, and others have introduced undergraduate service-learning research programs. For instance, Duke University provides a three-course offering of beginning, intermediate, and advanced community-based research methods. Given this increased interest and growing capacity in the academy for conducting research on the effects of community-based learning, one might expect a rise in both the quantity and quality of empirical research on this reform model.

Despite this growing capacity for research in the field of community-based learning, the various and somewhat disparate models represented within this reform and a lack of clearly delineated purpose or design present a challenge for researchers. For example, community-based models cut across a sometimes fluid continuum between whether the primary beneficiary of the learning approach is the student or the community, or whether these models provide mutual benefits. Similarly, there is a continuum between whether the program's experiential pedagogy focuses on volunteerism, internship, or some combination of service to the community and learning for the students (Kenworthy-U'Ren, Petri, & Taylor, 2006). As design and purpose tend to be fluid or unclear, researchers are hard-pressed to adequately select research designs, identify and define variables, or develop tools to collect measurable outcomes in the course of a study. For example, if a community-based learning program is designed around improving work ethic, could a shift in cultural responsiveness be anticipated as a measurable outcome? Conversely, a service program purposed to promote cultural empathy would not likely result in changes in classroom performance. Indeed, neither of these programs guarantees a social or academic shift for every student because those transformations largely depend upon each student's disposition. The program outcomes also vary based on the student's individual experience as well as the type and quality of relationships that may or may not organically emerge within a student's community experience. Despite these challenges, some research findings do point to common outcomes for students involved in various community-based learning designs. These studies can include cultural, personal, social, and academic outcomes and are reviewed in this chapter.

2   Research Findings

Despite the fact that community-based learning has been practiced in the United States since the early 1900s, researchers have conducted only a limited number of controlled studies on its impact (Billig, 2000; Carlisle, Gourd, Rajkhan, & Nitta, 2017; Furco & Root, 2010). Research that supports school-based community-based learning as an effective instructional method has lagged behind its growing popularity (Pedersen, Meyer, & Hargrave, 2015; Schamber & Mahoney, 2008; Shumer & Cook, 1999; Skinner & Chapman, 1999; Wade, 1997; Waterman, 1997). In addition, most studies focus on the social and psychological outcomes for postsecondary students (Cohen & Kinsey, 1994; Deeley, 2010; Giles & Eyler, 1994; Kretchmar, 2001; Simons & Cleary, 2006; Toews & Cerny, 2005), while only a few studies evaluate community-based learning in K–12 public education (Conrad & Hedin, 1981; Kinsley, 1992).

Studies on community-based learning in K–12 schools have yielded mixed results, particularly in establishing a relationship between the learning experience with student achievement (Conrad & Hedin, 1981; Melchior, 1998; Roberts & Moon, 1997; Scales, Blyth, Berkas, & Kielsmeier, 2000; Schollenberger, 1985). Reasons for these inconsistent results include focusing the study on diverse institutional settings (e.g., university, high school, middle school); single types of community-based learning programs (e.g., service-learning, work-based learning); and widely varying frameworks, outcomes, purposes, and definitions of community-based learning. In addition, most studies involve single or limited case studies, which don't allow for generalizations regarding the efficacy of community-based learning programs. Further, due to ethical considerations necessary in treatment-based research designs in schools, studies tend to lack comparison groups. Overall, studies reporting the effects of community-based learning on academic achievement, intellectual development, and school behavior are limited for both college students (e.g.,

Eyler & Giles, 1999; Markus, Howard, & King, 1993; Shumer, 1994) and middle and high school students (e.g., Melchior, 1998; Roberts & Moon, 1997; Scales et al., 2000; Schollenberger, 1985).

Indeed, most classroom-based learning programs differ in the type, content, and context of project assignments each student performs in the study, thus limiting analysis to single student cases and restricting overarching conclusions. One exception was a national empirical study Seitsinger (2005) conducted that sought to identify how community-based learning was implemented in middle-level schools across the United States. This study found that teachers who implemented service-learning regularly used standards-based instructional practices more often than their colleagues. One consistent finding in virtually every study on community-based learning is a high level of participant satisfaction (Conrad, 1991). Specifically, most studies in community-based learning found that student participants reported the experience as positive and helpful in terms of social awareness. Research has focused more intently on specific types of community-based learning, namely, work-based learning, service-learning, newcomer programs, and place-bound programs.

2.1 *Studies on Work-Based Learning*

Work-based learning is a type of community-based learning that emphasizes paid or unpaid workplace experiences. These programs are generally embedded into career-oriented vocational programs in secondary schools. The purpose of work-based learning is generally to (a) allow the student to experience what the work world is like, (b) provide the student with an overview of various work or career options open to them, (c) acquaint students with the education or skills needed to acquire certain kinds of work, (d) instill a work ethic in students, and (e) supply organizations with a pipeline of future workers. What does research tell us about the impacts of work-based learning experiences on students? Studies of urban high school students show that participation in work-based learning generated clearer career interests, increased confidence, and improved competencies to pursue a defined career, as well as better grades, improved school attendance, more academic motivation, and fewer at-risk behaviors (Scales et al., 2005).

2.1.1 Career Development Implications

Hawley and Marks (2006) surveyed over 1,700 high school students in a large urban Midwestern school district with 18 high schools. These schools required all students to complete 120 hours of combined work-based job shadowing and other community learning experiences, like paid and unpaid internships, in order to graduate. Students could enroll in a career class in ninth grade, perform community service in 10th grade, and then engage in volunteer or paid work in a local business. The focus of this program was on students gaining employable skills and thinking about career development. The study also measured whether students applied knowledge from their academic course work to their work internship. The study identified students' level of participation in the program as one variable. Specifically, students who participated least completed the career course and participated in a job shadow. In the next level of participation, students added volunteer time, which generally occurred at a nonprofit agency rather than in a business setting. The most intensive participation included a paid or unpaid internship on a worksite. The study surveyed graduating 12th graders, who were asked to measure the extent to which they applied classroom subject matter to their internship and about the most critical positive and negative elements of the experience. Hierarchical linear modeling analyses found that students who interacted more effectively with teacher mentors tended to participate more fully in the program, increased their application of classroom knowledge to the work experience, and were more motivated to pursue their career and academic goals after high school. This study speaks to the need to establish a positive teacher mentor component to the program to better ensure that work-based learning positively influences academic performance.

Bennett's (2007) empirical study concluded that the community-based learning experiences of high school students in a large urban district improved students' clarity regarding career interests and in continuing education after high school. Bennett's study looked at a single school district with 17 high schools that required all 11th- and 12th-grade students to earn a minimum of 60 hours in a community work-based internship in their intended career choice or interest. A teacher was assigned to assist the students with their internship placement, but the students picked the businesses themselves. The work-based program was designed to give students experience in the work world and help them determine a future career or job. No other requirements or training was provided for the students; the only requirement was completing the work hours. The study surveyed 1,741 students in 12th grade, who were asked about the program's most important features and outcomes. Hierarchal linear regression analyses indicated that an unpaid internship had a more positive influence on the students' engagement in learning about the career than a paid experience. Bennett (2007) suggested that the pay could have compelled students to select a particular placement rather than explore more diverse job interests. In addition, paid positions may have restricted the students to a narrow focus on the job site. Most significantly, the study found that engaging in a supportive relationship with the teacher mentor was more critical than any other component of the work-based program, including performance feedback from the worksite supervisor. The study concludes that supportive mentoring in work-based programs must be intentionally planned and implemented for outcomes to be maximized.

2.1.2 Effects on At-Risk Students

Work-based learning programs, while effective for all students, produced even more benefits with at-risk students. Scales et al. (2005) surveyed 429 mostly low-income Hispanic and African American students in an inner-city urban high school. In addition, 76 students, parents, school staff, and business partners participated in observations, interviews, and focus groups. The study purpose was to measure the impact of work-based learning experiences with the local business community. Students who actively participated in the work-based learning project and experienced higher levels of exposure to school–business partnerships reported improvements in social and cultural developmental assets (i.e., support, empowerment, safety, commitment to learning, positive identity) and reduced levels of risk behaviors (e.g., drug or alcohol use, sex, violence, overcoming adversity). Students with high levels of participation also reported improvement in academic skills, decision-making, and problem solving; higher grade point averages; more reflection on career and education plans; and increased motivation to graduate high school and pursue educational and career goals. The most successful work-based experiences were believed to result from the building of a productive relationship between the student and caring adults. The study results indicated that these relationships engaged, affirmed, and woke inner resources already imbued in some of the students and learned through the experience in others with less cultural capital. This particular community-based program focused on developing students' physical, cognitive, emotional, and social lives.

Gemici and Rojewski (2010) studied 1,752 at-risk high school students who were prone to excessive school absences, in-school suspension, probation, or disciplinary transfer. The researchers used propensity score matching to analyze data from the Educational Longitudinal Study of 2002, focusing the effects of participation in cooperative education on postsecondary transition readiness and the importance students placed on work. Work-based learning motivated at-risk students to plan and prepare for their future after high school, strengthened cognitive development, and enhanced psychological readiness to make important life decisions.

2.1.3 Social Justice Implications

While studies indicate academic and career benefits for students who actively participate in work-based learning, important social implications were also measured. For example, Avis (2004), in a review of literature on the effects of work-based learning programs, argued that while work-based learning was beneficial for all students, it was even more important for previously disaffected or marginalized students. Students in work-based learning experience the employee workplace at many levels within the organization and become more aware of workplace politics and issues surrounding employment relations. Work-based learning enables students to observe and reflect on the social and economic inequities in the larger society.

Bennett, Alsbury, and Fan (2015) conducted an empirical study of two large urban high schools implementing mandatory community-based learning programs focused on community services and work-based internships as a reform policy. Rawls' theory of justice as fairness was used to examine the capacity of the district's formal policy to achieve the fair equality of opportunity central to its democratic aims and purposes. Emergent themes through qualitative analysis indicated disparities in equity and access caused by an unclear program purpose and disparate implementation by key school personnel. Bennet et al. (2015) "warned that if a social justice lens was not purposely integrated into work-based learning experiences, students are otherwise learning little more than 'learning to labour,' which only serves to perpetuate inequities in the labor force and society" (para. 15).

2.2 Studies on Service-Learning

Another popular example of community-based learning is the use of service-learning. Service-learning can be described as a school-based program where classroom learning goals are combined with community service activities. The purpose of service-learning programs, in comparison to work-based learning, is to extend classroom learning in a more deliberative manner. These programs are generally developed by individual classroom teachers who provide projects for students in authentic learning that focus on developing student awareness and care about the community welfare and unjust social realities. Service-learning is intended to be less about providing assistance to the community and more about students immersing themselves in the community in order to learn about its challenges and to develop empathy and advocacy for societal inequities. Some proponents regard service-learning as vital to promoting and instilling democratic values of social responsibility and civic engagement within students, which is critical to the continuance of our democracy (e.g., Jennings, 2002; Kenny & Gallagher, 2003; Metz & Youniss, 2003, 2005; Schneider, 2004; Verba, Schlozman, & Brady, 1995).

2.2.1 Effects on Social Awareness and Civic Action

Metz and Youniss (2003) conducted a case study of 645 high school students in a suburban school district outside of Boston from 2000 to 2002. Students were required to perform community service to graduate from high school. Using an emergent theme analysis they found that service-learning, even when mandatory, improved student interest in and understanding of civic issues.

Metz and Youniss (2005) conducted an additional study on successive cohorts of high school students, one without (n=174) and two with a community service requirement (n=312). The two groups were compared longitudinally on measures of civic attitudes and behaviors. Each cohort was divided according to individual students' inclinations to serve voluntarily. Students already inclined to serve scored high on all measures of civic attitudes and showed no advantage after meeting the requirement. However, students who were less inclined to serve showed marked gains on three of four civic measures after completing their requirement. Schmidt, Shumow, and Kackar (2007) analyzed the National Household Education Survey, focusing on 4,306 high school students and one parent of each to describe characteristics of adolescents, the nature of their service activities, and academic, behavioral and civic outcomes associated with voluntary service. They concluded that students who worked directly with individuals in need had better academic adjustment and those who worked for organizations had better civic outcomes, regardless of whether the service was voluntary or required.

Bennett's (2009) studies of urban high school students indicated that students who engaged in service showed stronger inclinations for volunteer service, joining civic associations, support for nonprofit organizations, speaking out on issues, attending local or neighborhood meetings, contacting officials, and participating in action groups. Service-learning also influenced students to see service as more than just helping an individual but rather as a duty or responsibility essential to community membership.

Yates and Youniss (1998) reviewed previous empirical studies, and focused on data from a case study of black urban adolescents who participated in yearlong service-learning programs. This study examined the efficacy of mandatory community service for preparing all high school students in a large urban school district for civic engagement. The principal hypothesis asserted that mandatory community service was insufficient in influencing students' civic engagement orientations (CEO) unless accompanied by opportunities to receive social support. Survey data for this study were collected from all seniors in the district's 17 high schools (N=1,741) and ordinary least squares was applied in a hierarchical regression in four stages. Findings supported the moderating effect of social support in mandatory service-learning, especially having a mentor. Students' CEOs, however, were most affected by their perceptions of neighborhood vitality and civic discourse access. Recommendations centered on improving the urban district's mandatory community service policy by implementing systems and community partnerships that would enable equitable student access to socially supportive community adults and promote deeper integration of service-learning into the broader curriculum.

They noted that student capacity to analyze social complexities improved as a direct result of their service or field experiences and the growth of social consciousness. Students in service-learning developed specific steps to more fully engage in civil discourse about equity and access barriers and were more willing to participate in citizen action toward changes in public policy. Schwarz (2011) conducted an empirical study using a purposeful sample of 50 current and recently graduated high school students from a wide variety of socioeconomic classes who participated in 40 hours of required community service to graduate from an independent school in Ontario, Canada. Qualitative survey and focus group data were analyzed using an emergent theme approach. He found high-income students experienced personal change overcoming preconceived notions of other diverse social groups. Low-income students, however, did not experience as profound a personal transformation because they remained in their local communities to provide service and were already familiar with the circumstances they encountered.

An important factor determining whether students experienced personal transformation in their perceptions of social justice issues was the type of placement assigned to the student. Specifically, students placed in what Porfilio and Hickman (2011) called "critical service-learning" experienced more personal awareness and change regarding social equity issues. In traditional placements, students engaged in the charitable impact of their service, which more likely caused students to "swoop in and out without any learning occurring" (Porfilio & Hickman, 2011, p. xiii). Hayes (2011), through a review of literature, suggested that critical service-learning placements, which are formally structured, enable students to examine how "social institutions and policies reproduce and reinforce the root causes of social inequities" (p. 67). Bennett et al. (2015) noted:

> When students encountered these problems in their service-learning activities, they experience a *controlled dissonance* through mechanisms of reflection and dialogue that pushes them out of their comfort zones to question the distribution of power in society and to act toward social change. (p. 8)

Unlike critical service-learning, traditional forms of community service simply regard work as charity rather than prompting students to witness social inequities that may account for the problem they are working to alleviate (Yates & Youniss, 1996). Proponents argue that the lack of critical service-learning leaves students vulnerable to patterns of civic disengagement and disconnects them from social and systemic injustices that particular groups experience (e.g., Kirshner, Strobel, & Fernández, 2003; Sanchez-Jankowski, 2002). Furman (2004) noted that schooling in a democratic society must include opportunities for social discourse so that "voices of the marginalized can be heard and the inequities of the system can be exposed" (p. 6). In their empirical study, Bennett et al. (2015) noted that "students may be afforded opportunities to understand social problems through their CBL experiences that help students understand the structural causes of social problems and help them make informed decisions in the future that shape social policy" (p. 9).

2.2.2   Effects on Academic Performance

In addition to the effects of service-learning on civic responsibility and citizenship, researchers have examined the relationship between service-learning and performance on academic exams and school grades. Weiler, LaGoy, Crane, and Rovner (1998) conducted a study in California involving 775 primary and secondary students enrolled in 15 different classes that offered service-learning. These classes were selected because they provided well-designed and implemented programs. The students were compared to 310 students in eight classes that did not offer service-learning but that were otherwise comparable in grade level, student demographics, academic performance, and socioeconomic status. The study compared student scores on the standardized California Test of Basic Skills and surveyed the students to determine their attitudes toward school and community service. Study results report a statistically significant positive difference on reading and language test scores for students participating in service-learning. In addition, students in the service-learning class reported learning more.

Despite the potential for positive benefits for students participating in work-based learning, Hughes, Moore, and Bailey (1999) cautioned that one cannot easily generalize about its impact. They conducted a multiyear study investigating five different public school districts from across the United States representing suburban and urban settings. The program sites selected were purported to have a strong work-based learning program. Each of the programs included various requirements, but all provided a work placement, an internship class, and a teacher mentor. In addition, the 25 students in the study were required to keep a journal and produce a final paper reflecting on their experience. All of the programs were intended to (a) provide students with opportunity to learn more about employees' experiences and requirements, and (b) result in positive effects on academic learning. Using extensive observations and interviews, the study determined that nine of the students showed no evidence of academic reinforcement in the workplace, while 16 students were able to apply some school-based knowledge at work. Hughes, Moore, and Bailey (1999) concluded that it appeared that knowledge gained in the workplace could reinforce academic learning, but only if intentional instructor intervention connected the school and work experiences. They recommended that instead of placing students in internships and assuming they will learn something, the programs and teacher mentors must be strategic and fully involved so as to connect work activities with explicit classroom exercises. Indeed, they noted that poor student placements in the work-based experiences often led to "dismal, miseducative experiences," where students felt forced to complete meaningless service work and community businesses viewed the students as cheap labor (p. 37).

Davila and Mora (2007) conducted a large-scale longitudinal study involving 15,340 students and analyzed data from the 1988–2000 National Educational Longitudinal Study. They intended to determine if a significant relationship exists between high school student participation in unpaid service-learning and performance on standardized test scores in mathematics, reading, history, and science. Regression analyses revealed a positive significant correlation between engagement in school community service-learning programs and performance gains in mathematics, science, and history. No connection was found between community service and reading performance. In addition, the study found that high school students who engaged in community service-learning were more likely to graduate from college than their peers.

A study by Akujobi and Simmons (1997) focused on a single elementary school in southeast Michigan that had changed from being in a prosperous and homogenous middle-class neighborhood to a diverse and impoverished one as a result of the decline of the automotive industry. The school housed prekindergarten to sixth graders who lived in low-income housing projects, with 80% on free lunch programs and 82% from single-parent households. The community was plagued with many social problems, including high incidences of teenage pregnancy as well as alcohol and drug abuse. As a measure to help face these challenges, teachers established service-learning projects connected to lessons within their classrooms. The study included five fourth-grade classrooms in the school and involved interviews with the teachers, observations of students engaged in service-learning activities inside and outside the school, and test performance on the standardized Michigan Educational Assessment Program (MEAP) test. Most of the classroom service-learning activities were developed around civics or social studies and purposed primarily to improve student inter- and intrapersonal skills and provide social learning about their community issues. Projects included fund-raising for survivors of adverse events and serving in a local homeless shelter. In surveys, teachers reported that service-learning changed students' attitudes toward classwork and improved attentiveness and responsiveness to classroom instruction. Researchers compared the MEAP test results of two classes that participated in service-learning to three classes that did not. An analysis of variance indicated that students who participated in service-learning scored significantly higher in mathematics. No statistical improvement was evident in the area of reading. In addition, student grades in the class increased significantly.

A large-scale study of service-learning conducted by Klute and Billig (2003) focused on Michigan Learn and Serve grants provided to 70 teachers who agreed to integrate service-learning into their classroom instruction. The study included classrooms spanning grades three through 12 in mostly rural and suburban middle-class communities. Teachers in the program were allowed to develop the service projects independently, so the purpose and design of the projects varied. Surveys sent to over 150 students indicated little or no association between participation in service-learning and student engagement in the classroom. In addition, the quality of each program was measured and analyzed to determine if it moderated the relationship between the student participation level in the program and student engagement in school. No relationship was found, except when the service-learning participants reported enhanced student communication and interaction with the community. In addition to survey data, student performance was measured using the standardized MEAP test. The only significant findings were found in fifth-grade students who participated in service-learning and outperformed nonparticipants in writing and social studies test scores.

2.3   Alignment to Current Reform

Seitsinger's (2005) study not only is unique as one of a few national studies on this topic but sheds light on whether community-based learning is considered relevant and complementary with modern instructional best practices. This study examined teachers' self-perceptions of their (a) attitudes and beliefs toward educational practices in general and (b) the use of community-based learning as an instructional practice. Specific research questions included (a) what educational attitudes and beliefs were associated with the practices of community-based learning, (b) to what extent was this type of learning implemented in middle-level schools, and (c) what relationships, if any, existed between teachers' general educational attitudes and beliefs toward traditional instructional practice and community-based learning.

Seitsinger's (2005) findings included a correlation between teachers' support of community-based learning and other innovative instructional practices. Middle school teachers who supported innovative instructional techniques also included this approach as important for effective instruction. Unfortunately, the study could not correlate the level of endorsement for community-based learning to its implementation. Among innovative instructional practices, middle school teachers reported using this learning approach the least. However, teachers who used community-based learning also used instructional practices like critical thinking, authentic instruction, and cross-content standards-based instruction more frequently than traditional practices. In fact, Seitsinger found that teachers who used community-based learning strategies on a regular basis also used research-supported instructional best practices more often. This study supports conclusions by Waterman (1997), as well as by Bhaerman, Cordell, and Gomez (1998) and others, that this type of learning is aligned and complementary with other recommended instructional practices.

Conclusions in Seitsinger's (2005) study also included a link between the use of community-based learning and improvements in student performance in problem solving, mathematical reasoning, analysis of work, and self-reflection. These findings support Schollenberger's (1985) position that community-based learning has the potential to provide more opportunities for students to engage in higher order thinking. Seitsinger noted that even though the schools studied were atypical in their extensive support and use of innovative systemic reform, they still implemented community-based learning infrequently. As a result, Seitsinger suggested that this type of learning was probably almost nonexistent in most middle schools nationally.

2.4   *Language Course Applications*

One area of expansion in the application of community-based learning is in the area of language learning curriculum. In these community-based learning projects, students spend time conversing with community members who speak diverse languages and who may also live in culturally diverse families or neighborhoods. Research on these programs finds overwhelmingly positive benefits to this application of community-based learning.

One benefit reported in these studies is the students' improvement in language skills. Morris (2001) reported that students who engaged in community-based learning as an extension of their school language courses spoke the languages with less apprehension. Overfield (1997) also found that students' communicative competence improved. Researchers concluded that the target language used in a real-life context promoted proficiency, while the collaborative learning approach improved student self-confidence (Caldwell, 2008). One study of a community-based learning project in a Spanish course found that the experience energized the students to think critically, improved language skills both in Spanish and English, and lowered the students' affective filter (Dahms & Daniels, 2008).

Carney (2004) noted students who took community-based learning courses improved their Spanish skills more rapidly, experienced increased motivation in their study of the language and culture, and reported an increased appreciation for the complexities and challenges faced by the Latino community in the United States.

2.5   Cultural Competence

In addition to improving language acquisition, evidence suggests that the use of community-based learning approaches improved students' intercultural understanding, sensitivity, and responsiveness. Fitzgerald (2009) noted that issues of diversity and multiculturalism naturally emerged in the community-based learning experience. Many other researchers pointed to the opportunity provided by community-based learning to increase students' cultural competence (Jouët-Pastré & Braga, 2005; Muñoz-Christian, 2010; Weldon & Trautmann, 2003). The immersive nature of community-based learning uniquely lends itself to enhanced intercultural understanding, especially if the project includes structured reflection. Because students could observe or even share their experience of the real-world realities of cultural inequity with their community mentor, they had the opportunity to increase their intercultural sensitivity and decrease their ethnocentrism (Merrill & Pusch, 2007; Welch Borden, 2007). Hellebrandt, Arries, and Varona (2003) concluded that community-based learning can help develop intercultural communicative competence and that most students experience some intercultural learning. Polansky (2004) argued that

> through participation in the community beyond their campus, [the students] have interacted with age groups other than their own. They have found that language is useful beyond their own language classroom experiences and that their linguistic competence has enabled them to contribute beneficially to the lives of others. (p. 372)

Overall, studies concluded that community-based learning (a) provided the opportunity for strong transformative effects (Long, 2003; Morris, 2001; Varona & Bauluz, 2003), (b) increased intercultural awareness and sensitivity, (c) provided students with more authentic language practice, and (d) developed students' personal confidence and motivation to learn (Carmen, 2008).

2.6 *Student Perspectives*

Jones, Segar, and Gasiorski (2008) conducted a study of a diverse group of college students who had been required in high school to participate in community-based learning in order to graduate. Participants were asked to share stories of their experiences in completing the community-based learning requirement, what they had learned from it, and whether it had influenced their college experience. Results suggested that students were focused mainly on completing the requirement, which they perceived as a burden. However, once in college, students understood the value of the community-based learning project. This finding is typical of conclusions drawn by most studies of community-based learning projects. Namely, community-based learning provided opportunities for students to learn and grow in deep and meaningful ways but could not guarantee every student would take advantage of the opportunity to experience this growth. Consequently, the findings on the efficacy of community-based learning remain inconclusive in quantitative studies seeking a correlation between participation in a community experience and student performance or social growth measures.

2.7 *Program Variation within School Districts*

The district-wide efficacy of community-based learning projects in K–12 schools is generally thought to be due to particular designs or key implementation processes. However, recent studies indicate that community-based learning program success can vary broadly within a single school district. For example, Bennett (2007, 2009) and Hawley and Marks (2003, 2006) conducted a series of research studies on one large underperforming urban district they called "Midwestern City Schools." In this school district, a mandatory community-based learning project was implemented as part of comprehensive district reform efforts. The focus of the studies was to examine student experiences with the community-based learning project, and study data included surveys of 2,598 seniors and interviews with program coordinators and students. Findings in these studies included the importance of community-based mentors who provided encouragement, feedback, and information to students. Effective student–mentor relationships accounted for significant increases in student academic skills (Hawley & Marks, 2006), dispositions toward future occupational engagement (Bennett, 2007), and future civic engagement (Bennett, 2009).

In addition to these findings, the Bennett et al. (2015) study revealed significant differences in program success between schools within the study district. While the program was introduced and implemented as a district-wide initiative, significant differences occurred among the various district high schools in successfully completing community-based projects. In order to determine the possible cause of this discrepancy, a qualitative study was conducted to determine how students in the different schools within the district described their experience with the community-based learning project. Student participants were asked about their overall experience, their general impression of the program's purpose, their relationships with adult supervisors and mentors, and the academic and technical skills they used in the community-based learning activities. Findings in the study indicated that programs among schools within a single school district varied widely. The primary differences cited were in the type and quality of the teacher mentor relationship with students in the program. When mentors were more involved with students and elicited reflective discourse with them, students reported a much better experience and confirmed a change in social and civic awareness and empathy.

3 Conclusion

In reviewing research studies on student outcomes of participation in community-based learning, it is evident that the results of these programs are greatly influenced by variations in their purpose, design, and implementation quality. However, despite these program variations, common outcomes for students involved in various forms of community-based learning are evident, including cultural, personal, social, and academic benefits.

The effects of student participation in community-based learning are largely determined by the program's purpose and design. For example, work-based learning designs resulted in better clarity of student career interests, improved ability to find a job or career, improved school attendance, and increased motivation and engagement in the classroom. In addition, these positive outcomes were more pronounced for students who had previously displayed at-risk behaviors in school. Also notable is that these benefits of work-based learning were present despite the program's formal structures. Specifically, programs that required journaling, final papers, and completion of courses or seminars saw the same results as programs that did not require these elements. Indeed, it appears that the work experience itself, the relationships formed in the workplace, and, most importantly, the quality of the teacher mentor relationship with the student were most critical to achieving positive effects (Bennett, 2007; Bennett, Alsbury, & Fan, 2015).

Outcomes for students participating in service-learning designs were understandably different given the program's focus on developing social awareness through civic engagement and on the more intentional application of classroom work to community action. Consequently, service-learning experiences resulted in improved civic and social awareness, as reported by the students, although this only occurred when the students were strategically placed in critical service-learning settings (Porfilio & Hickman, 2011). In addition, student grades and test scores in math, language, science, and social studies were shown to improve across all studies, although improvements in reading were mixed. When service-learning programs focused on English language learning, students' confidence and ability to speak both English and the world language they were studying in the classroom improved.

Several results appear to be consistent regardless of the design or purpose of the community-based learning program. In all forms of this learning approach, students improved in civic and social awareness. However, consistent across all studies was the importance of the quality of the relationship between the teacher mentor and the student as well as the participating activities. Students displayed improved cultural competence when teacher mentors engaged in purposeful reflective discourse with them regarding their experiences in the community-based program and how that reflected on issues of social and cultural equity. When community-based learning did not include this type of intentional mentoring, social and civic outcomes were not evident. Finally, inconsistencies between schools within a single district point to the need for community-based learning programs to be structured, funded, and evaluated from a more central school district level to provide more consistent outcomes across the district. In the end, community-based learning can result in significant personal, cultural, and academic outcomes for students given effective program design, consistent implementation quality, and full student participation.

References

Akujobi, C., & Simmons, R. (1997). An assessment of elementary school service-learning teaching methods: Using service-learning goals. *NSEE Quarterly, 23*(2), 19–28.

Avis, J. (2004). Work-based learning and social justice: 'Learning to labour' and new vocationalism in England. *Journal of Education and Work, 17*(2), 197–217.

Bennett, J. V. (2007). Work-based learning and social support: Relative influences on high school seniors' occupational engagement orientations. *Career and Technical Education Research, 32*(3), 187–214.

Bennett, J. V. (2009). The impact of community service and social support on urban high school seniors' civic engagement orientations. *Theory & Research in Social Education, 37*(3), 298–342.

Bennett, J. V., Alsbury, T. L., & Fan, J. (2015). Mandatory community-based learning in U.S. urban high schools: Fair equality of opportunity? *International Journal of Leadership in Education: Theory and Practice.* doi:10.1080/13603124.2015.1034184

Bhaerman, R., Cordell, K., & Gomez, B. (1998). *The role of service learning in education reform.* Upper Saddle River, NJ: Pearson.

Billig, S. H. (2000). Research on K–12 school-based service-learning: The evidence builds. *Phi Delta Kappan, 81*(9), 658–664.

Caldwell, W. (2008). Taking Spanish outside the box: A model for integrating service learning into foreign language study. *Foreign Languages Annals, 40*(3), 463–471.

Carlisle, S. K., Gourd, K., Rajkhan, S., & Nitta, K. (2017). Assessing the impact of community-based learning on students: The community-Based Learning Impact Scale (CBLIS). *Journal of Service-Learning in Higher Education, 6.* Retrieved from http://journals.sfu.ca/jslhe/index.php/jslhe/article/view/104

Carmen, M. (2008). *Service learning and Spanish: Language proficiency and cultural awareness* (Doctoral dissertation). Retrieved from ProQuest Dissertations and Theses database. (UMI No. 3321893)

Carney, T. M. (2004). Reaching beyond borders through service learning. *Journal of Latinos and Education, 5*(4), 267–271.

Cohen, J., & Kinsey, D. (1994). Service experience and the moral development of college students. *Journalism Educator, 48*(4), 4–14.

Conrad, D. (1991). School-community participation for social studies. In J. P. Shaver (Ed.), *Handbook of research on social studies teaching and learning* (pp. 540–548). New York, NY: Macmillan.

Conrad, D., & Hedin, D. (1981). *Executive summary of the final report of the experiential education evaluation project.* St. Paul, MN: University of Minnesota Center for Youth Development and Research. Retrieved from ERIC database (ED 215 823)

Dahms, E., & Daniels, M. B. (2008). A case study of community-based learning: Centre College in Danville, Kentucky. *ADFL Bulletin, 39*(2–3), 61–65.

Davila, A., & Mora, M. (2007). *Civic engagement and high school academic progress: An analysis using NELS data.* College Park, MD: The Center for Information and Research on Civic Learning and Engagement.

Deeley, S. (2010). Service learning: Thinking outside of the box. *Active Learning in Higher Education, 11*(1), 43–53.

Eyler, J., & Giles, D. E. (1999). *Where's the learning in service-learning?* San Francisco, CA: Jossey-Bass.

Fitzgerald, C. M. (2009). Language and community: Using service learning to reconfigure the multicultural classroom. *Language and Education, 23*(3), 217–231.

Furco, A., & Root, S. (2010). Research demonstrates the value of service learning. *Phi Delta Kappan, 91*(5), 16–20.

Furman, G. C. (2004). The ethic of community. *Journal of Educational Administration, 42*(2), 215–235.

Gemici, S., & Rojewski, J. (2010). Contributions of cooperative education in preparing at-risk students for post-high school transition. *Journal of Education for Students Placed at Risk, 15*(3), 241–258. doi:10.1080/10824669.2010.495689

Giles Jr., D. E., & Eyler, J. (1994). The impact of a college community service laboratory on students' personal, social, and cognitive outcomes. *Journal of Adolescence, 17*(4), 327–339.

Hawley, J. D., & Marks, H. M. (2003). *Evaluating the Columbus public schools internship program.* Columbus, OH: The Ohio State University.

Hawley, J. D., & Marks, H. M. (2006, February). *Student use of academic knowledge and skills in work-based learning.* Paper presented at the Academy of Human Resource Development International Conference, Columbus, OH.

Hayes, K. (2011). Critical service-learning and the black freedom movement. In B. Porfilio & H. Hickman (Eds.), *Critical service learning as a revolutionary pedagogy: An international project of student agency in action* (pp. 47–70). Charlotte, NC: Information Age.

Hellebrandt, J., Arries, J., & Varona, E. T. (2003). *Juntos: Community partnerships in Spanish and Portuguese.* Boston, MA: Heinle.

Hughes, K. L., Moore, D. T., & Bailey, T. R. (1999). *Work-based learning and academic skills* (IEE Working Paper No. 15). New York, NY: Institute on Education and the Economy, Teachers College, Columbia University. Retrieved from ERIC database (ED 437 568)

Jennings, M. K. (2002). Generation units and the student protest movement in the United States: An intra- and intergenerational analysis. *Political Psychology, 23*(2), 303–324.

Jones, S. R., Segar, T. C., & Gasiorski, A. L. (2008). "A double-edged sword": College student perceptions of required high school service-learning. *Michigan Journal of Community Service Learning, 15*(1), 5–17.

Jouët-Pastré, C., & Braga, L. J. (2005). Community-based learning: A window into the Portuguese-speaking communities of New England. *Hispania, 88*(4), 863–872.

Kenny, M. E., & Gallagher, L. A. (2003). *Teenagers and community service: A guide to the issues.* Westport, CT: Praeger.

Kenworthy-U'Ren, A., Petri, A., & Taylor, M. L. (2006). Components of successful service-learning programs: Notes from Barbara Holland, Director of the U.S. National Service-Learning Clearinghouse. *International Journal of Case Method Research & Application, 18*(2), 120–129.

Kinsley, L. C. (1992). *A case study: The integration of community service learning into the curriculum by an interdisciplinary team of teachers at an urban middle school* (Doctoral dissertation). Retrieved from ProQuest Dissertations and Theses database. (UMI No. 9305850)

Kirshner, B., Strobel, K., & Fernández, M. (2003). Critical civic engagement among urban youth. *Penn GSE Perspectives on Urban Education, 2*(1), 1–20.

Klute, M. M., & Billig, S. (2003). *The impact of service learning on MEAP: A large-scale study of Michigan Learn and Serve grantees.* Denver, CO: RMC Research.

Kretchmar, M. (2001). Service learning in a general psychology class: Description, preliminary evaluation, and recommendations. *Teaching of Psychology, 28*(1), 5–10.

Long, D. R. (2003). Spanish in the community: Students reflect on Hispanic cultures in the United States. *Foreign Language Annals, 36*(2), 223–232.

Markus, G. B., Howard, J., & King, D. C. (1993). Integrating community service and classroom instruction enhances learning: Results from an experiment. *Educational Evaluation and Policy Analysis, 15*(4), 410–419.

Melchior, A. (1998). *National evaluation of Learn and Serve America school and community-based programs: Final report.* Waltham, MA: Brandeis University Center for Human Resources and Abt Associates.

Merrill, M. C., & Pusch, M. D. (2007). Apples, oranges, and kumys: Models for research on students doing intercultural service learning. In B. Shelley & S. Gelmon (Eds.), *From passion to objectivity: International and cross-disciplinary perspectives on service learning research* (pp. 21–40). Greenwich, CT: Information Age.

Metz, E., & Youniss, J. (2003). A demonstration that school-based required service does not deter—but heightens—volunteerism. *Political Science and Politics, 36*(2), 281–286.

Metz, E., & Youniss, J. (2005). Longitudinal gains in civic development through school-based required service. *Political Psychology, 26*(3), 413–437.

Morris, F. A. (2001). Serving the community and learning a foreign language: Evaluating a service-learning programme. *Language, Culture and Curriculum, 14*(3), 244–255.

Muñoz-Christian, K. (2010). Beyond the language lab: Serving and learning in dual immersion classrooms. *Information for Action Journal, 2*(1), 1–14.

Overfield, D. M. (1997). From the margins to the mainstream: Foreign language education and community-based learning. *Foreign Language Annals, 30*(4), 485–491.

Pedersen, P. J., Meyer, J. M., & Hargrave, M. (2015). Learn global; Serve local: Student outcomes from a community-based learning pedagogy. *Journal of Experiential Education, 38*(2), 189–206.

Polansky, S. (2004). Tutoring for community outreach: A course model for language learning and bridge building between universities and public schools. *Foreign Language Annals, 37*, 367–373.

Porfilio, B. J., & Hickman, H. (Eds.). (2011). *Critical service-learning as a revolutionary pedagogy: An international project of student agency in action.* Charlotte, NC: Information Age.

Roberts, L. P., & Moon, R. A. (1997). Community service learning methodology and academic growth in secondary school content disciplines: An action-research study. *The High School Journal, 80*(3), 202–209.

Sanchez-Jankowski, M. (2002). Minority youth and civic engagement: The impact of group relations. *Applied Developmental Science, 6*(4), 237–245.

Scales, P. C., Blyth, D. A., Berkas, T. H., & Kielsmeier, J. C. (2000). The effects of service-learning on middle school students' social responsibility and academic success. *Journal of Early Adolescence, 20*(3), 332–358.

Scales, P. C., Foster, K. C., Mannes, M., Horst, M. A., Pinto, K. C., & Rutherford, A. (2005). School-business partnerships, developmental assets, and positive outcomes among urban high school students: A mixed-methods study. *Urban Education, 40*(2), 144–189.

Schamber, J. F., & Mahoney, S. L. (2008). The development of political awareness and social justice citizenship through community-based learning in a first-year general education seminar. *The Journal of General Education, 57*(2), 75–99. doi:10.1353/jge.0.0016

Schmidt, J. A., Shumow, L., & Kackar, H. (2007). Adolescents' participation in service activities and its impact on academic, behavioral, and civic outcomes. *Journal of Youth and Adolescence, 36*(2), 127–140.

Schneider, C. G. (2004). Practicing liberal education: Formative themes in the reinvention of liberal learning. *Liberal Education, 90*(2), 6–11.

Schollenberger, J. W. (1985). *Opportunities for higher levels of thinking as they occur in service-learning* (Doctoral dissertation). Retrieved from ProQuest Dissertations and Theses database. (UMI No. 8512502)

Schwarz, K. C. (2011). Participants' interactions with recipients while completing Ontario's community involvement requirement. In B. Porfilio & H. Hickman (Eds.), *Critical service learning as a revolutionary pedagogy: An international project of student agency in action* (pp. 29–46). Charlotte, NC: Information Age.

Seitsinger, A. M. (2005). Service-learning and standards-based instruction in middle schools. *The Journal of Educational Research, 99*(1), 19–30.

Shumer, R. (1994). Community-based learning: Humanizing education. *Journal of Adolescence, 17*(4), 357–367.

Shumer, R., & Cook, C. C. (1999). *The status of service-learning in the United States: Some facts and figures.* Retrieved from https://digitalcommons.unomaha.edu/cgi/viewcontent.cgi?article=1143&context=slceslgen

Simons, L., & Cleary, B. (2006). The influence of service learning on students' personal and social development. *College Teaching, 54*(4), 307–319.

Skinner, R., & Chapman, C. (1999). *Service-learning and community service in K–12 public schools.* National Center for Education Statistics, Office of Educational Research and Improvement, U.S. Department of Education. Retrieved from https://nces.ed.gov/pubs99/1999043.pdf

Toews, M., & Cerny, J. (2005). The impact of service learning on student development: Students' reflections in a family diversity course. *Marriage & Family Review, 38*(4), 79–96.

Varona, L. T., & Bauluz, M. V. (2003). When everyday life becomes the focus of attention in intermediate Spanish courses. In J. Hellebrandt, J. Arries, & L. T. Varona (Eds.), *Juntos: Community partnerships in Spanish and Portuguese* (pp. 69–82). Boston, MA: Heinle.

Verba, S., Schlozman, K. L., & Brady, H. (1995). *Voice and equality: Civic voluntarism in America.* Cambridge, MA: Harvard University Press.

Wade, R. C. (Ed.). (1997). *Community service-learning: A guide to including service in the public school curriculum.* New York, NY: State University of New York Press.

Waterman, A. (Ed.). (1997). *Service-learning: Application from the research.* Mahwah, NJ: Erlbaum.

Weiler, D., LaGoy, A., Crane, E., & Rovner A. (1998). *An evaluation of K–12 service learning in California.* Emeryville, CA: RPP International.

Welch Borden, A. (2007). Impact of service-learning on ethnocentrism in an intercultural communication course. *Journal of Experiential Education, 30*(2), 171–183.

Weldon, A., & Trautmann, G. (2003). Spanish and service learning: Pedagogy and praxis. *Hispania, 86*(3), 574–585.

Yates, M., & Youniss, J. (1998). Community service and political identity development in adolescence. *Journal of Social Issues, 54*(3), 495–512.

PART 3

Community-Based Pedagogical Strategies with Students and for Educators

CHAPTER 4

Community-Based Pedagogical Strategies with Students

Lakia M. Scott, Karon N. LeCompte, Suzanne M. Nesmith and Susan K. Johnsen

Abstract

Community-based learning offers a multitude of benefits by deepening curriculum content while also providing opportunities to engage in the community through service and action. The purpose of this chapter is to highlight four community-based pedagogical approaches for K–16 classrooms. First, the pedagogical approach of independent investigation is utilized in a case involving elementary students seeking to address standards of care for animals at a local zoo. Next, Action Civics is explored in the context of providing middle-level students opportunities to identify a community issue, conduct research on the root causes, and propose solutions for change. Justice-oriented citizenship is another method discussed in which middle and secondary students participate in a public demonstration project where they marched to increase awareness about child hunger. In the final case, transdisciplinary learning is used in teaching college-level students how to examine local water quality issues and associated community concerns. From the cases presented and the extent of educational research demonstrating the value of this type of pedagogical approach, community-based pedagogical strategies can be recommended as a primary tool in educational spaces for transforming learning for students.

Keywords

community-based learning – independent investigation – action civics – justice-oriented citizenship – transdisciplinary learning

1 Introduction

This chapter describes community-based pedagogical strategies that engage K–16 students in independent investigations, action civics, justice-oriented citizenship, and transdisciplinary learning. The context for using each of these strategies is delineated, along with the strategy's characteristics and related research. Specific examples are organized by grade level and provide model cases in which these strategies were used within the community.

Students in today's schools need to learn a great deal in order to become contributing members of society as adults. They must learn content knowledge, they need to think critically and be able to solve complex problems, and they must prepare for college and career. Community-based learning provides opportunities for students to increase community engagement, make curriculum meaningful, and strengthen the connection between learning in schools and the community (Prast & Viegut, 2016). In addition, community-based learning provides opportunities for students to develop skills in order to take action on community issues. In consideration of the ways in which this pedagogical strategy can benefit both the immediate and long-term learning experiences of students, practitioners need to examine effective practices of community-based learning.

The Coalition for Community Schools, an alliance of nearly 200 national, state, and local organizations, represents community development and community building and provides a rationale for community-based learning in public schools. A Coalition for Community Schools report (2006, p. 2) postulates that community-based learning aims to "more fully engage young people, by harnessing their natural interest in where and how they live and by using their own community as a source of learning and action." The organization proposes that this type of pedagogical implementation values community influence, perspective, and input within academic settings, which in turn reinforce social and political acts from students and members. Presented here are examples of community-based pedagogical strategies in the forms of independent investigations, student-led projects, and engagement in global environmental issues.

2 Pedagogical Strategy: Independent Investigations

2.1 Context

The University for Young People (UYP) is a university-based summer enrichment program designed to develop talent in gifted students in grades 4–12.

University professors and local gifted-education teachers typically teach the summer UYP classes, which generally are 90-minutes long and offered over a one- to two-week period. Consistent with talent development frameworks (see Subotnik, Olszewski-Kubilius, & Worrell, 2011, pp. 27–29), course content is determined by students' interests, strengths, and career goals. Subjects taught serve to broaden exposure to topics not typically addressed in the general education program, deepen knowledge, develop creativity, and provide opportunities for independent investigations. Examples of classes offered include choices related to STEM (robotics, astronomy, computer game design, criminal science), fine arts (painting, drama, sculpture, music appreciation, video design), liberal arts (geography, logic, history, literature, poetry, chess), or life skills (cooking, public speaking, leadership, school safety, emergency life plans, money management). While UYP students find themselves learning about a new "community"—the university setting—they also focus on finding and solving problems within the local community using an independent investigation process.

2.2 Characteristics of Independent Investigations

Learning exists on a continuum ranging from more deductive, direct instruction, or prescriptive approaches, to more inductive, constructivist, or investigative approaches. For the most part, learning that takes place outside of formal school situations, such as in the community, is more investigative in nature. Renzulli (2012, p. 155) suggested that these types of investigations must meet three requirements: (a) students must be interested in the topic or problem, (b) they must use authentic methods of research, and (c) they must develop a meaningful product or service that will result in a desired effect on the intended audience—whether for self-fulfillment or, as in community-based learning, creative solutions to society's problems. Community-based investigations, therefore, are connected to the world outside the classroom and provide students with opportunities to apply authentic research methods and solve problems of interest to them.

A variety of models exist describing ways to guide students in independent investigations (Betts & Kercher, 1999; Moon, Kolloff, Robinson, Dixon, & Feldhusen, 2009; Johnsen & Johnson, 2007; Renzulli, 1976, 2012; Starko & Schack, 1992). Renzulli's Enrichment Triad Model (1976, 2012, p. 152) described three types of enrichment activities: (a) General Exploratory Activities (Type I), consisting of experiences and activities to introduce students to areas of personal interest; (b) Group or Individual Training Activities (Type II), involving instructional techniques and methods to develop the important skills related to the investigation; and (c) Individual or Small Group Investigations (Type III), providing students with opportunities to investigate a real problem or topic by using the acquired inquiry methods.

The specific investigation framework varies among researchers. Reis and Renzulli (1992) described a 12-step method, whereas Johnsen and Johnson (2007) proposed a nine-step cyclical process. Johnsen and Goree (2015) suggested that all of the steps may or may not be used in every investigation, since the instructor and the student may already have defined some steps. For example, the instructor may present a problem and the students are responsible primarily for gathering information and sharing their results. The steps are also not necessarily sequential but are more cyclical and based on each student's progress. For example, in the fourth step, Ask Questions, students are supposed to formulate questions, but if they haven't gathered enough information to articulate their questions, they may need to return to step 2, Organizing the Study. Similarly, students may begin to gather information about their questions and decide that they want to change or add another question to their study. Based on the student's performance, the instructor may also decide to skip steps, guide the student through some of the steps, and/or allow the students to do steps independently. The instructor will, therefore, use the independent study process as a framework based on the students' background and experiences.

Previous empirical research suggests that students who were involved in independent investigations felt more competent (Vallerand, Gagné, Senécal, & Pelletier, 1994, p. 174), had higher self-efficacy with regard to creative productivity (Starko, 1988, p. 296), were more motivated (Delcourt, 1993, pp. 29–30), pursued more creative projects outside of school (Starko, 1988, pp. 28–31), and were able to manage time and meet desired goals (Hébert, 1993, pp. 26–27). Selecting projects they enjoy tended to increase students' motivation and interest in future investigations (Collins & Amabile, 1999; Csikszentmihalyi, Rathunde, & Whalen, 1993). Diffily (2002, pp. 42–43) described how elementary students planned an intercultural festival for the community and gained not only knowledge about the culture but also skills related to collaborating with others, negotiating solutions to problems, and sharing information. She noted that these students' connection to the world outside the classroom encouraged their awareness of community resources and possibilities for finding answers to questions and solving problems.

2.3   *An Example of Using Independent Investigations*

One of the community problems addressed in a UYP course related to selecting a new animal for the local zoo. Since the zoo's opening in 1993, it had slowly built new attractions based on funding resources and community interest.

Fourth- and fifth-grade students selected this particular UYP course because they wanted to have an opportunity to express their opinions about the next animal exhibit. As one can imagine, each felt strongly about the possible choice.

Since the students were already interested in the topic, the instructor bypassed the Selecting a Topic step and developed an investigation plan with the students. The plan included a timeline for gathering information about the topic, organizing preliminary information to ask specific questions, collecting additional information, and developing a presentation for the zoo administrators.

Following the development of the plan, the instructor realized the students needed more information related to the zoo itself and new exhibits before they could formulate specific questions related to animal selection. They collected their information at this stage by exploring the zoo's virtual tour and developing questions to ask the zookeepers: How does the zoo select a new animal? What criteria are used? What animals might have the best chance of being selected for this zoo? When might we visit the zoo to share our choice?

After gathering this information, the students were ready to investigate possible future animal exhibits. They formulated their questions using the organization structure (Organizing the Topic or Problem): What are the characteristics of the animal's habitat (Descriptive Question)? How might this animal's compare to other animals that are already in the zoo (Comparison)? How might the local climate affect the animal (Cause and Effect)? How might the zoo build an exhibit that would protect the animal and encourage its adaptation (Problem and Solution)?

Next, individuals and small groups selected animals of interest to them and gathered information. The instructor shared with the students ways of ensuring that their information was factual by reviewing the importance of multiple and reliable sources (Study Method or Research Design). The students then conducted their independent investigations by examining books, visiting websites, and interviewing campus faculty from the environmental sciences and biology departments (Collecting Information). They then shared their information with one another, addressing the questions they had formulated as a class. The zookeepers' answers to their interview questions provided helpful criteria for selecting the final animal they would present when they visited the zoo.

After identifying the Komodo dragon as their animal of choice, the students developed PowerPoint slides and a diorama that showed a potential zoo exhibit (Organizing Information Into a Product and Performance). They practiced their talk and ultimately presented the information to the administrators at the zoo (Disseminating the Product). Following their presentation and an actual visit to the zoo, they reflected on their investigation and identified ways that they might have improved any of the steps in the process. Assessment questions addressed planning, time, depth of questions, varied resources, research method, product, and presentation. Following the UYP course, the class later learned that the Komodo dragon was selected as a future zoo exhibit! This result encouraged and empowered the students and the connections they created to the community.

3   Pedagogical Strategy: Action Civics

> For me, civic education is the key to inspiring kids to want to stay involved in making a difference. (Associate Justice Sonia Sotomayor, U.S. Supreme Court, iCivics, n.d.)

3.1   *Context*

Former U.S. Supreme Court Justice Sandra Day O'Connor championed an online civics resources website in 2008, entitled iCivics, that "works to ensure every student in America receives a quality and engaging civic education and graduates from high school well prepared and enthusiastic for citizenship" (iCivics, n.d.). This website contains free civics education games and supplemental curricular materials designed to promote civics knowledge and engagement for students in middle and secondary grades.

This website and consequent support gave life to the iEngage Summer Civics Institute, established at Baylor University in 2013, where fifth through ninth graders can learn about civic action and meet local leaders and officeholders before developing their own action plan for civic change. The one-week summer intensive has a twofold purpose: (a) provide teachers with free high-quality professional development focused on civics education, and (b) provide students with the opportunity to engage in meaningful civic learning through online gaming, live simulations, and action civics.

Action civics rooted in positive youth development (PYD) is an educational practice that holds promise for engaging students in activities that help them develop "voice" in the public arena and become informed about issues that affect their lives. Action civics "is a broad term used to describe curricula and programs that go beyond the traditional civics programs by combining learning and practice" (Center for Information and Research on Civic Learning and Engagement [CIRCLE], 2013b, p. 2). This approach insists that "students *do* and *behave* as citizens by engaging in a cycle of research, action, and reflection about problems they care about personally while learning about deeper principles of effective civics and especially political action" (Levinson, 2012, p. 224).

This model of civic education challenges the traditional instructional approach of memorizing government facts and processes and instead encourages teachers and students to engage in democratic action via technology and social networking. Action civics views young people as assets to the community in which they live and learn and rallies adult support in helping young people lead the process of personal development and community change (CIRCLE, 2013a, p. 7). Students find themselves positioned as knowledgeable insiders whose perspectives allow them to act as powerful agents of change (Levinson, 2012).

Levinson (2012) argued that this approach to civic learning stands in contrast to the way students, primarily low-income youth of color, are viewed as deficient and delinquent in their communities. Action civics empowers youth through the acquisition of civic knowledge and skills, thereby increasing student motivation and engagement. Action civics is intentionally political and policy-oriented (Levinson, 2012). Research suggests that engagement in participatory civic opportunities exposes students to factors that will increase their academic achievement, allow them to develop collegial relationships with adults and peers, and boost their self-esteem (Levine, 2013; Levinson, 2012).

Although action civics programs vary in scope, content, and duration, they do share the following key elements: (a) student voice, experience, and decision-making is valued; (b) students learn by engaging in civic activities in the classroom or beyond; (c) students choose an issue important to them and work to make a difference; and (d) students reflect on their own actions, successes, and challenges throughout the project (CIRCLE, 2013b, pp. 2–3).

3.2 *Characteristics of Action Civics*

In order to make civics education meaningful and relevant to civil society, we need a combination of "deliberation, collaboration, and civic relationships" (Levine, 2013, p. 3) In addition to reforming social studies/civics standards and creating better assessments, researchers have suggested a number of possible solutions related to civics education curricula and pedagogy—particularly those that are experience-based (Levinson, 2012). Participating in student government, civic-related extracurricular activities (Kahne & Middaugh, 2008), and local government have all shown to have positive effects on students' propensity for civic action. Additionally, classroom pedagogy such as simulations (Lin, 2015), discussing current and controversial issues (Youniss, 2011), exposure to civic role models (Kahne, Chi, & Middaugh, 2006), and service-learning (Lin, 2015) are key to a high-quality civics curriculum.

With its early roots in the work of John Dewey, community-based learning has a strong theoretical foundation. Dewey argued that civics engagement would provide an educational framework for community-based experiential learning linked to public problem solving (Saltmarsh, 2008). This kind of experiential learning is particularly powerful because, as Dewey (1927/2010) noted, "The level of action fixed by embodied intelligence is always the important thing" (p. 50). Learning is active and the learner investigates, inquires, and creates solutions.

Levinson (2012) argued that action civics empowers young people because it addresses three causal components of an individual's civic engagement, including ability and resources, motivation or engagement, and opportunity or recruitment. Through an action civics experience, students have meaningful opportunities to develop their civic knowledge, participation skills, and attitudes while simultaneously making a positive impact on their community. Students can make the connections between the individual, isolated problems they choose to investigate and the larger world of public policy, including more systematic solutions to issues (Delli Carpini & Keeter, 1996). By spending time immersed in learning civic principles, meeting civic leaders, and engaging in civic activities, students not only gain valuable civics content knowledge, but they are also able to apply this knowledge to real-world civic issues.

Erbstein (2013) supported this notion and added, "Effective outreach to marginalized youth [relies] on locally grounded, culturally specific understandings" of these youth (p. 111). Erbstein (2013, pp. 119–122) related this idea to PYD by sharing key components of a culturally relevant PYD: (a) engaging adult allies; (b) respect, care, and high expectations; (c) a critical stance toward systems; (d) communication; and (e) shared culture, language, and experience. Moreover, Williams and Le Menestrel (2013) suggested that "youth development practitioners may have to increase their knowledge base of different cultures to begin the journey to accomplishing cross-cultural competence so programs may be designed for cultural inclusion of diverse youth and volunteers" (para. 16).

3.3 An Example of Implementing Action Civics

During an iteration of the program, middle school students participated in social action projects and advocacy campaigns in small groups. After deciding on an issue to address, students researched information via the Internet and newspaper articles in addition to contacting community members, local organizations, and support networks. Working collaboratively, students developed an advocacy campaign to showcase their issue and proposed solutions. Participants were asked to discuss community issues that plagued them and then, after learning and rediscovering citizenship and civil rights, students developed advocacy campaigns. By spending time immersed in learning civic principles and engaging in civic activities, students gained valuable content knowledge and were also able to apply information to real-world civic issues.

From the action civics project, students became keenly aware that, even as a young person, they have rights. Elaborate conversations emerged about instances in which students' rights had been violated at school or in a public setting. After learning and having a better understanding of the first 10 amendments to the U.S. Constitution, students felt empowered to "plead the Fifth" or to state, "No, I know my rights!" These salient themes exemplify the notion of navigational and resistance capital. Students gained an understanding of how to navigate through various institutions, such as schools or neighborhoods, using a critically aware lens into the social and racial inequities that continue to persist (Yosso, 2005).

Students also demonstrated an increased knowledge, expanded understanding, and direct application of civic engagement. Part of the focus for the action civics unit was to help students understand ways in which to "let their voices be heard." In doing so, most participants demonstrated mastery in understanding how to identify root causes of community issues as well as conduct research on how to propose solutions. For example, one group of students examined the impact of open carry (the right to bear arms) in lower-income neighborhoods. Gathering information from the Centers for Disease Control, they found that in poorer communities (such as the ones in which they live), guns increase the rate of premature deaths among youths and young adults. With this information, students decided to create a social media campaign to "Stop the Gun Rage" by increasing neighborhood surveillance and encouraging business owners to refuse services to those who carry weapons.

As another example of student engagement in the community, one group of middle school students expressed an idea of police officer and church membership. Their proposal was that police officers and their families should attend a church in the same community that they patrol. This is an example of students "thinking outside" of the political and social restraints to enhance community engagement and communication. One youth commented, "If the police came to my church, they would recognize me, and know my family."

Findings from this action civics experience suggest that students demonstrated civic engagement and efficacy by drawing attention to local and national issues through their advocacy projects, researching places where they could volunteer, and contacting state and national officials. Moreover, students felt an increased sense of power in their ability to make a difference in their community.

4   Pedagogical Strategy: Justice-Oriented Citizenship

4.1   *Context*

The Children's Defense Fund (CDF) continues the legacy of the Freedom Summer of 1964 through a summer literacy program called Freedom Schools. This national movement has impacted over 137,000 pre–K–12 youth in its 20-plus years and is sustained primarily through churches in schools in lower-income neighborhoods (CDF, 2016). The CDF Freedom School model focuses on teamwork, conflict resolution, and history in addition to building self-esteem and teaching respect. Using principles of Afrocentricity and critical pedagogy practices such as call response, critical reflection, and social consciousness, students are highly engaged using black cultural traditions.

CDF Freedom Schools provide summer and after-school enrichment through a research-based and multicultural curriculum that supports children and families through five essential components: (a) high-quality academic and character-building enrichment, (b) parent and family involvement, (c) civic engagement and social action, (d) intergenerational servant leadership development, and (e) nutrition, health, and mental health. CDF Freedom Schools incorporate the totality of CDF's mission by fostering environments that support children and young adults in excelling and believing in their ability to make a difference in themselves and in their families, schools, communities, country, and the world with hope, education, and action.

Freedom Schools curricula originally focused on rejecting traditional teaching practices of rote memorization and little student interaction by relying on teaching and learning practices that promoted "student participation in learning, a sense of the worth and equality among students, and the need to connect lessons to life" (Perlstein, 1990, p. 319). They are schools for questioning, for exposing students to meaningful discussion experiences, and for helping them understand the social forces influencing their lives, with the hope that they might achieve some management of social conditions under which they lived (CDF, 2016). Students' questioning their experiences and their personal situations was a first step toward overcoming the pattern of passively accepting authority and learning to think, to inquire, and ultimately to convert learning and inquiry into action (Chilcoat & Ligon, 2001, p. 218).

The Freedom Schools model also incorporates a National Day of Social Action (NDSA), which is a major component that incorporates civic engagement and social justice advocacy. The goals of the NDSA are to: (a) amplify children's voices on issues that matter to them, (b) encourage Freedom School participants and their families to make a difference in the country by becoming involved in civic engagement and principles of nonviolent social action, and

(c) influence the national discussion by taking collective action that amplifies the message around critical areas impacting children, specifically health, poverty, and nutrition. In this model, students work together to intensely research the topic or focus of the summer and to enact suggestions and plans to "make a difference." Critical thinking and problem-solving skills are developed as students become responsive to community issues. Each year, thousands of children and teens from CDF Freedom School sites in the United States take part in a variety of actions, including writing letters to and visiting elected officials, and joining together for marches, rallies, and other initiatives in order to generate awareness. In years prior, topics for the NDSA have included neighborhood safety, health care, homelessness, gun violence, and voter registration, to name a few. Participants learn that they are not merely citizens awaiting change but are empowered to make a difference now. In this way, various forms of social capital, such as participatory and justice-oriented citizenship, are emphasized (Westheimer & Kahne, 2004, p. 240).

4.2 Types of Citizens

Westheimer and Kahne (2004, p. 240) recognized the bridge between civic education, service-learning, and instructional pedagogies in promoting democratic values for students. In a longitudinal study, they examined the concept of citizenship and provided a prescriptive lens for educating students about democratic theory. In their framework, three kinds of citizens are identified: personally responsible, participatory, and justice-oriented.

They describe the personally responsible citizen as one who "acts responsible in his/her community" (Westheimer & Kahne, 2004, p. 240). This kind of citizen obeys laws, rules, and regulations, but to the extent that actions are individually minded and personally based on interests and commitment. They further assume that "to solve social problems and improve society, citizens must have good character; they must be honest, responsible, and law-abiding members of the community" (Westheimer & Kahne, 2004, p. 240). Examples of service such as volunteering for a blood drive, recycling, or donating clothing are tangible acts of the personally responsible citizen that stem from perspectives of character education and morality. Westheimer and Kahne (2004, p. 241) noted that these acts build personal responsibility and a character that emphasizes honesty, integrity, self-discipline, and hard work.

Next, they conceptualize the participatory citizen as one who is "an active member of community organizations and/or improvement efforts, knows how government agencies work, and knows strategies for accomplishing tasks" (Westheimer & Kahne, 2004, p. 240). This kind of citizen demonstrates leadership by facilitating community efforts based on community needs at local, state, and national levels. Underlying values are based on this type of citizen's ability to "actively participate and take leadership positions within established systems and community structures" (Westheimer & Kahne, 2004, p. 240). At the school level, programs that seek to educate students about how governmental and community-based programs work and to train students on being part of organized efforts encourage participatory citizenship. Westheimer and Kahne (2004, pp. 241–242) emphasized that participatory citizens go beyond the call of engaging in community matters by leading, facilitating, and/or organizing efforts.

Finally, the justice-oriented citizen is conceptualized as one who "critically assesses social, political, and economic structures to see beyond surface causes [and] knows about democratic social movements and how to effect systematic change" (Westheimer & Kahne, 2004, p. 240). This kind of citizen explores root causes in order to "question, debate, and change established systems and structures that reproduce patterns of injustice over time" (Westheimer & Kahne, 2004, p. 240). Stemming from critical theorists like Antonio Gramsci, Paulo Freire, and Derrick Bell, justice-oriented citizens place similar emphasis on collective work-related community issues alongside the participatory citizen, however, this type of citizen goes beyond charity support and volunteerism by learning about social movements and how to affect systemic change. Within the educational context, programs that prepare students to better society by critically analyzing and addressing social issues and injustices encourage justice-oriented citizens (Westheimer & Kahne, 2004, pp. 242–243). However, they mention that this type of perspective on citizenship is less commonly developed because of the need for ongoing critical analyses and discussions of social, political, and economic structures and the procurement of voice to promote collective goals in political arenas. Notwithstanding, of the three types, justice-oriented citizens have the greatest impact in enacting change at the local, state, or national level.

4.3 An Example of Justice-Oriented Citizenship

As mentioned earlier, the CDF Freedom School model incorporates citizenship values in the NDSA programming. Specifically, the participatory and justice-oriented citizen types are recognized and highlighted for promoting leadership, collective responsibility, and critical analyses of societal problems and issues. The following example of the 2017 National Day of Social Action will provide further connection to Westheimer and Kahne's (2004) notion of justice-oriented citizenship.

In 2017, the topic for the NDSA was child hunger across America. At each Freedom School site, middle and secondary students planned a march that ended at a targeted destination where groups delivered and displayed symbolic empty plates to represent the population of children who go hungry each day. It was critical to emphasize the need for programs and funding to support child health, nutrition, and development. Students, parents, and community supporters also joined in the march and demonstration by holding visuals or posters with statements or quotes that provided a strong message to support the importance of food. The goal of this campaign was to bring attention to the 2018 U.S. federal congressional budget and to support of maintaining and improving programs like the Supplemental Nutrition Assistance Program (SNAP), Women, Infants, and Children (WIC) programs, free school meals, and summer feeding programs.

Prior to planning and implementing the Child Hunger March, students researched the issue and how it affected local, state, and national youth populations. Students were provided with access to technology to look up national statistics, and community members specializing in social welfare programming and hunger initiatives spoke with students about child hunger. After the initial research period and discussions with community networks, some students worked in teams to create statements and speeches in preparation for the march. Others worked to create signage and visuals to pass out to spectators during the event.

To prepare for this event, students followed procedural guidelines, as guided by the CDF's National Social Action Planning Committee. First, students targeted a specific location and audience. With the goal in mind to march around four blocks of city hall, where legislation and governmental matters take place, students notified city officials to gain approval to occupy space for a demonstration following the march. Next, students mapped their march route, which included stopping points to share information with spectators. This portion of the planning was also helpful because students were able to provide parents and community supporters with meeting points and locations to join. Then, students finalized display materials. One of the most powerful visuals used was empty paper plates with painted forks and spoons. In the center of the plate was a number that represented a portion of the 13.1 million children living in America who are food insecure—children who are not certain when they might have their next meal. Since the student group averaged 50 participants, each student held a plate with the number 262,000 in order to highlight that each plate stood for the number of kids who go hungry each day. Afterward, students finalized the slogan to use on posters and in verbal chants: No Child Hungry. Finally, students voted on march leaders and demonstration speakers in order to maximize the event's timetable. Staff members also helped to coordinate the events by notifying local media contacts and supporting students in the march and demonstration activities.

The march and demonstration were well received by community members. In fact, some local policymakers attended and participated in advocating programs to prevent or alleviate child hunger. Students also became widely recognized in the local community, as all media outlets were present to highlight their actions. In particular, the local news cited how informative the event was for community constituents and how students were making a difference in their community (Conlon, 2017). To date, the program and students involved have received citywide recognition for their efforts in eliminating child hunger.

This example deeply resonates with Westheimer and Kahne's (2004, pp. 242–243) notion of justice-oriented citizenship because of the students' abilities to identify the problem's root causes and to take collective action at the local (and national) level to solve the issue. What seems to be one of the most meaningful aspects of the NDSA is the inquiry-based lessons that facilitate action regarding community issues. In a brief survey after the conclusion of the Freedom Schools program, students shared how they felt empowered to make a difference in their communities as a result of the skills learned and implemented in the NDSA event. Additionally, most students also commented that they would continue to advocate for issues such as child hunger through further organizing and rallying of support in the community. In fact, some wrote letters to members of Congress and attended local city meetings in efforts to continue to bring about awareness of the issue. From these experiences, students are deeply compelled not only to become informed citizens but also justice-oriented and action driven. By spending time immersed in learning civic principles and engaging in social action activities, students gained valuable content knowledge and were also able to apply information to real-world issues.

5   Pedagogical Strategy: Transdisciplinary Learning Experience

5.1   *Context*

The Social Innovation Collaborative (SIC) brings together university faculty, staff, and undergraduate students in efforts to discover and develop innovative ways to promote human fulfillment. The Healthy River, Healthy Community SIC project consists of a semester-long course designed and taught by eight university faculty members representing seven departments. Recognizing industry and employer demands for graduates equipped with competencies from multiple disciplines necessary for solving complex, real-world problems, the course incorporates a transdisciplinary, inquiry-based approach with numerous field-based and community-embedded components. Examples of course components include a canoe trip on a local river; exploration of the natural history collection at a local museum; a tour of an urban water-cycle facility; interactions with environmental lawyers; panel discussions involving federal, state, and national water experts; water-quality chemical analyses; cost-benefit assessments; and collaborations with education specialists in designing and sharing water activities with local children. Though focused on the local river and associated community-specific water issues, the adoption of a transdisciplinary approach provides a means of moving beyond a university's institutional boundaries and local community boundaries into a wider community of stakeholders capable of working together to approach complex wicked problems that defy easy resolution (Brown, Harris, & Russell, 2010, pp. 61–83; Brundiers, Wiek, & Redman, 2010, pp. 311–313; Scholz, Lang, Wiek, Walter, & Stauffacher, 2006, pp. 231–232).

5.2   *Transdisciplinary and Community-Based Learning*

The integration of disciplinary knowledge is referred to as multidisciplinary, interdisciplinary, or transdisciplinary, and students often illustrate these term designations based on degree of knowledge integration. Marinova and McGrath (2004) defined *multidisciplinary* as the examination of a topic "not only in one discipline but in several at the same time," *interdisciplinary* as "the links and the transfer of knowledge, methods, concepts and models from one discipline to another," and *transdisciplinarity* as involving "what is between the disciplines, across the disciplines and beyond the disciplines" (p. 3). Moreover, transdisciplinary understanding moves beyond interdisciplinary understanding in that knowledge and the modes of thinking of stakeholders outside of the academic arena are included in the knowledge integration. The distinctions between forms of knowledge integration support using a transdisciplinary approach to solve real-world community-based wicked problems because "academic knowledge alone has failed to solve society's most pressing problems" (Remington-Doucette, Hiller Connell, Armstrong, & Musgrove, 2013, p. 407; Fischer, 2000, chapter 2).

Three key competencies of transdisciplinary, drawn from Wiek, Withycombe, and Redman (2011, pp. 207–211), include systems, normative, and strategic thinking. A systems thinking approach focuses on building understanding of the system by exploring both the whole and the many levels of interrelationships of the system, as opposed to a mechanistic/reductionist approach that focuses on explaining a system through the isolated analysis of all system components. Wicked problems encompass diverse perspectives borne of different value and belief systems, thereby leading to conflict in reaching solutions to the problem. It is through systems thinking that individuals can recognize and critically analyze the values associated with these perspectives.

Additionally, competence in systems thinking builds capacity to recognize the values underlying the structure of social systems and the actions of individuals. At a personal level, systems thinking enhances an individual's ability to integrate multiple perspectives into one's viewpoints (Ellis & Weekes, 2008, p. 493; Porter & Cordoba, 2008, pp. 323–324; Remington-Doucette et al., 2013, pp. 408–409; Warburton, 2003, pp. 44–45).

Normative thinking generally refers to an ideal standard or model and is typically associated with an assertion of values relative to what the world should look like, whereas positive knowledge is generally associated with facts and reality. In terms of wicked community-based environmental problems such as water quality and quantity, possessing a normative competence allows an individual to move beyond the ability to understand and describe a current system and how it might continue to develop in the future given the continuation of existing conditions, to thinking about how the current system should be developed in the future to enhance economic, social, and environmental systems.

Closely associated with normative thinking competence is strategic competence. When confronted with real-world challenges, individuals will propose varying courses of action based on their preferences, values, and beliefs. Often referred to as an ability to "get things done," competence in strategic thinking provides the means to "collectively design and implement interventions, transitions, and transformative strategies to redirect current systems towards a sustainable future state" (Remington-Doucette et al., 2013, p. 410; Wiek, Withycombe, & Redman, 2011, p. 210).

Recent research has revealed the impact of a transdisciplinary approach in relation to community-based problems. Vogel, Scott, Culwick, and Sutherland (2016, p. 526) determined that utilizing a transdisciplinary approach together with reflexive examination resulted in participants' wider, more realistic views of local environments that allowed for an enhanced world view and better solutions to wicked problems. Remington-Doucette and her colleagues (2013) found that university students enrolled in a semester-long transdisciplinary real-world sustainability course exhibited enhanced competence in systems thinking compared to their normative and strategic competencies. Additionally, findings revealed a connection between students' majors/disciplinary affiliations and their capacities for developing the transdisciplinary competencies (Remington-Doucette et al., 2013, pp. 417–422). A university in Taiwan implemented a policy that considerably reduced the number of compulsory module credits while simultaneously establishing transdisciplinary climate-focused courses to guide students in their choice of compulsory modules. Results revealed that the small number of students who chose modules from other disciplines performed better in projects associated with climate change issues and made module choices that addressed their real interests (Yu & Chiang, 2018, Conclusions section, para. 1).

5.3   An Example of a Learning Experience

As rivers flow across the land, they are used and managed by multiple stakeholders and user groups, including a myriad of human and nonhuman uses. These user groups often present conflicting demands and perspectives in terms of both quantity and quality of water needed. On a local, national, and global scale, water is inextricably linked to critical social issues such as energy use, health and human development, poverty, food scarcity, and environmental degradation. As such, water serves as a wicked problem that is complex in scope and requires technological solutions alongside equity and ethical considerations. Additionally, water presents an environmental conflict that is often so heavily value-based that "not even the strongest possible evidence can settle differences between stakeholders or avoid triggering major political conflicts" (Crowley & Head, 2017, p. 543; Van de Kerkhof, 2006, p. 282). With recognition of these factors, a group of university faculty members from across the university (the schools/departments of Environmental Science, Business, Religion, Education, and English; the university aquatic systems center; and the local natural science and cultural history museums) gathered to design a river-focused, real-world, inquiry-based, community-embedded transdisciplinary learning experience for undergraduate students.

Students from across the university were invited to enroll in the course, and the course met a variety of degree requirements. For example, depending on the student's major, the course could meet requirements for general science, environmental science, social science, and informal education. Decisions about degree requirements were made and provided to students well in advance of registration deadlines to allow for well-founded course choices.

Class was held once a week for 2.5 hours with four required Saturday field/community experiences. Specific course instructors assumed the lead for each class, yet all instructors tried to be present and participate in every class session and community experience. This structure allowed each instructor to utilize his or her unique expertise, experiences, and perspectives in addressing a water-related topic while also allowing all students and co-instructors to explore and discuss the issue through their own personal lenses. During numerous class sessions, course instructors chose to include other individuals to further expand students' exposure to varying perspectives and areas of expertise. To name a few, guest speakers included a former U.S. Secretary of the Interior, a branch chief from the state Parks and Wildlife Department, a member of the U.S. Army Corp of Engineers, a manager from the state Commission on Environmental Quality, a manager from the local river authority, and the local city manager. During the entirety of the course, students were asked to reflect upon and respond to the following questions: What is a river? Why are rivers important? What is the relationship between a river's health and a community's health? How can the health of a river and a community be explored and expressed? What actions can be taken to improve the health of a river and community? Who can take this action?

In addition to readings, discussions, and field experiences, students participated in two major course projects: (a) designing and sharing with local children a hands-on, field-based, and/or collections-based river activity; and (b) designing, piloting, administering, and evaluating the results of a Contingent Valuation Modeling (CVM) survey specific to the local river. The interactive activities occurred on the banks of the local river and addressed water pollution and filtering, biotic and abiotic factors of river habitats, and adaptations (beaks and mouth structures) of river species. CVM-proposed survey projects included a "river festival" to promote appreciation and awareness of the river environment and river health, a revitalization of the creek that runs through the city and university campus, and development of a campus-wide water filtration system. Ultimately, students chose to pursue the creek revitalization project and developed surveys to determine university students' and community members' likelihood of paying a fee/tax in support of the project. Results revealed that most of those surveyed would be willing to pay a minimal fee/tax for a short period of time to clean and revitalize the creek.

While the course did not include the actual implementation of a CVM project, numerous class members pursued the creek revitalization project by taking the idea to university officials. To date, the university has not acted on the students' proposal, yet these students continue their interest in the project.

6   Conclusion

Under the administration of U.S. President Barack Obama, the Every Student Succeeds Act (ESSA) became law in the United States in 2015 and included initiatives to create school and community partnerships. This federal legislation supports the value of communities in schools and their influence on accountability and educational equity for all students. As such, this chapter presented four cases in which community-based learning was implemented in K–16 schooling environments.

To summarize, one case presented opportunities for gifted and talented students to develop independent investigations via student projects. Elementary students from low-income and diverse backgrounds were mentored in small groups with peers of similar ability. While the students found themselves learning about a new "community"—the university setting—they also focused on finding and solving problems within the local community. These course-related community problems ranged from identifying a new animal for the zoo to identifying "safe" places in the community for interacting with friends. The second case highlighted the impact of action civics by providing students with opportunities to examine root causes using research and to develop solutions to community problems. This example showcased middle school students who conducted inquiry-based projects that reflected civic dispositions in action. Next, historically, the CDF Freedom Schools program was examined for its practice of justice-oriented citizenship. Through the local and national days of social action, the program also expands tenets of community-based learning through civic engagement and social advocacy. Finally, Healthy River, Healthy Community, an SIC course, provided undergraduate students with an opportunity to engage in a real-world, problem-based, community-embedded transdisciplinary learning experience involving faculty members from multiple schools and departments. Addressing the community-based problem of access to safe and affordable water provided students with an opportunity to investigate a wicked problem that is difficult to define, socially complex, lacks a clear solution, and involves many interdependencies.

Community-based learning is a means for educators to expand and bridge concepts through opportunities of critical inquiry and civic engagement. Pedagogies associated with community-based learning promote stronger relationships between the school and community, while also encouraging instructional connectivity, community integration and participation, and active citizenship. While community-based learning is not an easy task, it is hoped that this chapter has provided tangible examples for its integration into today's K–16 classrooms.

References

Betts, G. T., & Kercher, J. K. (1999). *The autonomous learner model: Optimizing ability*. Greeley, CO: Association of Learned & Professional Society Publishers.

Brown, V. A., Harris, J. A., & Russell, J. Y. (2010). Collective inquiry and its wicked problems. In V. A. Brown, J. A. Harris, & C. L. Russell (Eds.), *Tackling wicked problems through the transdisciplinary imagination* (pp. 61–83). London, U.K.: Routledge Earthscan.

Brundiers, K., Wiek, A., & Redman, C. L. (2010). Real-world learning opportunities in sustainability: From classroom into the real world. *International Journal of Sustainability in Higher Education, 11*, 308–324.

Center for Information & Research on Civic Learning and Engagement (CIRCLE). (2013a). *All together now: Collaboration and innovation for youth engagement. The Report of the Commission on Youth Voting and Civic Knowledge*. Medford, MA: Author. Retrieved from https://civicyouth.org/wp-content/uploads/2013/09/CIRCLE-youthvoting-individualPages.pdf

Center for Information & Research on Civic Learning and Engagement (CIRCLE). (2013b). *Civic learning through action: The case of generation citizen*. Medford, MA: Author. Retrieved from https://civicyouth.org/wp-content/uploads/2013/07/Generation-Citizen-Fact-Sheet-July-1-Final.pdf

Chilcoat, G. W., & Ligon, J. A. (2001). Discussion as a means for transformative change: Social studies lessons from the Mississippi Freedom Schools. *The Social Studies, 92*(5), 213–219. doi:10.1080/00377990109604006

Children's Defense Fund. (2016). *The Children's Defense Fund Freedom Schools Model*. Washington, DC: Author. Retrieved from https://www.childrensdefense.org/programs/cdf-freedom-schools/

Coalition for Community Schools. (2006). *Community-based learning: Engaging students for success and citizenship*. Washington, DC: Author.

Collins, M., & Amabile, T. (1999). Motivation and creativity. In R. J. Sternberg (Ed.), *Handbook of creativity* (pp. 297–312). New York, NY: Cambridge University Press.

Conlon, S. (2017, July 19). Freedom School students protest federal budget proposals in National Day of Social Action. *Waco Tribune-Herald*. Retrieved from https://www.wacotrib.com/news/downtown_waco/freedom-school-students-protest-federal-budget-proposals-in-national-day/article_ee1a8ce3-5f11-5768-8ee5-2995369957cf.html

Crowley, K., & Head, B. W. (2017). The enduring challenge of 'wicked problems': Revisiting Rittel and Webber. *Policy Sciences, 50*, 539–547.

Csikszentmihalyi, M., Rathunde, K., & Whalen, S. (1993). *Talented teenagers: The roots of success and failure*. New York, NY: Cambridge University Press.

Delcourt, M. A. B. (1993). Creative productivity among secondary school students: Combining energy, interest, and imagination. *Gifted Child Quarterly, 37*, 23–31.

Delli Carpini, M., & Keeter, S. (1996). *What Americans know about politics and why it matters*. New Haven, CT: Yale University Press.

Dewey, J. (2010). Excerpt from the public and its problems. In J. Gripsrud, H. Moe, A. Molander, & G. Murdock (Eds.), *The idea of the public sphere: A reader* (pp. 43–53). Plymouth, U.K.: Lexington Books, Roman & Littlefield. (Original work published in 1927)

Diffily, D. (2002). Project-based learning: Meeting social studies standards and the needs of gifted learners. *Gifted Child Today, 25*(3), 40–59.

Ellis, G., & Weekes, T. (2008). Making sustainability 'real': Using group-enquiry to promote education for sustainable development. *Environmental Education Research, 14*, 482–500.

Erbstein, N. (2013). Engaging underrepresented youth populations in community youth development: Tapping social capital as a critical resource. In M. Calvert, M. Emery, & S. Kinsey (Eds.), *New directions for youth development* (pp. 109–124). Hoboken, NJ: Wiley Periodicals.

Fischer, F. (2000). *Citizens, experts, and the environment.* Durham, NC: Duke University Press.

Hébert, T. P. (1993). Reflection at graduation: The long-term impact of elementary school experiences in creative productivity. *Roeper Review, 16*, 22–28.

iCivics (n.d.). *iCivics is reimagining civic learning.* Retrieved from https://www.icivics.org/about

Johnsen, S. K. (2015). Practical strategies for teaching independent study. In H. E. Vidergor & C. R. Harris (Eds.), *Applied practice for educators of gifted and able learners* (pp. 251–272). Rotterdam, The Netherlands: Sense Publishers.

Johnsen, S. K., & Goree, K. K. (2015). Teaching gifted students through independent study. In F. Karnes & S. Bean (Eds.), *Methods and materials for teaching the gifted* (4th ed., pp. 445–478). Waco, TX: Prufrock Press.

Johnsen, S. K., & Johnson, K. (2007). *Independent study program* (2nd ed.). Waco, TX: Prufrock Press.

Kahne, J., Chi, B., & Middaugh, E. (2006). Building social capital for civic and political engagement: The potential of high-school civics courses. *Canadian Journal of Education, 29*(2), 387–409.

Kahne, J., & Middaugh, E. (2008). High quality civic education: What is it and who gets it? *Social Education, 72*(1), 34–39.

Levine, P. (2013). *We are the ones we have been waiting for: The promise of civic renewal in America.* New York, NY: Oxford University Press.

Levinson, M. (2012). *No citizen left behind.* Cambridge, MA: Harvard Education Press.

Lin, A. (2015). Citizenship education in American schools and its role in developing civic engagement: A review of the research. *Educational Review, 67*(1), 35–63.

Marinova, D., & McGrath, N. (2004). A transdisciplinary approach to teaching and learning sustainability: A pedagogy for life. In *Seeking educational excellence: Proceedings of the 13th Annual Teaching Learning Forum*, February 9–10, 2004, Perth, Australia: Murdoch University. Retrieved from http://otl.curtin.edu.au/tlf/tlf2004/marinova.html

Moon, S. M., Kolloff, P., Robinson, A., Dixon, F., & Feldhusen, J. F. (2009). The Purdue three-stage model. In J. S. Renzulli, E. J. Gubbins, K. S. McMillen, R. D. Eckert, & C. A. Little (Eds.), *Systems & models for developing programs for the gifted and talented* (2nd ed., pp. 289–322). Waco, TX: Prufrock Press.

National Action Civics Collaborative. (2013). *Why action civics?* Retrieved from https://actioncivicscollaborative.org/why-action-civics/?

Perlstein, D. (1990). Teaching freedom: SNCC and the creation of the Mississippi Freedom Schools. *History of Education Quarterly, 30,* 297–324.

Porter, T., & Cordoba, J. (2008). Three views of systems theories and their implications for sustainability education. *Journal of Management Education, 33,* 323–347.

Prast, H. A., & Viegut D. J. (2016). *Community-based learning: Awakening the mission of public schools.* Thousand Oaks, CA: Corwin Press.

Reis, S. M., & Renzulli, J. S. (1992). The library media specialist's role in teaching independent study skills to high ability students. *School Library Media Quarterly, 21,* 27–35.

Remington-Doucette, S. M., Hiller Connell, K. Y., Armstrong, C. M., & Musgrove, S. L. (2013). Assessing sustainability education in a transdisciplinary undergraduate course focused on real-world problem solving: A case for disciplinary grounding. *International Journal of Sustainability in Higher Education, 14*(4), 404–433.

Renzulli, J. S. (1976). The enrichment triad model: A guide for developing defensible programs for the gifted and talented. *Gifted Child Quarterly, 20,* 303–326.

Renzulli, J. S. (2012). Reexamining the role of gifted education and talent development for the 21st century: A four-part theoretical approach. *Gifted Child Quarterly, 56,* 150–159.

Saltmarsh, J. (2008). Why Dewey matters. *The Good Society, 17*(2), 63–68.

Scholz, R. W., Lang, D. J., Wiek, A., Walter, A. I., & Stauffacher, J. (2006). Transdisciplinary case studies as a means of sustainability learning: Historical framework and theory. *International Journal of Sustainability in Higher Education, 7,* 226–251.

Starko, A. J. (1988). Effects of the revolving door identification model on creative productivity and self-efficacy. *Gifted Child Quarterly, 32,* 291–297.

Starko, A. J., & Schack, G. D. (1992). *Looking for data in all the right places: A guidebook for conducting original research with young investigators.* Waco, TX: Prufrock Press.

Subotnik, R. F., Olszewski-Kubilius, P., & Worrell, F. C. (2011). Rethinking giftedness and gifted education: A proposed direction forward based on psychological science. *Psychological Science in the Public Interest, 12*(1), 3–54.

Vallerand, R. J., Gagné, F., Senécal, C., & Pelletier, L. G. (1994). A comparison of the school intrinsic motivation and perceived competence of gifted and regular students. *Gifted Child Quarterly, 38,* 172–175.

Van de Kerkhof, M. (2006). Making a difference: On the constraints of consensus building and the relevance of deliberation in stakeholder dialogues. *Policy Sciences, 39,* 279–299.

Vogel, C., Scott, D., Culwick, C. E., & Sutherland, C. (2016). Environmental problem-solving in South Africa: Harnessing creative imaginaries to address 'wicked' challenges and opportunities. *South African Geographical Journal, 98,* 515–530.

Warburton, K. (2003). Deep learning and education for sustainability. *International Journal of Sustainability in Higher Education, 4*(1), 44–56.

Westheimer, J., & Kahne, J. (2004). What kind of citizen? The politics of educating for democracy. *American Educational Research Journal, 41,* 237–269.

Wiek, A., Withycombe, L., & Redman, C. L. (2011). Key competencies in sustainability: A reference framework for academic program development. *Sustainability Science, 6,* 203–218.

Williams, B., & Le Menestrel, S. (2013). Social capital and vulnerability from the family, neighborhood, school, and community perspectives. In M. Calvert, M. Emery, & S. Kinsey (Eds.), *New directions for youth development* (pp. 97–107). Hoboken, NJ: Wiley Periodicals.

Yosso, T. J. (2005). Whose culture has capital? *Race Ethnicity and Education, 8*(1), 69–91.

Youniss, J. (2011). Civic education: What schools can do to encourage civic identity and action. *Applied Developmental Science, 15*(2), 98–103. doi:10.1080/10888691.2011.560814

Yu, C.-Y., & Chiang, Y.-C. (2018). Designing a climate-resilient environmental curriculum—A transdisciplinary challenge. *Sustainability, 10*(1), 77.

CHAPTER 5

Connecting Learning to the Community: Pedagogical Strategies for Educators

Suzanne M. Nesmith, Lakia M. Scott, Karon N. LeCompte and Susan K. Johnsen

Abstract

Community-based pedagogical approaches come in many styles and structures, with the singular commonality being a strategy that moves class-based learning and thinking beyond the school walls and into the community in support of action and service. This chapter examines how community-based learning involving educators promotes transformation in school settings, and the four highlighted pedagogical cases provide evidence of the manner and impacts of addressing and implementing community-based approaches. Creative problem solving in community learning explores how a preservice educator guided elementary-age students in examining and devising solutions to community-based problems associated with stray animals. The case of field-based environmental issues focuses on immersing educators within a local wetland environment to enhance their environmental efficacy and implementation of environmental education curricula centered on community stewardship. Action civics presents as a case wherein a preservice educator developed and incorporated a personally meaningful, inquiry-based project to address hunger in the local community. Literacy serves as the focus of a service-learning case that provided preservice educators the opportunity to develop, share, and gift specially designed book bags with children at a local community center. The presented cases, alongside supporting research specific to each pedagogical case, confirm the transformational power that results from sharing community-based learning approaches with educators.

Keywords

community-based learning – community-based pedagogy – creative problem solving – field-based environmental education – action civics – service-learning

1 Introduction

"The education system faces irrelevance unless we bridge the gap between how students live and how they learn" (Melaville, Berg, & Blank, 2006, p. 1). One means of bridging this gap is through community-based learning. This chapter describes community-based pedagogical strategies that engage educators in creative problem solving, field-based environmental education, action civics, and service-learning through literacy. The context for using each of these strategies is defined, along with the strategy's characteristics and related research, and the examples provide how each of the strategies were used within the community.

In its broadest sense, community-based learning refers to any learning that moves class-based learning beyond the school walls or that includes children in community projects. Yet in order to successfully bridge the gap between students' lives and learning, community-based learning must connect learning and thinking and not simply provide opportunities in some form of community involvement or participation.

Community-based pedagogies include civic engagement, academically based community service, environmental education, service-learning, work-based learning, and place-based learning. Regardless of nomenclature, community-based pedagogies share common characteristics: meaningful content (learning focuses on places and issues that have meaning for students), voice and choice (learning tasks require students to take active roles), personal and public purpose (learning objectives connect personal outcomes with public purposes), and assessment and feedback (learning tasks enhance students' community-based relationships and resources) (Melaville et al., 2006). Additionally, though appropriate to view community narrowly as place or neighborhood-based, the description of community may extend across a range of varied spaces and scales (Valentine, 2004).

An intentional focus on community-based learning helps students develop the knowledge, skills, and attributes of effective citizenship through identifying and acting on community-specific issues. Additional benefits of community-based learning include increased student motivation and engagement, family–school involvement, and an appreciation of local resources as curriculum resources (Sharkey, Olarte, & Ramirez, 2016). Community-based learning outcomes vary; one reason for the variance is educators' prior exposures, experiences, and comfort levels with community-based learning. Educators who are products of traditional learning environments often express unfamiliarity, dissonance, discomfort, and uncertainty when exposed to or asked to implement community-based pedagogies (Clayton & Ash, 2004). Moreover, educators working with children and families whose cultures, languages, and socioeconomic backgrounds do not match their own often struggle with developing and utilizing pedagogies that connect with students' lives and/or local resources, interests, and realities (Bomer & Maloch, 2012; Garcia, Arias, Murri, & Serna, 2010).

Challenges to community-based learning are numerous, yet thoughtful, realistic exposure to and utilization of community-based pedagogies allows educators to become more adept at interpreting and enacting the pedagogies and recognizing that community-based pedagogies are flexible enough to allow multiple entry points, varying trajectories, and autonomous teaching. Educators cannot ignore the realities of cultural disconnects, or standards and testing requirements that restrict their autonomy and intellectual authority. This recognition, however, does not mean that curriculum should be shared in an uncritical way that fails to engage students in meaningful and purposeful learning. Community-based learning offers a means to confront, address, and overcome these realities to move beyond reform to ultimately transform education. What follows are examples of community-based learning pedagogical strategies utilized for and with educators.

2   Pedagogical Strategy: Creative Problem Solving

2.1   *Context*

Preservice educators in the School of Education at Baylor University who are seeking certificates in both elementary and gifted education are required to take a course on differentiating the curriculum. In this course, preservice educators create and implement an interdisciplinary curricular unit that addresses differences among learners in their classrooms. These learner differences are described in terms of *content, rate, preference,* and *environment* (Johnsen, Haensly, Ryser, & Ford, 2002). *Content* is defined as the learning progressions of subject matter, processes, and products/performances that need to be learned. Learners will vary in terms of the content they know and can demonstrate proficiently as well as their talents and interests. *Rate* is defined as the amount of time it takes for a student to learn the content. In this area, some learners may need only a few examples to learn the content, whereas others may need many examples. *Preference* is characterized as the student's choice in available learning resources. Some students prefer using pictures, graphics, and reading materials, whereas others might prefer oral and auditory approaches, such as tapes, videos, and small group discussions. *Environment* is also related to student choice and the kinds of physical arrangements and opportunities for interaction within and outside the classroom setting. Student preferences will vary in terms of structure, group engagement, and independent work. To address these differences, preservice educators learn a variety of pedagogical strategies for differentiating their curricular units. One of these strategies is the *creative problem-solving process*, which provides preservice educators with ways to adapt to individual differences and opportunities for engaging their students in investigating community-based problems.

2.2   *The Creative Problem-Solving Process*

Creative problem solving in educational settings has evolved over 60 years (Isaksen & Treffinger, 2004). It is distinctly different from problem solving where students find solutions to known problems because creative problem solving incorporates a stage that requires students to identify the problem to solve. Osborn (1953) initially identified seven steps in the Creative Problem Solving model (orientation, preparation, analysis, hypothesis, incubation, synthesis, and verification). Sidney J. Parnes and his colleagues (Noller, Parnes, & Biondi, 1976) later modified Osborn's original Creative Problem Solving method and created five stages (fact-finding, problem-finding, information-finding, solution-finding, and acceptance-finding), which was widely disseminated in the 1970s and 1980s. Concerned about the balance between creative and critical thinking and its linear presentation, Isaksen and Treffinger (1985) enhanced the Osborn-Parnes model by adding another stage (mess-finding), changing the titles of two of the stages (fact-finding to data-finding and solution-finding to idea-finding) and emphasizing its flexibility and cyclical aspects. In other words, every step might not be used or they might be rearranged or repeated based on the needs of the problem-solvers (Isaksen & Treffinger, 1985). Their stages also stressed the convergent and divergent aspects of each stage in the Creative Problem Solving framework. For example, in the data-finding stage, students might brainstorm possible underlying problems (divergent) and use criteria to examine those problems that are most relevant to an ill-defined problem—the "Mess" (convergent).

More recently, based on research and how individuals are more likely to use the creative problem-solving strategies, Treffinger and Isaksen (1992) have clustered the creative problem-solving stages into three main problem-solving components. In each of the stages, the individual focuses on divergent thinking, and then convergent thinking. Each stage therefore forms the creative foundation for the next stage. Treffinger, Isaksen, and their colleagues have continued to modify the model by adding a Planning Your Approach component (which includes appraising tasks and designing process stages) to the three other components and six stages so that creative problem solving addresses more systemic challenges (see Isaksen, Dorval, & Treffinger, 2011). Since action plans may typically take more than one year to implement and thus appraise (Bohnenberger & Terry, 2002), the preservice educators in the differentiation course primarily used the three-component, six-stage Creative Problem Solving framework. In their classrooms they created an ill-defined problem, or a "mess," for the students to examine that was related to content standards, integrated multiple disciplines and perspectives, engaged students in areas of interest, and varied the complexity of the content. These ill-defined problems varied, with some relating to historical problems (such as how Native Americans survived in wilderness areas), some to future problems (such as global warming and its effects on animals), and some to current school or community problems (such as school safety or recycling trash). The breadth of the problem allowed them to incorporate differentiation and address all aspects of individual differences.

Research evidence suggests that creative problem solving is a viable method for developing creative behaviors and engaging students in community learning activities (Isaksen & Treffinger, 2004). When creative problem solving is centered on individual interests and integrated into service-learning, students not only learn how to work collaboratively but also become more involved and connected to the community (Terry, 2003). Beason-Manes (2018) described how middle school students developed a solution to a community issue. From a variety of problems, her students identified the challenge of community members who appeared to lack access to financial guidance (i.e., understanding the problem). They generated ideas and decided they would host a free public event where community members could discuss financial issues with local financial advisors (i.e., generating ideas). They finally developed their action plan (i.e., planning for action) by locating a downtown venue (the library), soliciting the commitment of financial advisors to provide free services to families and community members in need, and marketing the event. In this example, the middle school students actually implemented their plan and were able to evaluate the results.

2.3   *An Example of Using Creative Problem Solving*

In the differentiation course, preservice educators designed and implemented a variety of units in their classroom related to challenges within the community, such as bullying, community transportation, global warming, homeless animals, and a variety of other topics related to student interests. To increase the fidelity of implementation, the course instructor reviewed each preservice educator's unit and lesson plans prior to implementation and then coached the preservice educator through the implementation process with students.

In this way, the preservice educators could immediately practice the newly learned process and solve problems as they occurred. One preservice educator's unit related to homeless animals is presented in more detail below.

2.3.1 Understanding the Problem

After visiting with directors of local animal shelters and reading local newspapers, the preservice educator developed and presented this "mess" to her grade three elementary students:

> In the community, there is a problem with stray animals who are lost or who do not have a home. To take care of these animals, we have two non-profit organizations whose purposes are to provide shelter to these stray animals—Fuzzy Friends and the Humane Society. Fuzzy Friends operates strictly on donations from people like you and me. You can adopt, volunteer, and foster animals for the night. The City funds the other shelter—The Humane Society. It provides opportunities for adoption, rescue, and fostering. You have been asked by these organizations to identify possible problems and solutions that may arise when operating an animal shelter. Following your studies, they are interested in learning about your findings and possible action plans.

After presenting the problem to the class, the preservice educator then facilitated and taught the students how to brainstorm the who, what, when, where, why, and how related to the problem (mess-finding). Some of their questions included: What is the purpose of a shelter? Who is involved with the shelters? Where are they located? How many stray animals are in the shelters? What influences the number of stray animals? What are the effects on the community when there are stray animals looking for food? How many people know about the shelters and what they do? How does the community support them? To assist the students in organizing the information, the preservice educator listed them on a classroom visual web chart. The preservice educator encouraged the students to examine all aspects of the problem—data-finding (e.g., economic, social, political, educational, environmental). Using the visual web chart of underlying problems, the preservice educator assisted the students in selecting one of these problems for further research and taught them how to collect information in small groups using technology, websites, books, videos, newspapers, and interviews with the animal shelter directors. Observing that some students had limited research experience, the preservice educator modified her lesson plans and developed research guides with the assistance of the instructor. Following this data-finding stage, the preservice educator taught the students how to collaborate so they would be able to identify the main problem together (problem-finding). The preservice educator provided a framework for the problem (i.e., In what ways might we + action verb + solution) and the students filled in the important elements: In what ways might we communicate the purposes of the animal shelters to the community so that the shelters have sufficient resources for reducing the number of stray animals?

The preservice educator was particularly careful to ensure that students had opportunities to research a problem that was related to their interest. In this case, the preservice educator assisted in identifying related topics such as pet care and responsibilities, the cost of pet care, animal protection, reasons people abandon pets, nonprofit organizations, and wild versus domestic animals in the environment.

2.3.2 Generating Ideas

Following the data- and problem-finding stages, the preservice educator facilitated another session brainstorming many different solutions to the main problem (idea-finding). Some of their solutions included making presentations to the community about the shelters, creating videos and posters, producing a play for the school about pets, crafting a model pet care center, and selling pet toys in the school.

2.3.3 Planning for Action

The preservice educator taught the students how to develop criteria and guided them in evaluating the solutions (solution-finding): Which is best for communicating the needs of the shelter? Which is most likely to improve resources? Which is most likely to have the desired effects, that is, reduce stray animals? Which is easiest to implement within our timeline? Using an evaluation matrix, the preservice educator guided the students in evaluating each solution against each criterion. After the solution was selected, the preservice educator assisted the students in elaborating the most promising solution: "We will present our research about reducing the number of stray animals to the other classes in our school, the staff of the nonprofit organizations, and to the City Council." The final step in the process required the preservice educator to teach the students how to prepare their presentations, and she coached them so that they would be more successful at the city council meeting (acceptance-finding). As a positive outcome, the local television station was at the city council meeting and interviewed the preservice educator and her students on the next news program, which resulted in additional resource allocations for the Humane Society and more donations for Fuzzy Friends. These effects reinforced the preservice educator's use of creative problem solving as a pedagogical strategy and the students' continued involvement and connection to their community. The reciprocal coaching approach between the instructor, preservice educator, and students assisted the preservice educator in learning how to successfully implement a complex pedagogical strategy.

3   Pedagogical Strategy: Field-Based Environmental Education

3.1   *Context*

Field-based environmental education capitalizes on children's natural curiosity about the world and uses the environment to give voice to students' prior knowledge and natural interests. Recognizing the benefits of this pedagogical strategy, an environmental education workshop embedded in a local wetland habitat was developed, and local educators were invited to attend. The Wetland Environmental Academy took place at a local Wetland Center situated outside a large urban area. This location was purposefully chosen for the academy because it is one of the largest water reuse projects in the United States and provides an appropriate context for exploring general water issues as well as issues specific to urban water conservation, reclamation, and reuse. Five Baylor University scientists and educators, as well as the director of the Wetland Center, worked together to develop the field-based professional development opportunity that addressed the state's unique water issues and provided practical hands-on experiences for K–12 educators from areas that receive reclaimed water from the wetland facility. The academy spanned a complete year, with educators attending three-day workshops in two consecutive summers.

The academy included daytime and evening activities, such as a Wetland Center tour, identifying wetland species based on prints/dung/sounds, gathering water and biological samples, measuring water quality parameters based on chemistry and biological evidence, designing experiments related to water quality, and discussions and opportunities specific to modifying and applying academy content to meet various grade levels, course standards, and community needs. The academy's unique design and setting assured inclusion of the four key aspects of environmental education professional development: (a) immersion in student experiences, (b) community-based learning and networking opportunities, (c) reflection on teaching experiences, and (d) familiarity with a variety of methods for teaching specific content (Klein & Riordan, 2011). Moreover, by employing the community-based learning strategies of environmental education and place-based learning, the academy provided the educators with firsthand experiences they could use to capitalize on students' natural curiosity. The educators could use the community as a framework for students to construct their own learning, while also providing a context and resources for focusing on community needs and interests (Melaville et al., 2006).

3.2 Field-Based Environmental Education

Appropriately designed and implemented environmental education curricula allow educators to provide students with experiences that will increase environmental understanding and develop necessary environmentally based skills (Klein & Riordan, 2011). Yet in order to be well rounded in environmental education, students need to apply their environmental understanding and skills in exploring environmental issues, making decisions, and acting upon these issues. This expanded perspective of environmental education has led many environmental educators to view the development of responsible environmental behaviors and citizenship as the ultimate goal of environmental education (Forbes & Zint, 2011).

Hungerford, Peyton, and Wilke's *Goals for Curriculum Development in Environmental Education* (1980) guides the development of curricula that attend to all essential environmental education components so as to aid students in becoming environmentally knowledgeable, skilled, and dedicated citizens who are willing to work toward achieving a dynamic equilibrium between quality of life and quality of the environment. Hungerford et al.'s four-level curriculum framework places an equal emphasis on developing learners' knowledge about the environment, conceptual awareness of how their actions impact the environment, skills for investigating and evaluating environmental issues, and capabilities for taking positive actions. Specifically, Level I (Ecological Foundations) focuses on providing students with the knowledge needed to make sound decisions about environmental issues; Level II (Conceptual Awareness) promotes developing student awareness regarding how their actions affect the environment and may ultimately result in awareness of issues requiring resolution; Level III (Investigation and Evaluation) involves the skills needed to investigate environmental issues and provide alternate solutions; and Level IV (Environmental Action Skills) emphasizes developing the skills necessary for taking action and providing opportunities for students to make decisions about environmental actions, apply skills to specific issues, and evaluate the impact of their actions.

Though not mentioned specifically within Hungerford et al.'s (1980) framework, if educators want to provide students with experiences at all four levels, they must develop environmental education curricula that move learning beyond the classroom and into the environment. The science education community typically refers to place-based education as on-site fieldwork or field-based education, yet all these terms refer to a pedagogy that combines discipline- and community-specific practices to involve individuals in educational activities that connect academic content to a local setting (Zimmerman & Weible, 2017).

Research supports using field-based environmental education in prompting students to become stewards of their community. Jensen (2010) posits that learner-centered, action-oriented education is the key to learning about environmental issues so that people can make a difference in their community: actions should be directed at solving a problem, and these actions should be decided upon by those preparing to carry out the action. Jensen further argues that educators often fail to present environmental topics in such a way as to foster knowledge of stewardship action. In support of Jensen's perspective about the current state of school-based environmental education, Kollmuss and Agyeman (2002) found that extensive education about environmental issues increases student knowledge, but this knowledge does not always correlate with increases in students' pro-environmental behaviors. Zimmerman and Weible (2017) conducted a study involving high school students in a rural, poverty-impacted school engaged with place-based understanding of their everyday activities and community through watershed and water quality experiences. Results revealed students' increased understanding of connections between the watershed and their community alongside unanswered questions regarding actions that could and should be taken by themselves and community members. Based on their findings, Zimmerman & Weible (2017) further suggested that research is needed on how to prepare science educators in creating learning communities that produce action-oriented science knowledge—as opposed to static knowledge of environmental problems—during place-based education experiences.

3.3 *An Example of a Field-Based Environmental Experience*

Educators in the Wetland Academy were recruited from school districts and education centers surrounding the Wetland Center, and all educators and their students received reclaimed water from the wetland facility. The academy was limited to 15 educators to assure that each educator had the necessary individualized attention to successfully attain the project objectives, namely, to positively impact the educators' environmental education attitudes, efficacy, and instructional practices so they could, in turn, possess the skills and desire to construct curricula aligned with the four levels of the environmental education framework.

Participating educators had access to the Wetland Center during the three-day period each consecutive summer, and then contact with the academy facilitators throughout the academic year. Over half the educators were able to return for the second summer, with no new educators included. All events occurred on-site at the Wetland Center facility, and educators and project partners were invited and encouraged to stay overnight at the center, as the facility had housing. This overnight component allowed educators to explore the Wetland nightlife and enhanced the development of an environmental education community.

In designing the academy, project partners worked to address the needs cited in environmental education literature (e.g., lack of science knowledge and research skills, perceived weaknesses in environmental education–related attitudes and teaching practices, and lack of action-oriented knowledge and experiences). Hence, the academy sought to encourage an inquiry-based approach where the educators worked alongside scientists and science educators to develop a deeper understanding of urban water reclamation and reuse via a local, community-based, constructed wetland. Essential components of the academy included: (a) learning about worldwide water resources, regional water resource challenges, and wetland systems; (b) touring the Wetland Center; (c) gathering water samples and measuring water quality parameters (temperature, dissolved oxygen, turbidity, pH, specific conductivity, hardness, orthophosphate, and dissolved inorganic nitrogen); (d) an overview of experimental design components specific to physical/chemical/biological water quality parameters (i.e., discussing questions that can be investigated specific to water quality, wetland systems, and other water resources; exploring the tests/experiments that can be performed to address these questions; discussing the equipment/supplies necessary for conducting said investigations and answering said questions); (e) small group research focused on physical/chemical/biological components of the wetland system; and (f) learning about value-belief-norm theory and place attachment in relation to why people choose to participate in behaviors that protect or improve the natural environment and the role of place attachment in enhancing concern for the environment (Stern, Kalof, Dietz, & Guagnano, 1995; Wynveen, Connally, & Kyle, 2013).

During the group research, educators utilized the experimental design process to determine a research question, identify variables, and select study sites across the wetland gradient. Educators then gathered and analyzed samples, evaluated data, and formulated conclusions relevant to gradients of water quality, water reuse, and wetland systems. Thus, instead of teaching how to simply monitor common water quality parameters, the educators focused on asking research questions related to environmental gradients using these water quality indicators. The educators then discussed correlating and applying the academy content to grade level–specific/science course–specific standards and including community-based experiences.

The goal of the second summer at the academy was to build upon the first summer by increasing the educators' understanding of the ecological structure and function of wetlands and water reuse, along with skills related to designing and conducting research and experiences relevant to ecological components of wetland systems. Additionally, the second academy provided an opportunity for the educators and the project partners to explore the relationship between the first academy and the long-term impact of the academy on the educators' environmental attitudes, efficacy, teaching practices, and classroom curricula.

An examination of surveys and group interviews revealed that participation in the academy positively impacted the educators' environmental attitudes and significantly impacted their efficacy in teaching environmental education. Specifically, the educators indicated enhanced abilities in bringing about positive student change in the areas of environmental knowledge, attitudes, and skills (Nesmith et al., 2015). Moreover, the educators expressed all four levels and corresponding components of the environmental education curriculum development goals Hungerford et al. (1980) outlined, and they revealed numerous field-based, community-embedded experiences, with one educator indicating:

> We [students and educator] went to our little creek. I just had them walk around and smell the sulfur, and they're like, "This is so nasty." We went ahead and put in our little aquatic plants, and we gave them a month. We went back and you could already tell a difference. They're like, "Look at the clarity of the water. We're not smelling the smells that were here a month ago. That's amazing." Now we're ... getting some aquatic plants and helping to try to remediate some other water bodies around us.

4   Pedagogical Strategy: Action Civics

4.1   *Context*

Inquiry-based instruction fosters students' investigations of essential topics through scaffolded and collaborative learning opportunities (Nenadal & Mistry, 2018). It provides educators and students a venue in which to study a subject deeply with a focus on self-generated questions and purposeful discovery (Gardner, 2011). During the era of progressivism, John Dewey (1916/2013) and others recognized the importance of such study. However, most classrooms across the country have dropped this type of learning because it takes too much time and is challenging to manage. International, national, and state accountability measures have likewise resulted in a decline of thoughtful inquiry-based experiences due to an emphasis on test preparation (Lunenburg, 2011). Elementary preservice educators in the School of Education at Baylor University are required to enroll in a social studies methods course. One course requirement highlights inquiry-based investigations and community change through an action civics project. The purpose of the course project is to engage preservice educators by asking them to design and implement an inquiry-based service-learning project that is meaningful to them and, ultimately, to prepare them to initiate such projects in their future classrooms. To do so, the preservice educators begin with a question that focuses on a community issue, conduct research specific to the issue, personally interview individuals associated with the issue (typically, individuals within issue-related organizations), and, finally, advocate a solution to the issue in the form of a persuasive letter. This advocacy aspect of service-learning is what Levinson (2012) refers to as action civics.

4.2   Action Civics as Community-Based Service-Learning

Voices in the world of education are not silent about the merits of service-learning. It has long been in the curricula of educational courses and in the social and behavioral sciences. Service-learning is defined as a research-based teaching method that applies classroom learning through action addressing an authentic community need. It allows for student initiative and provides structured time to reflect on the service experience and to demonstrate acquired skills and knowledge (Kaye, 2010). Freeman and Swick (2003) described service-learning as encompassing attributes developed by the National and Community Service Trust Act of 1993. These include involving students in pre-arranged service that meets a community need, nurturing civic responsibilities, integrating the curriculum, and providing students the opportunity to reflect upon their projects. Service-learning is purposefully designed to emphasize the integration of outside community service with academic instruction.

Though service-learning in the traditional sense represents a concerted effort to meet a community need, providing active inquiry-based investigation and change in a community issue propels the service-learning to action civics. Service-learning that incorporates action civics has the propensity to engage students in citizenship that is purposeful and active (Levinson, 2012). Moreover, thoughtfully structured action civics experiences provide meaningful opportunities to develop individuals' civic knowledge, participation skills, and attitudes while simultaneously making a positive impact on the community. By its very nature, action civics utilizes crucial civic skills, including critical thinking, elaborated communication, and collaboration, which are essential to individuals' permanent roles as civic actors.

Action civics projects are representative of "New Civics," a term from the report on civics learning from the National Association of Scholars (Randall, 2017). The New Civics report identifies best practices for civic education, and service-learning within the New Civics framework encourages the design and implementation of programs that provide students with application opportunities. In reality, New Civics programs connect what students learn in the classroom with authentic community issues, allowing students to incorporate knowledge, skills, and dispositions needed for lifetime civic engagement.

Successful service-learning within educator-preparation programs provides preservice educators opportunities to participate in community service projects that allow them to acquire the necessary skills and knowledge to become 21st-century practicing educators (Briody, 2005). To prepare preservice educators to become fluent in developing and utilizing service-learning projects such as action civics, they need opportunities to plan and execute these projects as scholars in an educator-preparation program (Wade, 2007). Moreover, in designing the projects, the preservice educators need to be mindful of standards. In the current educational climate for accountability, new standards are calling for an increased focus on inquiry-based learning. Development of service-learning with an action civics component in educator-preparation programs, in this case, resulted from a statewide initiative that purposely focused on the rigorous standards aligned with inquiry-based learning.

4.3 *An Example of an Inquiry-Based Action Civics Project*

Preservice educators enrolled in an elementary social studies methods course were assigned the task of developing and incorporating an inquiry-based action civics project. Assignment parameters included a focus on a personally meaningful community issue, and Ashley (pseudonym), a preservice educator, decided to explore Campus Kitchens, a campus-wide initiative at Baylor University to eliminate hunger. The student-led organization focuses on donating leftover food from the campus dining halls to the hungry. In her project introduction, Ashley wrote, "The issue of feeding the hungry has always been something near my heart. That is the reason I chose Campus Kitchens." Ashley indicated that she finds it nearly impossible to drive through town and not notice the number of homeless men and women. Additionally, when she steps outside her front door, she sees that her neighbors have no air conditioning, and just a few minutes from her house, people living in low-income housing don't have the money to feed their families. She states, "If I could just get the idea into people's heads and hearts, then I know the passion for building up the community surrounding the University would spread like wildfire. I will work on educating others, and by this time next year I will hopefully be changing the lives of many who call this community home." This preservice educator wrote her letter to the head of Campus Kitchens, and her PowerPoint included eight slides that summarized hunger in the Waco community, illuminating the positive impacts of the Campus Kitchen program. In her reflection, Ashley wrote, "I feel so blessed to have completed this project with much more knowledge of the hunger facing our community. My research has shown me what is necessary of me in order to align my life goals with my current behaviors and efforts. My efforts in this community will become even more meaningful."

The standards that Ashley used to guide her project included: (a) assessing different governmental systems and functions; (b) explaining and analyzing the importance of civic engagement; and (c) evaluating how major philosophical and intellectual concepts influence human behavior or identity (Texas Education Agency, 2018). By using these standards as a framework for inquiry-based action civics, Ashley found a new respect for her community and the struggles facing people in her neighborhood. Critical thinking about poverty will hopefully change the way that Ashley teaches through increased awareness and compassion for children in impoverished environments.

Examining all the preservice educators' project descriptions, lesson plans, and artifacts revealed that they felt empowered by the ability to have their voices heard, and they learned important research skills in finding information related to their projects. They took action and proposed solutions for their community issues. In essence, through their authentic, inquiry-based action learning in a community setting, these preservice educators will step into classrooms well prepared to serve as model citizens capable of designing experiences for students so that they, in turn, will move closer to becoming the kind of action-oriented, informed citizens we want and need in our 21st-century communities.

5   Pedagogical Strategy: Service-Learning through Literacy

5.1   Context

During their time in the undergraduate educator-preparation program at Baylor University, preservice educators in the elementary program are required to complete a one-semester designated Literacy block in their junior year. The block includes two courses (Elementary Literacy Methods and English Language Arts Methods) and a concurrent Integrated Language Arts and Reading teaching field experience. Before the Literacy block, students must have taken the Early Literacy course, which addresses oral language development, phonological and phonemic awareness, alphabetic principle, and the beginning stages of literacy development and practice.

In alignment with statewide preservice educator competencies, the Literacy block centers on elementary grade level pedagogy and instruction in English Language Arts and Reading. The Elementary Literacy Methods course focuses keenly on upper elementary literacy practices (grades 3–6). This course addresses the following topics, as guided by the Texas State Board for Educator Certification (TSBEC): Literacy Development and Practice, Word Analysis and Decoding, Reading Fluency, Reading Comprehension, and Assessment and Instruction of Developing Literacy (TSBEC, 2007). Since the course is built with an integrated field experience component, preservice educators typically spend their mornings working in elementary schools, and in the afternoons throughout the course of the semester, they partake in nine hours of preservice educator courses.

Baylor University's undergraduate educator-preparation program model has received national recognition for the program's features, most notably, the numerous field experiences preservice educators receive prior to graduation. By embedding clinical experiences into a majority of the courses, learning and academic outcomes are magnified for those entering the teaching field. Additionally, the sequence provides opportunities for students to engage in community-based learning via addressing social and cultural topics that are specific to the Central Texas area, which can be termed as an urban-emergent site (Milner, 2006). Along with the program course sequence, students participate in a plethora of workshops and seminars that address other pertinent educational issues, such as parental involvement, language differences, classroom management, learning disabilities, and community demographics. These topics are further explored in content area courses to provide continuity in understanding the cyclical relationship between theory and practice. In this way, the undergraduate educator-preparation program model succeeds in providing direct and indirect encounters for community-based learning and pedagogy to occur.

5.2   *The Service-Learning Experience*

Jacoby (1996) defined service-learning as "a form of experiential education in which students engage in activities that address human and community needs together with structured opportunities intentionally designed to promote student learning and development. Reflection and reciprocity are key concepts of service-learning" (pp. 1–2). In this model, service and learning share a focus and should be seen as equal and reciprocal, wherein both the recipient and the provider benefit from the experience. Jacoby differentiates service-learning as the culmination of volunteerism, community service, field experiences, and internships because of the intentional acts of reflection and reciprocity that are designed to promote student learning and development. Service-learning opportunities expose students to cultural and social contexts present and prevalent in community spaces, while also reducing stereotype threat and prejudice. Specific to higher education, Jacoby asserts that service-learning engages students in moral, spiritual, and leadership development through critical thinking opportunities that are action-oriented and socially just. Similar theorists have also highlighted the significance of service-learning opportunities and potential models for higher education students (Arias & Poynor, 2001; Clark & Medina, 2000; Hollins & Guzman, 2005; Miller & Gonzalez, 2010).

In discussing how preservice educator service-learning experiences can lead to informed engagement between students and community constituents, Boggs (2013) shared:

> First, teacher educators, preservice teachers, and teachers can use service-learning pedagogies to listen to the interests of students and their communities as prerequisites to or, in Vygotskian terms, histories of instruction, planning, and assessment. Second, all stakeholders, including students, families, and school administrators, can use service-learning practices to repurpose or resituate academic tools to work against the wind of structural marginalization of community goals. (pp. 32–33)

In this way, the author emphasizes the importance of community building through student service-learning encounters, and the analogy of "working against the wind" is used to show that pedagogy can be part of the transformation process of rebuilding for the sake of social justice and equity in educational environments.

Tinkler and Tinkler (2013) also examined how service-learning experiences helped to develop cultural and linguistic responsiveness in educator-preparation program models. In a reading and writing content area course that included tutoring refugee students, preservice educators were able to better understand how literacy practices enhanced student engagement—particularly for students marginalized in traditional classrooms. A major finding of the study revealed that through the experience preservice educators were better equipped to make decisions regarding instructional content as well as become more effective in working with refugee and immigrant student populations. Many of the students became more empathetic as a result of the increased awareness of background factors and personal challenges for this demographic.

The components of Melaville et al.'s (2006) community-based learning are indeed present in the preservice educator service-learning model. Preservice educators are provided with opportunities to engage students in content that is meaningful and relevant while also reflecting on personal and public purposes. Jacoby's (1996) notion of reciprocity between the provider (preservice educator) and the recipient (student) also yields positive outcomes for both to become autonomous in the experience. Feedback in the form of individual or small group reflections can help to shape perspectives about teaching in schools with diverse student populations.

5.3 An Example of a Service-Learning Project

Each fall semester, preservice educators enrolled in the Elementary Literacy Methods course participate in the Book in a Bag service-learning project. During this project, preservice educators are asked to select a children's book whose text emphasizes an instructional strategy or approach. After selecting the book, the preservice educators must formalize a 30-minute lesson plan that addresses textual and content features. For example, Katie Smith Milway's *One Hen* is based on a true story of how reaching out to help someone can have a big impact. The story, set in a small, rural town in Ghana, is told through the narrative of a young boy named Kojo. Throughout the text, new words and places are introduced to readers. If this were a selected children's book, the lesson plan could focus on acquiring vocabulary, and development or instruction could emphasize comparing and contrasting geographic locations and features. Preservice educators are familiar with lesson plan components and instructional strategies and are asked to reinforce these items to demonstrate understanding and competency of course content.

After preservice educators select the children's book and create an accompanying lesson plan, the fun begins. During a class period, the preservice educators share their book selections and provide summary points of the lesson plan. The course instructor then provides canvas tote bags and art materials (paint, hot glue, glitter, feathers, etc.) to decorate the bags in anticipation of gifting the book and bag to a school-age student at the local community center. Preservice educators are asked to design one bag to be given with the book. Creativity and uniqueness are encouraged by challenging preservice educators to focus on significant details from the book that make the story come alive for readers.

Once the bags are designed, the children's book, along with other toiletries, are put inside and the course instructor designates a day and time for the entire class to deliver the bags and teach the lessons. When preservice educators arrive at the community center, they are given ample space to set up a display of their book in preparation for reading and teaching the lesson to one student. When students enter the space, they choose which text they want to read (or be read to) by sitting in front of the book. After all students are seated, preservice educators introduce themselves and proceed with reading the book. Following the reading, preservice educators implement their lesson plans and, finally, gift the book and bag to the student. The bag is an unexpected surprise for students and they are often overjoyed by the item's decorative aspects, along with its contents. After the lesson, light refreshments provide an opportunity for further discussions between the preservice educator and student.

After the experience, preservice educators revisit the lesson and provide a reflection. Specifically, they are asked to reexamine the implementation of each lesson plan component (before, during, and after activities) and discuss strengths and challenges. They are also asked to reflect on their experience of selecting a children's text, crafting and gifting the canvas tote, and learning more about the student they encountered. From the past few years of employing this activity, learning outcomes and themes have been fairly consistent. Though brief, most preservice educators shared that the experience had a profound impact on their perceptions about the learners. Many also commented that the experience was fulfilling in that it encouraged reading for pleasure or enjoyment and inspired students to build and grow home libraries. Others highlighted how students felt "special" when they learned that the bag was intentionally and uniquely designed and created in preparation for meeting them. And, finally, some highlighted how the experience fostered reciprocal acts of service; though preservice educators gifted items, they also felt like recipients themselves because they gained a greater understanding of the backgrounds of the community's students.

6 Conclusion

Engaged learners work harder, care more deeply about their learning, and achieve their goals at rates and levels that surpass those of unengaged learners. Learners engaged in community-based experiences are more likely to recognize the relevance of course work, transfer knowledge and skills to new settings, and view themselves as citizens willing and able to impact their communities, schools, states, and nations. Community-based learning may thus be classified as transformational in that the experience contributes to the student's academic learning, personal growth, and civic engagement while concurrently benefiting the community in which the experience occurs. The onus for designing and implementing engaging community-based learning experiences into the curriculum lies with the educator. It behooves educators to seek opportunities to build their understanding and abilities relevant to community-based learning, and it's essential that educator-preparation programs recognize their responsibility in promoting and providing community-based learning experiences for preservice educators. As the examples illustrate, a wide range of styles, formats, and structures exist for community-based learning, and there is no single way to share community-based pedagogies with educators. The commonality of the shared examples and, indeed, all community-based pedagogies lies in their potential to transform school settings into places that empower students to gain a clearer vision of real-world social issues alongside a sharper sense of how they can serve as agents of community change.

References

Arias, B., & Poynor, L. (2001). A good start: A progressive, transactional approach to diversity in pre-service teacher education. *Bilingual Research Journal, 25*(4), 417–434.

Beason-Manes, A. D. (2018). Community activism as curriculum: How to meet gifted students' needs while creating change. *Gifted Child Today, 41*(1), 19–27.

Boggs, G. (2013). Teacher education as partnership: Service-learning and the audacity of listening. In V. M. Jagla, J. A. Erickson, & A. S. Tinkler (Eds.), *Transforming teacher education through service-learning* (pp. 31–50). Charlotte, NC: Information Age.

Bohnenberger, J. E., & Terry, A. W. (2002). Community problem solving works for middle level students. *Middle School Journal, 34*(1), 5–12.

Bomer, R., & Maloch, B. (2012). Diverse local literacies and standardizing policies. *Language Arts, 90*(1), 44–52.

Briody, J. (2005). Infusing preservice teacher preparation with service-learning. *Journal of Early Childhood Teacher Education, 26*, 149–155. doi:10.1080/10901020591001335

Clark, C., & Medina, C. (2000). How reading and writing literacy narratives affect preservice teachers' understanding of literacy, pedagogy, and multiculturalism. *Journal of Teacher Education, 51*(1), 63–76.

Clayton, P. H., & Ash, S. L. (2004). Shifts in perspective: Capitalizing on the counternormative nature of service-learning. *Michigan Journal of Community Service-Learning, 11*(1), 59–70.

Dewey, J. (1916/2013). *Experience in education: An introduction to the philosophy of education*. Retrieved from http://www.gutenberg.org/files/852/852-h/852-h.htmt

Forbes, C. T., & Zint, M. (2011). Elementary teachers' beliefs about, perceived competencies for, and reported use of scientific inquiry to promote student learning about and for the environment. *The Journal of Environmental Education, 42*, 30–42. doi:10.1080/00958961003674673

Freeman, N., & Swick, K. (2003). Preservice interns implement service-learning: Helping young children reach out to their community. *Early Childhood Education Journal, 31*(2), 107–112.

Garcia, E., Arias, M. B., Murri, N. J. H., & Serna, C. (2010). Developing responsive teachers: A challenge for a demographic reality. *Journal of Teacher Education, 61*(1–2), 132–142.

Gardner, H. (2011). *The unschooled mind: How children think and how schools should teach.* New York, NY: Basic Books.

Hollins, E. R., & Guzman, M. T. (2005). Research on preparing teachers for diverse populations. In M. Cochran-Smith & K. M. Zeichner (Eds.), *Studying teacher education: The report of the AERA panel on research and teacher education* (pp. 477–548). Mahwah, NJ: Erlbaum.

Hungerford, H., Peyton, R. B., & Wilke, R. J. (1980). Goals for curriculum development in environmental education. *The Journal of Environmental Education, 11*, 42–47. doi:10.1080/00958964.1980.9941381

Isaksen, S. G., Dorval, K. B., & Treffinger, D. J. (2011). *Creative approaches to problem solving: A framework for innovation and change* (3rd ed.). Thousand Oaks, CA: Sage.

Isaksen, S. G., & Treffinger, D. J. (1985). *Creative problem solving: The basic course.* Buffalo, NY: Bearly.

Isaksen, S. G., & Treffinger, D. J. (2004). Celebrating 50 years of reflective practice: Versions of creative problem solving. *Journal of Creative Behavior, 38*(2), 75–101.

Jacoby, B. (1996). *Service-learning in higher education: Concepts and practices.* San Francisco, CA: Jossey-Bass.

Jensen, B. B. (2010). Knowledge, action, and pro-environmental behaviour. *Environmental Education Research, 8*, 325–334. doi:10.1080/13504620220145474

Johnsen, S. K., Haensly, P., Ryser, G., & Ford, R. (2002). Changing general education classroom practices to adapt for gifted students. *Gifted Child Quarterly, 46*(1), 45–63.

Kaye, C. B. (2010). *The complete guide to service-learning*: Proven, practical ways to engage students in civic responsibility, academic curriculum, and social action. Minneapolis, MN: Free Spirit.

Klein, E. J., & Riordan, M. (2011). Wearing the "student hat": Experiential professional development in expeditionary learning schools. *Journal of Experiential Education, 34*, 35–54. doi:10.5193/JEE34.1.35

Kollmuss, A., & Agyeman, J. (2002). Mind the gap: Why do people act environmentally and what are the barriers to pro-environmental behaviour? *Environmental Education Research, 8*, 239–260. doi:10.1080/13504620220145401

Levinson, M. (2012). *No citizen left behind.* Cambridge, MA: Harvard University Press.

Lunenburg, F. (2011). Critical thinking and constructivism techniques for improving student achievement. *National Forum of Teacher Education Journal, 21*(3), 1–9.

Melaville, A., Berg, A. C., & Blank, M. J. (2006). *Community-based learning: Engaging students for success and citizenship*. Washington, DC: Coalition for Community Schools.

Miller, K., & Gonzalez, A. (2010). Domestic and international service-learning experiences: A comparative study of pre-service teacher outcomes. *Teacher Education Quarterly, 28*(4), 51–70.

Milner, H. R. (2006). Preservice teachers' learning about cultural and racial diversity: Implications for urban education. *Urban Education, 41*(4), 343–375.

Nenadal, L., & Mistry, R. S. (2018). Teacher reflections on using inquiry-based instruction to engage young children in conversations about wealth and poverty. *Early Childhood Research Quarterly, 42*, 44–54. doi:10.1016/j.ecresq.2017.07.008

Nesmith, S. M., Wynveen, C. J., Dixon, E. M., Brooks, B. W., Matson, C. W., Hockaday, W. C., ... DeFillipo, J. E. (2015). Exploring educators' environmental education attitudes and efficacy: Insights gleaned from a Texas wetland academy. *International Journal of Science Education, 6*. doi:10.1080/21548455.2015.1078519

Noller, R. B., Parnes, S. J., & Biondi, A. M. (1976). *Creative action book*. New York, NY: Scribner's.

Osborn, A. F. (1953). *Applied imagination: Principles and procedures of creative thinking*. New York, NY: Scribner's.

Randall, D. (2017, January). *Making citizens: How American universities teach civics*. National Association of Scholars. Retrieved from http://www.nas.org/images/documents/NAS_makingCitizens_fullReport.pdf

Sharkey, J., Olarte, A. C., & Ramirez, L. M. (2016). Developing a deeper understanding of community-based pedagogies with teachers: Learning with and from teachers in Columbia. *Journal of Teacher Education, 67*(4), 306–319.

Stern, P. C., Kalof, L., Dietz, T., & Guagnano, G. A. (1995). Values, beliefs, and proenvironmental action: Attitude formation toward emergent attitude objects. *Journal of Applied Social Psychology, 25*(18), 1611–1636.

Terry, A. W. (2003). Effects of service learning on young, gifted adolescents and their community. *Gifted Child Quarterly, 47*, 295–308. doi:10.1177/001698620304700406

Texas Education Agency. (2018). *Texas college and career readiness standards*. Retrieved from http://www.thecb.state.tx.us/reports/PDF/10337.PDF?CFID=74910347&CFTOKEN=99315967

Texas State Board for Educator Certification. (2007). *Approved educator standards*. Texas Education Agency. Retrieved from https://tea.texas.gov/Texas_Educators/Preparation_and_Continuing_Education/Approved_Educator_Standards/

Tinkler, A., & Tinkler, B. (2013). Teaching across the community: Using service-learning field experiences to develop culturally and linguistically responsive teachers. In V. M. Jagla, J. A. Erickson, & A. S. Tinkler (Eds.), *Transforming teacher education through service-learning* (pp. 99–118). Charlotte, NC: Information Age.

Treffinger, D. J., & Isaksen, S. G. (1992). *Creative problem solving: An introduction.* Sarasota, FL: Center for Creative Learning.

Valentine, G. (2004). *Public space and the culture of childhood.* Aldershot, U.K.: Ashgate.

Wade, R. C. (Ed.) (2007). *Community action rooted in history: The civiconnections model of service-learning.* Silver Spring, MD: National Council for the Social Studies.

Wynveen, C. J., Connally, W. D., & Kyle, G. T. (2013). Pro-environmental behavior in marine protected areas: The cases of the Great Barrier Reef Marine Park and the Florida Keys National Marine Sanctuary. *Journal of Park & Recreation Administration, 31*(2), 28–49.

Zimmerman, H. T., & Weible, J. L. (2017). Learning in and about rural places: Connections and tensions between students' everyday experiences and environmental quality issues in their community. *Cultural Studies of Science Education, 12,* 7–31. doi:10.1007/s11422-016-9757-1

PART 4

Global Approaches for Community-Based Learning

CHAPTER 6

Toward Learning in the Community: Insights from the U.S.A., India, and China

Eija Kimonen and Raimo Nevalainen

Abstract

The aim of this chapter is to examine the changing nature of the pedagogical activities of community-based learning and their authentic learning environments in the United States, India, and China. This analysis, based on a previous historico-hermeneutical study in comparative education, concentrates particularly on the activities of community-based learning and their central pedagogical approaches in a context of social change. With respect to the United States, the primary focus is on experiential education, while in India it is on vocationally productive education, and in China it is on productive labor education. This chapter demonstrates that community-based learning can take place in a variety of learning environments prioritizing the Naturalistic, Sociocultural, Productive, Economic, Martial, Ecological, or Scientific-Technical Dimensions, in accordance with the general direction of political, economic, and social development. The chapter shows that by the mid-20th century these three countries had started to focus efforts on expanding learning environments from schools to the real world outside of schools. In the past five decades, pedagogical approaches and their learning environments have increasingly given special importance to the use of technology-based applications. The study concludes that approaches to community-based learning could provide a way for teachers and communities to prepare students to participate and become engaged in solving local problems.

Keywords

community-based learning – pedagogical activities – pedagogical approaches – learning environments – experiential education – vocationally productive education – productive labor education – United States – India – China

1   Introduction

The present chapter explores the pedagogical activities of community-based learning in the United States, India, and China at different times. Firstly, special attention is paid to authentic learning environments that are connected to physical, mental, or cultural dimensions of the reality outside of the school. Secondly, the properties of pedagogical activities are compared in light of the approaches to community-based learning and their links to the dimensions of the learning environments at different times in the context of social change. Finally, this chapter concludes by comparing the various activities of community-based learning from the perspective of the learning environments in these three countries at different times.

This study is part of a broader research project, the aim of which is to examine the interplay between education and society throughout the course of the 20th century. It applies the historico-hermeneutical approach to comparative education (for methodological decisions, see Kimonen, 2015). The overall aim is to demonstrate the existence of fundamental educational patterns, policies, and practices in a social context.

1.1   *Dimensions of School Culture*

The school organization can be examined as a collaborative system that gathers and integrates different resources in order to implement desired objectives. The theory of organizations viewed as cultures provides a new perspective on the internal reality of organizations. Every organization has its own deep mental structure that guides people's thinking, choices, and actions. Culture represents an organization's prevailing ways of thinking and acting, which have been created and strengthened through shared experiences (Harisalo, 2008, pp. 31, 40, 265–266). Arends (2009) defined "school culture" as the philosophies that members of the school community use to justify their actions. It reflects their beliefs, values, and history (p. 488).

A school culture is a multidimensional entity. Schoen (2013) noted that the following four dimensions must be examined when changing a school culture: the school staff's professional orientation, the school organization's structure, the student-centered focus, and the quality of the learning environments. Developing the professional orientation and quality of the learning environment are integral dimensions of the teacher's work. All staff members must participate in development work in order to achieve real changes in the school's internal reality as well as to develop the school organization and learning environments and make its activities increasingly student centered (pp. 13, 29–31).

1.2   Key Features of the Learning Environments
A school culture has a significant impact on education and instruction at the school and thus on learning environments. The concept of a "learning environment" has been characterized by a wide diversity of definitions, depending on the learning approach:
- Wilson (1998) defined a constructivist learning environment as "a place where learners may work together and support each other as they use a variety of tools and information sources in their guided pursuit of learning goals and problem-solving activities" (p. 5).
- Stein (1998) believed that situated learning environments place students in authentic learning situations, where they are actively immersed in an activity while using problem-solving skills. These opportunities should involve a social community that replicates real-world situations (para. 3).
- Based on the contextual learning approach, Kauppi (1996) suggested that the contextual learning environment moves learning out of the classroom into authentic environments or environments that imitate reality (p. 95).

Land and Hannafin (2009) stated that "learner-centered environments provide interactive, complimentary activities that enable individuals to address unique learning interest and needs, study multiple levels of complexity, and deepen understanding" (p. 2). Learning environments are based on the following five core foundations:
- Psychological foundations that emphasize theories and research related to thinking and learning;
- Pedagogical foundations that include the qualities that exist and can be developed in the environment;
- Technological foundations that influence how information technology supports, constrains, or enhances the learning environment;
- Cultural foundations that reflect the prevailing values in a learning community; and
- Pragmatic foundations that emphasize the reconciling of available resources and restrictions when teachers are designing a learning environment (Land & Hannafin, 2009, p. 3).

The concept of a learning environment can be understood comprehensively as a socialization environment. The family has traditionally been regarded as the most important environment for primary socialization, however, the family's role as a child's primary socializer has decreased over time (Gauvain & Parke, 2010, pp. 239–240). The main environment for secondary socialization is linked to the contexts of pedagogical processes inside the school as well as to the physical, personal, and/or sociocultural contexts outside the school that are connected with these processes (for the learning contexts, see Braund & Reiss,

2004, p. 7). The world of work after the years spent at school can be seen as a tertiary environment for socialization (Jarvis, 2009, p. 45). The study at hand has demonstrated that the Naturalistic, Sociocultural, Productive, Economic, Martial, Ecological, and/or Scientific-Technical Dimensions are emphasized in accordance with social trends in environments that are geared toward secondary socialization.

The following sections provide a more detailed interpretation of the activities of community-based learning from the perspective offered by central pedagogical approaches and the dimensions of the learning environment with which they are intertwined. With respect to the United States, the primary focus is on experiential education, while in India the focus is on vocationally productive education and in China on productive labor education. The nature of pedagogical activities in these countries is examined through earlier case studies and program descriptions, a further object of interest being the means, content, and settings of action.

2   Early Pedagogical Ideas of Community-Based Learning

2.1   *American Progressive Schools*

The post-World War I decades (1920–1940) were the most vigorous era of progressive education in the United States. The pedagogical activities of the progressive school resembled those that had been implemented in the Indian neo-traditional school from the 1940s until the mid-1960s. The central challenge of pedagogical progressivism was to use education to adjust the citizenry to the new industrialized society. The Americans adopted a pioneering approach to meet this obligation: they combined teaching with practice, direct experience, and the actual life of the community in a methodological manner. During those times, different methods of reform-pedagogical teaching were applied in schools, following the use of the fundamentals of correlated, fused, core, comprehensive, and experience-based curricula (for curriculum-focused approaches, see, e.g., Spears, 1940, p. 53). Characteristics of experience-based curricula include concentrating on the student, real-life content, and comprehensive themes, as well as on actual problem-solving activities. The primary pedagogical activities in the school context were working in shops and gardens, in addition to activity-based classes. Typical forms of teaching and learning in the out-of-school context were collaborative and individual study projects, visits, and field trips, as well as school camps.

The progressive schools that applied activity-pedagogical approaches had a tendency to emphasize the Sociocultural Dimension of the learning environment in their community-based learning. This was evidenced in such activities as study visits to factories, laboratories, and other places in the community, as well as projects devoted to local housing conditions, means of livelihood, or serious social problems (for the pedagogical activities in selected schools, see, e.g., Dewey & Dewey, 1915, p. 52; de Lima, 1944, pp. 246–248; Wegner & Langworthy, 1936, p. 86). The following summary about teachers and students at one Kansas high school who were involved in a project regarding local housing conditions provides an example of applying these activity-pedagogical procedures in more detail:

> The ninth graders of Holton High School in Holton, Kansas, carried out a study of city planning and the prevailing housing conditions. They also surveyed the utilities in and the modern conveniences of houses on the basis of a questionnaire they had created. Drawing on this data, they made tables and graphs, as well as a map, in which the houses of the city were classified according to their convenience level. Finally, the students wrote an analysis describing the execution of the study and providing the study's findings and conclusions (Green, 1936, pp. 192–194).

While activities such as nature study, school gardening, and school camping certainly emphasized the Naturalistic Dimension of the learning environment, closeness to nature was also favored in other activity-pedagogical undertakings. In nature study, the students explored plants and observed animals in fields, forests, and on shores (for the pedagogical activities in one school, see, e.g., Rice, 1969, pp. 243–246). The school garden provided them with a place for learning from spring until fall. They plowed and prepared the soil, sowed seeds, planted and took care of plants, and reaped the harvest (for the pedagogical activities in one school, see, e.g., Lauderdale, 1981, pp. 47–48). The following summary illustrates these activity-pedagogical processes at one high school in the town of Ellerbe, North Carolina:

> The students of Ellerbe High School grew trees and bushes in the school's nursery. They sowed seeds in beds to germinate and grow into seedlings, rooted cuttings, and planted them to continue growing in a nursery garden, as well as transplanted seedlings that were growing too densely to more open ground before planting them in their final location. As the work gradually progressed, the students became acquainted with the growth factors connected with such things as germination, the promotion of rooting, and transplanting. They also sold plants, planned gardens, and did planting jobs (Merritt, 1938, pp. 122–125).

Characteristic of an experience-based curriculum was a focus on problem solving in the active functioning of the school workshops. There, students became familiar with raw materials, methods, and equipment through different activities, such as woodcraft, weaving, sewing, and cooking. Simultaneously, all school subjects were integrated. Dewey (1899/1953) viewed the ideal activities in the school workshops as being closely connected with the economy, sciences, arts, and communication in the surrounding community. Working in the school kitchen and garden were to be associated with the countryside, its processes and its products. Then the students could work on projects to study topics such as factors related to growth, the role of agriculture in human history, and life in contemporary society. Activities on field trips and study visits were linked to the topics being treated at school (pp. 66–67). The following overview based on the work of Mayhew and Edwards (1936/1966) describes the pedagogical applications carried out at the Dewey school in Chicago:

> The students of Group 8 at the University of Chicago Laboratory School visited the Armour Institute, where they studied the electric bell and motor. The purpose of the course was to re-create Faraday's classic electromagnetic experiment with an iron core and a coil. The students planned the visit to the Armour Institute in order to familiarize themselves with a motor, a dynamo, a battery, and a telegraph, as well as a galvanometer for measuring weak electric currents. To conclude their course, the students constructed a dynamo motor.
>
> The next year, the same students visited the Armour Institute again during their course dealing with electric machines. During the visit, they familiarized themselves with a galvanometer, an ammeter, a voltmeter, and an electric magnet, as well as an electric-powered plane and jigsaw. Additionally, they had the opportunity to see direct and alternating dynamos as well as electric motors equipped with two kinds of armatures. In practice, the students thus learned that a dynamo is a machine that can be used to generate mechanical energy or, conversely, can be used to convert energy into electric energy. After the visit, the students decided to construct a galvanometer in the shop as well as considered constructing both a motor and dynamo as well if they could find the necessary components (Mayhew & Edwards, 1936/1966, pp. 208–209).

Even if Dewey (1916/1950) argued that the objective of activity-pedagogical work at a school shop has neither economic nor vocational benefit (pp. 234–235), as had been the case with Gandhi's craft-related activities, the Productive Dimension of the learning environment was still emphasized in schools where the students worked for the benefit of the school and community. The students worked on the school premises in such places as the printing shop, the hatchery, the farm maintenance shop, the barber shop, or the beauty parlor, or engaged in activities such as canning fruit and vegetables for sale and doing electrical wiring on contract (for the pedagogical activities in one school, see, e.g., Freeman, 1938, p. 123).

This can be interpreted to mean that the Productive Dimension was justified by the neo-evolutionary theories which were holistically integrated with Deweyan activity-pedagogical methods and processes, and their associated meanings. By virtue of these strategies, the progressive school oriented itself in a deliberate manner toward a transaction process with the early industrial society in accordance with the classical liberal trend of thought. An effort was made to adjust Americans to an unprecedented social situation that included a rapid change from a traditional agrarian society to one that was modern, urbanized, and industrialized. The following exemplifies how the selected schools in Indiana, Kansas, and Alabama applied the Productive Dimension in their learning environments during the peak of pedagogical progressivism:

> The students of Public School 26 in Indianapolis, Indiana, renovated and furnished old buildings for use by the school and instructed community inhabitants in gardening. The students of Interlaken School, near LaPorte, Indiana, planned and constructed buildings for the school, tended the school farm, and edited a local newspaper (Dewey & Dewey, 1915, pp. 87–89, 214–216, 220). In Kansas, the students of Holton High School took part in drawing up a housing program with the city housing committee. In this work, they made use of an earlier study done by students on housing conditions (Green, 1936, pp. 194–195). Near Montgomery, Alabama, the students of Holtville School offered a variety of meat processing and soil transportation services. They canned fruits and vegetables for sale and did electrical wiring on contract. The school had a hatchery, a farm maintenance shop, a barber shop, and a beauty parlor (Lauderdale, 1981, pp. 47–49).

During the 1930s and 1940s, American public school camps were principally summer camps with programs that followed traditional camp programs. The Naturalistic Dimension was emphasized in this learning environment most strongly when students were practicing their camping skills out in the open or engaging in recreational activities at the camp center (for more details, see Hammerman, 1961, p. 134). The following describes the school activities and the community camp program at one school district in Washington State in the late 1930s:

> The school and community camp program for 1939 in the Highline School District in King County offered genuine camping close to nature at a campsite on Lake Wilderness. The summer camps for fifth and sixth graders of Highline Public Schools lasted for six days, in which students lived in tents, practiced camping skills, and hiked in the great outdoors. They learned such camp crafts as outdoor cooking, using knives and axes, and tying knots. They swam, played, did handicrafts, and spent nights around the campfire. They could also row and try riding (Jensen & Burgess, 1952, pp. 7–8, 111, 113, 126–127, 129–131, 133–134, 153, 161).

The quality of the Naturalistic Dimension of the learning environment was, however, to change by the 1950s. This decade saw the establishment of numerous resident outdoor schools whose programs were gradually supplemented, in addition to outdoor life experiences, with curriculum content: the study of nature, the environment, and conservation (Hammerman, 1961, pp. 148–150, 151, 161–162; for a closer examination of two resident outdoor education programs, see, e.g., Holland, 1955, pp. 16–18; Holland & Lewis, 1950, pp. 539–540). The following description of Camp Cuyamaca serves as an example of a late 1940s resident outdoor education program based on conservation studies for San Diego teachers and their sixth graders:

> Camp Cuyamaca, whose program for the academic year 1947–1948 focused on conservation studies in particular, was set up in a California state park. The school camps for sixth graders from San Diego public schools usually lasted five days, in which students studied in groups at a campsite and in neighboring fields, forests, and mountains. The students worked in the arts and crafts shops, visited the natural history museum, and spent time in the library. They planted seedling trees, took long hikes, and observed how nature functioned (Clarke, 1951, pp. 8–10, 27–28, 30, 51–105).

This type of change in the nature of the Naturalistic Dimension was also seen in other community-based teaching, which was increasing in many out-of-school sites, such as the school yard, garden, forest, and farm (Smith, 1955, 1970). Freeberg and Taylor (1963) reported that by the 1960s more than half of the states had public school forestry programs, and in several states many high schools offered practical agriculture education (pp. 170–171, 202). The following exemplifies pedagogical applications of practical agriculture education that were carried out by teachers and their students at selected schools in Missouri, Texas, and Michigan during the late 1950s:

> In Steelville, Missouri, the students of Steelville School District hiked in the school's 250-acre forest. They familiarized themselves with forestry methods and conservation practices, planted trees, and studied natural organisms. The public school students in Tyler, Texas, visited the school farm, where they observed the farmer in his daily work. They became acquainted with growing legumes, repairing fences, feeding penned animals, and other farm activities. The school farm of Battle Creek Public Schools, near Battle Creek, Michigan, also had a garden in which the fifth and sixth graders took care of their plants from spring to fall (Freeberg & Taylor, 1963, pp. 171–173, 209).

2.2 Indian Neo-Traditional Schools

A reform-pedagogical process paralleling that of the United States began in India in the 1940s when the neo-traditional school attempted to comprehensively integrate education and other social activity by utilizing the occupations and means of livelihood within the community. In addition to connecting teaching with the child's social and physical environment, it was also linked specifically to the community's traditional handicraft production and agriculture (see Zakir Husain Committee, 1938, p. 203). The following brief summary, based on the government publication *Experiments in Primary and Basic Education* (1956), further clarifies the different pedagogical activities of handicraft production and agriculture. It shows how teachers and students in junior basic schools in the former state of Hyderabad in the late 1940s engaged in local crafts or other traditional work:

> In Hyderabad, junior basic school instruction was linked to local handicraft production. Gardening and growing vegetables were also typical areas of expertise. At Subzimandi Junior Basic School, spinning and weaving were chosen as the main crafts, with gardening as the auxiliary craft. Pottery was selected as the main craft at Kunta Road Junior Basic School. At Somjiguda Junior Basic School, the main crafts were sewing and making artificial flowers. At Adikamet Junior Basic School, carpentry was the main area, but since small boys were unable to carry heavy tools, cardboard work was taught in addition to carpentry. At Nala Kunta Junior Basic School, basket making was chosen as the main craft. At Choodi

Bazar Junior Basic School, the main area was leatherwork (Ministry of Education, 1956, p. 13).

The curriculum was based on correlating the subjects and integrating the teaching, which meant that community-centeredness and real-life content and themes, in addition to actively practicing craft-related processes, were characteristics of the pedagogical procedures. Within the school context, the curriculum benefited from the use of projects carried out independently or cooperatively, from work-related lessons and vocational activities, and from on-premises work and cultivating land near the school as forms of teaching and learning. Gandhi (1962a) described that the entire work process in a school such as this—growing, picking, carding, spinning, and weaving cotton—was designed to train students in the specific abilities and methods for achieving a particular objective. During the various phases of the work, questions connected with the subjects were to be discussed in different ways. For example, elementary arithmetic was to be correlated with spinning and weaving so that the length of the spun thread was measured in yards, the correct number of threads was determined using hanks as the unit of measure, or the number of cross threads was calculated in the warp of a specific cloth (pp. 11–12). The following demonstrates the correlated craft-related processes in the basic schools of a district in Bihar in the 1940s:

> The basic schools of the village communities in the Champaran District chose spinning as their main craft. The students participated in the entire spinning process: cleaning the cotton, ginning, opening up the cotton, preparing it for spinning, carding and preparing slivers, as well as spinning on the *takli* and the *charkha*. They learned the names of the raw materials, the equipment used, and the finished products, and practiced recognizing the count, strength, and evenness of yarn. They estimated the maximum and minimum speed of spinning in class on a daily basis, and calculated the average speed for the whole class per day, week, fortnight, month, and year, in addition to comparing the average speed of the class with the speed prescribed in the syllabus. Likewise, they calculated the cost of the raw materials and supplies used as well as the daily, weekly, and monthly earnings from spinning.
>
> When they were spinning, the students sang songs about cotton, the carding bow, the *takli*, and their work. After the period spent spinning, they often presented short plays about the different phases of the work or drew pictures of the equipment used during the work. They wrote in their diaries what they had done or learned, and read what they had written to

each other and to the teacher. The class monitor organized the necessary equipment and supplies. At the end of the day, the students cleaned their cupboards (*almirah*), their classroom, and the entire school compound (Prasad, 1949, pp. 135–140).

Work and service activities, study visits, field trips, and festivals were the main pedagogical approaches included in the out-of-school context. Using these methods, the neo-traditional school integrated itself with society in a planned and coordinated manner. Its function can thus be seen as the process of social transformation. Students became familiar with using local traditional methods, work tools, and raw materials in order to strengthen the entire Indian preindustrial agrarian society. The properties of such procedures were justified by the Gandhian idea of truth (*satya*) and nonviolence (*ahimsa*). This comprehensively encompassed the systems of concepts referring to humankind and, more widely, the values guiding the lives of the individual and society, and beliefs concerning the world. Schools made efforts to raise the vocationally productive work processes of community-based learning and associated meanings, especially emphasizing traditional Indian cultural values rather than material values as a strategy for helping India attain social and economic self-sufficiency.

Social service activities within the school curriculum also targeted, at their best, social transformation, with attempts at raising the quality of housing, health, and hygiene; stimulating economic life; or promoting literacy (for the pedagogical activities in selected schools, e.g., see Arunachalam, 1949, p. 103; Devi, 1940, pp. 183–185; Salamat, 1970, pp. 38, 71–72). For example, the basic school students in the villages of the Champaran District, Bihar, studied local housing conditions under the guidance of their teacher. They discovered that the local houses were mostly made of bamboo, with thatched roofs and no windows, and lacked any planned layout or systematic arrangement of the interiors. During this learning process, they realized that the houses easily caught fire, but that they could be protected during the hot season from dangerous east-west winds by building them in a north-south direction (Prasad, 1949, pp. 135, 143). Thus, the students, besides understanding that simple innovations could prevent the houses from catching fire each year, also understood how changes affecting the whole society could be based on Indian national cultural values and customs.

This type of social service is intended to benefit the school and community in many ways. The following illustrates some of the pedagogical applications of social service that teachers and their students carried out in selected schools in Gujarat, Bihar, and Rajasthan:

The students of the Thamna village school in Gujarat were responsible for the cleanliness of the school building and the surrounding community, in addition to arranging evening prayers and telling the participants the news of the day (Parikh, 1940, pp. 167, 172, 178–179). The students at Mihijam Senior Basic School in Santhal Pargana, Bihar, constructed soak pits for sewage removal and trench latrines for preparing manure in the nearby villages, in addition to explaining the importance of manure to the villagers. The students at Gram Vidyalaya School in Suwana, near Bhilwara, Rajasthan, took part in various kinds of postal services: acquiring postcards, envelopes, and money order forms for the public; writing letters for the villagers who were illiterate; and ensuring that everything to be sent was taken to the Bhilwara post office (Salamat, 1970, pp. 9–10, 67, 69, 71).

The Productive Dimension of the learning environment characteristic of craft-related education was emphasized in pedagogical activities in which students worked at the school's spinning and weaving facilities; in the leather, pottery, and other workshops; at the cowshed (*goshala*), dairy, or its store; and in the garden and areas under cultivation (for school-specific pedagogical activities, see, e.g., Kulkarni, 1940, pp. 126–128; Ministry of Education, 1956, p. 29; Prasad, 1949, p. 140). The following brief description provides an example of applying the Productive Dimension in the activities of craft-related education at two schools, one in Gujarat and the other in Rajasthan:

> The students of the national school in Rajkot, Gujarat, ran a dairy and produced nutritive foodstuffs, such as hand-ground flour, hand-pounded rice, pulses, and pure *ghani* oil (Gandhi, 1962b, pp. 93–94). The students at Gram Vidyalaya School in Suwana, Rajasthan, worked in the school's cowshed (*goshala*), store, and bank (Salamat, 1970, pp. 67, 69, 72).

The Sociocultural Dimension was particularly stressed when the students were acquainted with work linked to the processes of craft-related education at the community bazaar areas and plantations, or when they were involved in social service at the local markets and festivals, or within contexts such as the sanitation program and construction projects (for school-specific pedagogical activities, see, e.g., Prasad, 1949, pp. 143–144). Such emphasis could still be seen with the establishment of the first multipurpose higher secondary schools in the mid-1950s, when the modernization process was launched in India. Even if cooperation between the multipurpose school and the community tended to be modest in scale (D'Souza & Chaudhury, 1965, p. 121), there were Indian schools that were in contact with the local culture, attempting to promote its traditions and means of livelihood. The following description clarifies the manner in which the Sociocultural Dimension was emphasized in the pedagogical activities of social service at one multipurpose higher secondary school in Rajasthan:

> In 1959, a multipurpose higher secondary school was established in the town of Rajgarh. The students of the school participated in community activities, developed the conditions at the school, and supplied articles produced by the craft-related courses to commercial outlets for sale. In the community, they ran the drinking water huts at the Jagannathji fair (*Jagannathji mela*), guided pilgrims, and maintained general order. The school orchestra played in the fair chariot (*mela rath*) and at various events arranged by the rural local government (*panchayat samiti*). In the school area, the students participated in the construction of roads and an open-air theater, in addition to assuming responsibility for the cleanliness of the playgrounds. They bound books, dipped candles, and produced articles for sale in woodcraft and tailoring classes. In the evenings, they held literacy courses for the inhabitants of the community (Salamat, 1970, pp. 62–65).

2.3   *Chinese Revolutionary Schools*
2.3.1   Radical Reforms and Tragic Events

China implemented a major educational reform during the Great Leap Forward (1958–1961) that instituted a radical change to students' studies and teachers' work. The revolutionary school intended to teach children and young people respect for the principles of socialist consciousness and culture. The means to achieve this was a course of productive labor in each school in which students would participate. Schools would run factories and farms and, similarly, industrial and agricultural cooperatives would run schools.

At the beginning of the Great Leap, the work-study school was established according to the ideas of Mao Zedong (1893–1976) in order to implement the fundamentals of education that would serve proletarian politics and be combined with productive labor. Schools were encouraged to set up factories or workshops and to create contracts with local agricultural cooperatives, factories, or different production units. The purpose was to enhance the ability of students to participate in productive labor (Mao, 1991/1998a, p. 797). Studying and performing productive labor were to be integral parts of the school program, usually consisting of half-time study and half-time work in agricultural production, the handicraft industry, or public service. The intention was to combine theory with reality, and manual labor with mental labor (Ministry of Education of the C.P.G., 1998d, p. 800).

Work-related activities varied according to the grade level, from cleaning the school premises to various activities in local villages and communes. Working and studying could also alternate on a daily and weekly basis or even longer at harvesting time. Work-based learning took place in many kinds of settings. It included labor courses and units of study in the school, working after school for the benefit of the school and the community, and working in factories and on farms at the school as well as at local cooperatives and production units. For example, Wang et al. (1996) reported that between 1957 and 1959, the schools in Ningbo, Zhejiang, developed their productive labor program with academic studies. Many high school students in the old city area were engaged in building animal breeding farms on Jin'E Mountain. Jiangdong High School was the first to build a factory and arrange for its students to work there. They studied three days and performed labor three days a week, with four hours of studying and four hours of work a day. Later, the high school in the village of Zhangchun opened a school farm for forestry programs, built an electric maintenance workshop, and served local farmers. Wang et al. also reported that the Young Pioneer drug-manufacturing factory of Cang Shui Jie Primary School was considered very profitable, and that some rural elementary schools opened rabbit farms that offered many kinds of labor and service activities (Wang et al., 1996, pp. 290–291).

During learning processes, the students were guided by teachers, workers, and peasants. Labor was divided among the students according to their abilities. Everyone was considered to be important and beneficial in the process of advancing a socialist society through labor and productive work (for requirements for students' work in each grade in two schools, see, e.g., Guang ya zhong xue, 1959, p. 9; Si ping shi yi ma lu xiao xue, 1959, p. 19). The following explains how labor-related activities were organized at one high school in Shanghai in the late 1950s:

> No. 2 High School in Jiading County built chemical, casting, and electric factories as well as factories for wood- and metalworking. The older and stronger students worked in the electric and chemical factories, in the smithy or forge, and in front of the furnace in the casting factory. The girls and less strong boys helped with filtering, fitting molds, and as firefighters. Often these students were, however, involved with various activities in experimental fields and farming. They took care of vegetable and fruit gardens and reaped the harvest (Jia ding xian di er zhong xue, 1959, pp. 13–14).

The integrated labor-related activities naturally varied according to the students' readiness and class studies. In conjunction with their courses, the students applied the subject matter learned at school to their practice in school factories or local cooperatives. Ke (1958) reported that No. 1 High School, for example, had contracts with the factories, farms, and stations of the villages in Qin County, Shanxi. The teachers arranged opportunities for students to work in local production units, and their technical workers taught production skills to the teachers and students (p. 30). The relevant courses at school were closely connected with the practical activities that took place on the school premises and at local establishments. The Productive Dimension was emphasized in learning environments where the students practiced the subject matter during the production processes, when they made such tools as hammers and drills to be used at the school. They worked with cutting tools to make metal parts, shaped them with the machine, made speed changes, and stopped the machine when the work was done. The production could consist of cutting, drilling, welding, installing rivets, and other processes (for pedagogical activities at specific high schools, see, e.g., Liu, 1956, pp. 31–32). The following exemplifies the manner in which the Productive Dimension was prioritized in the process of combining study with work at one high school in Changchun, Jilin, at the time:

> The junior students of Shiyan High School studied zoology and botany in class and applied the subject matter when they practiced agriculture and husbandry. The first- and second-grade seniors studied mechanics and machinery during the physics course and applied what they learned to making machines and casting. In the chemistry course, third graders studied how heat can change iron and steel from a solid to a liquid state, and they applied this knowledge when practicing iron- and steelwork. The school also organized research groups. The physics research group studied how to make a simple computer, and the biology group learned how to grow plants and make new varieties (Ji lin sheng shi yan zhong xue, 1959, p. 20).

The dimensions of the learning environment were especially connected with sociocultural values and methods when the projects students carried out were oriented toward life outside of the school. During visits and field excursions, the students could observe the activities of the surrounding community as well as participate in various activities for the benefit of the community. The Sociocultural Dimension was emphasized in learning environments where the students constructed and afforested a martyrs' cemetery, carried water to the fields during a serious drought, or dug up sweet potatoes and harvested grain or pulse for the village (for the pedagogical activities in selected schools, see, e.g., Huang, 1959, p. 17; Sun, 1957, pp. 43–44). The following illustrates the pedagogical applications that were carried out at one high school in Lankao, Henan:

> The students of Lankao No. 2 High School familiarized themselves with work on local farms. The students took notes and studied the basic skills of field farming, the development of cultivated plants, and the influence of the seasons on the harvest. They collected documents related to local history, nature, and different kinds of productive processes. During their farm visits, the students learned about farming production methods and helped the farmers with their work. Yunsan Shi and Zengyu Zhang, for instance, taught one farmer how to plow the field, and Jinghua Yang taught a village woman how to grow cotton. Fude Guo helped the villagers to plant, grow, and harvest sweet potatoes and taught them how to grow tubers (Lian, 1958, pp. 9–10).

During the Great Leap Forward, the dimensions of the learning environment were tightly linked with the country's economic productivity, as the goal was to save educational expenses while carrying out the principles of labor and productive work (for self-sufficiency at all schools, see Bo, 1958/1998, p. 798). Social reform based on revolutionary thinking was intended to promote the adaptation of education to the new needs of the socialist society. It also aimed to have a sudden and major impact on schooling and educators' work. This form of revolutionary education, the efforts of which were directed toward the society-centered transformation of knowledge, was integrated with society in an organized manner. Chen (1981) wrote that revolutionary education "contained potent ideas of an educational program rising from the needs and problems of contemporary society and was designed to produce immediate changes in contemporary living" (p. 221). The conclusion can be drawn that, from the perspective of community-based learning, the orientation of the interrelationship between education and society was radical and contextual. Fouts and Chan (1997) stated that "the inclusion of labour into the school curriculum was based on an ideological position held by the Communists, and that ideology ran contrary to traditional Chinese educational thought and practice" (p. 31).

The Productive and Economic Dimensions of the learning environments, characteristic of productive labor education, gave importance to pedagogical activities when the students made school tables and chairs, agricultural chemicals and tools, and drilling machines in the school's workshops and factories; when they grew local crops in gardens and on farms on the school premises; or worked in local cooperatives and their production units (for pedagogical activities in selected schools, see, e.g., Cui, 1959, p. 21; Jia ding xian di er zhong xue, 1959, p. 13; Ke, 1958, p. 30; Lian, 1958, p. 7; Shang hai shi jiao yu yu sheng chan lao dong xiang jie he zhan lan hui, 1958, pp. 1–2). The Sociocultural Dimension was especially emphasized in learning environments where the students were involved in voluntary and social welfare work within such contexts as local construction projects and natural-disaster programs (for school-specific pedagogical activities, see, e.g., Chu xiong zhuan shu bian, 1958, pp. 6–7; Wang, 1958, pp. 35–36). The following provides an example of applying the Productive Dimension in the activities of labor-related education at one primary school in the area of Baicheng, Jilin:

> In the town of Taonan, Jingren Primary School started to build school farms and factories in 1958. The students participated in agricultural work according to both their abilities and the prevailing seasons. The rice-planting program for 1959 included many activities for all students. The students in higher grades turned over piles of manure; plowed, harrowed, and leveled the land; constructed irrigation canals; performed springtime sowing and summertime hoeing and weeding; transplanted rice seedlings; and did grafting. Students in the middle grades mainly selected seedlings and did weeding and pollination. All students in the school were engaged in harvesting and plowing the field in the fall (Cui, 1959, p. 21).

The Great Leap Forward was an economic and social campaign led by Mao during the second five-year period (1958–1963). The intention was to transform the country's economy through rapid industrialization and collectivization. However, it is commonly considered to have created poorly organized economic, agricultural, and industrial reforms without Soviet experts and, within the context of natural disasters between 1959 and 1961, resulted in widespread famine (for these difficulties, see, e.g., Palese, 2009, p. 30; Zhou, 1984/1998, p. 1083).

In the middle of this disastrous time, the work-study students were needed to help on the farms and save the harvest (Ministry of Education of the C.P.G., 1998e, p. 1028). Teachers were inexperienced, unqualified, and strained by the Great Leap changes (Ministry of Education of the C.P.G., 1998a, p. 1079). Consequently, school days were combined with time for rest instead of labor (C.P.C. Central Committee, 1998b, p. 989), and many rural middle schools were integrated with spare-time schools (Ministry of Education of the C.P.G., 1998e, p. 1028). Despite these difficulties, some schools intended to increase working time and production capacity as well as encourage teachers and students to improve production tools and modify techniques and skills. In many cases, the reasons for teachers' willingness to assist the society in crisis were based on how experienced a certain school community and its region was with the Communist Party's moral-political values. The following illustrates how teachers at one primary school in Jiutai County, Jilin, tried to serve society when working with their students:

> Shiyan Primary School improved the school's workshops and working schedule in 1960. Now the first and second graders had one hour for study and six hours for work per week. The teachers arranged for the students to take care of themselves and to collect food for the pigs and rabbits. They were shown how to do some agricultural work in local places with their third-grade mates. The school repaired the sewing, woodworking, and metalworking factories and built a new workshop with an electric saw. A greater number of students could now make wooden boxes, sew facial masks, saw wooden plates, or make articles using a metal press for the local factory. In the school's metalworking factory, the students and their teachers also studied and developed a nut-punching machine for more efficient production and safer work (Jiu tai xian shi yan xiao xue, 1960, p. 23).

By 1963, the importance of academic schools and spare-time schools increased considerably, as Liu Shaoqi (1898–1969) had become Mao's designated successor, after the unsuccessful Great Leap Forward in 1961, and new curriculum work had begun (Ministry of Education of the C.P.G., 1998b, pp. 1202, 1204–1205). The reduction in work-study schools led to conflict in 1963 and 1964 between the adherents of work-study schools and those of academic schools (see, e.g., Liu, 1998, pp. 1253–1254). As a consequence of this conflict, Mao renewed his 1955 campaign in which urban intellectuals were resettled in rural areas to perform labor and study his ideas (Gong qing tuan, 1998, p. 1274).

In 1965, on the eve of the Cultural Revolution, the revolutionary regime organized a conference at the Political Bureau of the Central Party Committee on urban work-study schools. Liu stated in his conference speech that work-study schools should be established in urban and rural areas and that the emphasis should be on developing lower secondary schools and institutions of higher education. The aims documented at the conference included (a) increasing farm and factory production, (b) strengthening the interaction between theory and practice in teaching, (c) decreasing parents' educational expenses, (d) settling urban students in rural areas, and (e) increasing students' motivation to study. This plan was to be implemented within 10 years after a five-year trial (see, e.g., Liu, 1993/1998, pp. 1369–1370). Through the era of political changes and conflicts, many schools continued to perform labor during their work-related studies. Schools were engaged in production so that they could attain the goal of self-sufficiency. Especially at rural schools, students helped the village people and, in turn, the villagers helped teachers to run the school. The following demonstrates these processes at some rural schools in Yangquan County, Hebei:

> At the Wang Jia Liang village school, the fourth and fifth graders had only three hours to study at school. The morning and afternoon hours were reserved for working in the village. After studying the use of an abacus at school, the fifth graders taught their family members to calculate the working hours with an abacus. Similarly, the higher grade students helped the village accountants to do food and payment calculations using this tool. The students of Shi Jia Hui School collected lime, a natural substance that improves growth, and made fertilizer by burning it. The school received economic support from peasant families for schoolbooks and tuition. About 30 village schools, such as Heiyan and Wang Jia Gou, found some local solution to the lack of schoolbooks and other things for students (Jin, 1965, pp. 25–26).

2.3.2   Sweeping Changes and Conflicts

The Great Proletarian Cultural Revolution (1966–1976) was preceded by a campaign started at the beginning of the 1960s in the People's Liberation Army to promote the study of Mao's ideas. In the mid-1960s, Mao strongly criticized the inequality of both the educational system and academic leadership in higher education institutions. He condemned the exclusive attention paid to theoretical studies in the curriculum, the fact that book-centered learning was too dominant, and the burden of an examination system. He demanded that work-study schools should be standardized throughout the nation (Mao, 1967/1998b, pp. 1249–1250; Mao, 1967/1998c, p. 1383). Mao's criticism is connected with the larger social disapproval—the criticism of bourgeois ideology and revisionist thinking. Mao's school reform was part of transforming the superstructure of society, including the Party, existing administrative bodies, and production machinery. The following quotation, based on Mao's (1969/1990) pivotal 1964 speech, included the basic elements for the upcoming educational revolution:

> Our general policy is correct, but our methods are wrong. There are quite a few problems regarding the present school system, curriculum,

methods of teaching, and examination methods, and all this must be changed. They are all exceedingly destructive of people. ... Nowadays, first, there are too many classes; second, there are too many books. ... Real understanding must be acquired gradually through experience at work. (pp. 45–46)

In June 1966, the C.P.C. Central Committee and the State Council directed that, in order to forward the Cultural Revolution, all lower level institutions of higher learning not take any new students (Ministry of Higher Education of the C.P.G., 1998, p. 1403). This caused the closure of all schools in the nation. In August 1966, the C.P.C. Central Committee official decided to start the Cultural Revolution (C.P.C. Central Committee, 1966/1998a, pp. 1406–1408). An editorial on January 22, 1967, in the *People's Daily* had an enormous effect on the masses, inspiring them to action. After this, new organizations began to take power, causing chaos throughout the country (Ren min ri bao she lun 1967–1–22, 1967/1998, p. 1411). Young people formed groups of Red Guards that freely roamed the country and destroyed everything that represented old thoughts, old culture, old traditions, and old habits. This resulted in demolishing old temples and burning books, paintings, and sedan carriages used at weddings and funerals (Han, 2000, p. 53). Primary schools gradually reopened in late 1967, secondary schools a couple of years later. Universities were closed more than four years during the Cultural Revolution. Academic classes were completely closed and plans for the revolutionary education started to emerge.

The Cultural Revolution regime intended to integrate labor-related work with teaching at all school levels and types according to prevailing political and social needs. Education was regarded as connected with other cultural and human activity and thus intimately linked to society and its economic and political power structure. This social reform required that ideological teaching, accompanied by book reading, was to be given in close connection with production. The means to achieve this goal was that the school and a factory, a commune, and the army should form a coherent whole. Hong (1975) described that during this era, primary schools, middle schools, and higher institutions were to function in conjunction with the local factories, people's communes, or army units. Small factories and farms were to be set up in primary and secondary schools, where workers, peasants, and soldiers were part-time teachers (p. 482).

Wang's (1975) investigation evaluating education in China at that time revealed that secondary and higher institutions set up local factories within schools for the purpose of training students in practical work and engaging them in production. Students also worked at local factories for practical training. Veteran workers were often invited to teach certain parts or aspects of their work at school (p. 763). The dimensions of the learning environment were intimately linked with productivity, and students participated in the work processes of local factories and construction sites. Their work was valued, since it was seen to increase productivity that benefited the entire socialist society. Productive labor education gave importance to pedagogical activities when the students and teachers were working in a local factory for several months. The students learned how to use a windlass or plate roller and how to do riveting and electric welding. They could learn a skilled trade, such as being a welder, carpenter, or electrician (for industrial work-study programs in a local factory and school factory, see, e.g., Tian jing shi si shi er zhong ge ming wei yuan hui, 1970, pp. 58–60). The following exemplifies the manner in which the Productive Dimension was emphasized in the learning environment when the students of one primary school worked in the Xinhua Lock Factory and at a construction site in Harbin, Helongjiang:

> Anguang Primary School intended to combine teaching with production in the late 1960s. The higher grades took turns working in an assembly workshop of the Xinhua Lock Factory. The school also invited the workers to give lectures at the school. The teachers and students wrote material for the Industrial Learning course, which included experiences and ideas about lock-assembly work. The students felt that they had learned a lot from the workers, could exchange their ideas with them, and were encouraged to apply the material learned at school to practice in the assembly workshop. Similarly, the school arranged for the students to work at a construction site. There, the workers showed them how to mix concrete and how to determine the proportions of cement, sand, pebble, and water (Har bin shi an guang xiao xue, 1971, p. 22).

During the Cultural Revolution, learning was to be intimately linked to the economic life of the local community. This was possible since productive work in factories and on farms formed a major part of the schools' curriculum. Schools utilized a system consisting of an integrated curriculum that was built around productive labor. This type of appreciation for work was intertwined with moral-political values, which served to accentuate patriotism and loyalty toward a socialist system and the various virtues it represented. These could be obtained when students were engaged in different types of work-study programs in schools. Wang (1975) reported in his Chinese investigation that some factories even established schools of their own where teachers and students worked. It is also possible that these educational reforms, designed to achieve economic goals, offered students more practical training and actual work in production than the previous educational system (p. 764). The following shows how teachers and students implemented labor-related education at one factory-run middle school in Lanzhou, Gansu:

> Wu Qi Middle School arranged for teachers and students to be involved in activities in the School of Lanzhou Steelworks. The school program comprised Mao's thinking, industrial and agricultural studies, and military training. About half of the teachers and students worked in the factory while about half worked on the farm. Normally, they changed places every second year. The workers, peasants, and soldiers taught with the schoolteachers. During the work, the students had an overseer to guide them. They had to learn to do certain factory work and to use certain methods on the farm alongside the workers and peasants. The military course included Mao's war strategies and general knowledge of military training (Gan su he lan zhou ge ming wei yuan hui, 1969/1998, p. 1441).

In the agrarian areas, students worked in the gardens and fields together with the peasants. The learning programs included such activities as clearing unproductive lands, planting and harvesting, and helping with the construction of irrigation systems. The specific objectives depended on the particular needs of the local community (Wang, 1975, p. 763). Tchen (1977) reported that Peking No. 12 Middle School, for instance, decided to set up an affiliated boarding school in a village several kilometers from the school where the students could study the entire term and work for a month alongside the peasants in the fields (p. 414). Similarly, productivity was emphasized in the learning environment when the school in Nanning, Guangxi, built an affiliated school in a rural area. Combined with their studies, the students were involved in agricultural work in the fields. They leveled the field, turned over the earth using a plow so that seeds could be planted, and improved the soil (for the pedagogical activities, see, e.g., Guang xi nan ning shi di er zhong xue dang zhi bu, 1976, pp. 42–43). The following illustrates how the Productive Dimension of the learning environment was stressed when the students of one high school worked on the school premises and on a tea farm in Wuyuan County, Jiangxi:

> Wukou Tea Cultivation High School was founded in 1965. The learning program included such areas as planning a tea farm, designing a tea factory, growing tea, and transplanting tea. The school had a tea workshop, garden, field, and regular classrooms. The busiest working time

was from August to April, when the students grew tea on the Wukou tea farm, cleared marginal lands for the farm, and took care of tea bushes and transplants. The farmers and workers taught students as they performed labor in the farm's fields. At harvest time, they picked tea and volunteered to produce tea after practicing for two months (Wu yuan xian ge ming wei yuan hui, 1968, pp. 25, 27–28).

The educational and social reform at the time required that political and ideological education be taught during learning processes in the factories, farms, and army units. The military courses were normally organized according to similar militia groups. Students took part in military activities, during which they were involved in such exercises as marksmanship, bayonet handling, and guerrilla warfare. They learned about true Chinese qualities when they studied the principles of the People's Liberation Army. They also received further political lessons, as was typical of all military training in China at that time (Ong, 1970, p. 172). The Martial Dimension was stressed in the learning environment in which the students participated in artillery measurement programs in an army unit (for the pedagogical program that included military training, and industrial and agricultural work, see, e.g., Bei jing shi di shi san zhong xue dang zhi bu, 1975, pp. 40–43). The following shows how military training was integrated with the learning program carried out by a factory, a farm, and an army unit in Lanzhou, Gansu:

> No. 5 High School was transformed into the High School of Lanzhou Casting Factory. The teaching program included productive work at the casting factory, agricultural work at the Gaolan People's Commune, and military training in a local army unit. The teachers arranged the work according to the students' age and health. Some teachers and their students worked in rural areas while others worked in the factory. They changed places once a year. In small groups at the factory, the students learned how to use tools and equipment for making metal objects by melting metal and pouring it into molds under the guidance and instruction of specific workers. In the countryside, the work and study times were organized according to the farming seasons. The students were to work full-time during sowing and harvesting days, but at other times they could concentrate more on studies. At the army unit, the students engaged in similar military training, with military exercises and political lessons typical of common military training in the Chinese army at that time (Gan su he lan zhou ge ming wei yuan hui, 1969, pp. 30–34).

During the Cultural Revolution, school education was connected more firmly with the life of the community outside the school than most educational systems had before. The revolutionary schools intended to attain the goals and values inherent in the neighboring community directed by the local Party organizations. During work processes, teachers and students also engaged in production in order to become self-sufficient and avoid needing the support of the local leadership body. This economic value of the work-study schools was emphasized in China, while the central government and Party maintained authority over the teachers' work and school activities. The Sociocultural and Economic Dimensions were stressed in the processes in which the students especially benefited the school and the community. Together with their teachers, they cleared marginal lands for buildings and fields; built their own schoolhouses, factories, and farms; and helped local people, who, in turn, helped teachers to run the school (for the pedagogical activities in selected schools, see, e.g., Nei meng gu wu yuan xian min zu gong she, 1973, pp. 75–77; Liao ning sheng ge ming wei yuan hui, 1968, pp. 50–51; Zhao yuan he sui hua ge wei hui, 1971, p. 48). The following exemplifies how the students at the agricultural high school in Wuyuan County, Jiangxi, benefited their own school and nearby community members:

> The students of Wukou Tea Cultivation High School were involved in work that benefited the community and the school. Some students took part in the repair work on the road from the school to the stream. Some students of the Wukou production team helped an old woman by bringing water, cutting firewood, and growing vegetables for her. Some students helped farmers to draw their carts along the muddy road near the school. Apart from these, the school students and teachers made their own teaching materials, washed and repaired clothes, maintained desks and chairs, grew vegetables, and raised pigs. This made it possible for them to attain the goal of self-sufficiency (Wu yuan xian ge ming wei yuan hui, 1968, p. 29).

3   Challenges

Comparing community-based learning practices in American progressive schools and in Indian neo-traditional schools reveals that both school environments inevitably encountered the same types of problems. These problems were contextual, procedural, and resource-linked. After the Second World War, American society experienced sweeping changes. The conservative political and social thinking typical of the period exacerbated criticism of reform-pedagogical movements, particularly from the late 1940s (Cremin, 1968, pp. 348–351). This also meant a downfall in the popularity of progressive education. The final setback occurred in 1957, when the treatment of themes connected with national defense was suddenly linked to international competition in the fields of science and technology (see National Defense Education Act of 1958, 1958, Section 101). In a comparable manner, the political and economic changes that took place in India weakened the neo-traditional educational thinking of the 1950s and 1960s when the innovations in economic strategy that the central administration implemented failed to emphasize local activities in the countryside aimed at ensuring self-sufficiency. Urbanization increased alienation. At the same time, there was little academic study of curriculum planning and implementation (Holmes & McLean, 1989, pp. 156–157). One possible interpretation of this is that the American progressive and the Indian neo-traditional movements in education were incapable of reforming themselves within the context of these types of social changes.

These world-renowned school reforms failed to change the fundamentals of the pedagogical work of teachers. For example, progressive teaching procedures in the United States were only combined with traditional teacher-centered instruction externally. The teachers tended to implement procedures unevenly and only for certain parts of the school day. The large groups of students were heterogeneous and often weakly motivated to study (Cuban, 1993, pp. 142–144). In India, the teachers were broadly opposed to the neo-traditional school curricula and primarily utilized traditional teaching methods in their correlation-based teaching. The schools were unable to change their curriculum in the direction of vocational education. At the same time, many of the manual occupations associated with craft related education, such as spinning and weaving, actually seemed irrelevant from the perspective of economic development. In particular, various demographic segments in large cities felt no connection with Gandhian neo-traditional education (Holmes & McLean, 1989, pp. 156–157).

Additionally, both schools of reform pedagogics suffered as a consequence of poor economic, mental, and physical resources. The fact is that sufficient economic resources were simply not allocated for the school reforms. Insufficient teacher education, in particular, was reflected in the low quality of the instruction the schools provided. Teachers did not know how to implement reformist procedures, and school furnishings were old-fashioned, with inadequate teaching premises and equipment (Cuban, 1993, pp. 142–144; Subbarao, 1958, pp. 13–15, 154).

The challenges and problems of the Chinese educational reforms were completely different during the Great Leap Forward and the Cultural Revolution than in the United States and India described above. The opposite reform efforts to solve the prevailing educational problems in China caused a pendulum swing between revolutionary education and academic education. Chen (1981) argued that the problem with the revolutionary education was weak planning, with a lack of understanding about academic education. The revolutionary politicians did not know the particulars of pedagogical processes in applying theories to practice and, instead, they emphasized political dogma and wording. The ultimate purpose of revolutionary educational reform was to create an educational form based on Maoism that superseded the intellectual and cultural elites. The following quotation, based on Chen's book *Chinese Education Since 1949* (1981), illustrates this in more detail:

> The ideologues-radicals fashioned a program that diminished the importance of formal schooling, threw systematic learning and the acquisition of knowledge out the window, and gave no significant role for the intellectuals to play. The management of revolutionary education was left in the hands of … ideologues, functionaries, and cadres of limited or no educational experience, and unschooled workers-peasants-soldiers who were barely literate but had learned to repeat the dogmas and clichés and were given authority to demand that students and teachers follow their example of ideological devotion. (p. 223)

For teachers' work, revolutionary education produced many challenges, since teachers were forced to follow the Party's instructions on what, where, and how to teach students. Many factors regarding contexts and resources were beyond the teachers' authority and fell under the responsibility of people who were active in Party politics. The main obligations should have been to design and maintain a physical learning environment that would promote students' health, safety, well-being, and learning. However, in many cases, this type of educational reform did not succeed in providing learning environments that would meet at least minimum requirements. This was evidenced in such activities as working in the front of furnaces in the casting factory, where metal objects were made by melting and pouring hot liquid metal into molds. Additionally, organizing appropriate training for the teachers and workers who participated in the teaching was inadequate.

Through this revolutionary era, the school-specific studies used in this chapter suggest that it is possible that the revolutionary regime forced teachers to do their work in accordance with the all-powerful value objectives that constituted the background for the revolutionary society of that time. In this demanding situation, many teachers, guided by their practical ethics, were willing to work effectively and cooperate multiprofessionally. Chinese teachers seem to have been committed to their work despite the prevailing difficult circumstances. Han (2000) even described that teachers "learned to respect villagers and other working people. ... Farmers no longer viewed the educated elite with mystic feelings because they knew the educated teachers better after working with them" (p. 116).

Chen (1981) wrote that dissatisfaction with the revolutionary education in China did not arise in a moment or accidentally. Although many people were interested in the theoretical background and concepts of this approach to education in the beginning, opposition grew, especially among those who felt that the function of education is not to transmit political ideology but to develop various skills and abilities (p. 125).

4   Pedagogical Changes and New Directions

4.1   *American Essentialist and Neo-Essentialist Schools*

In 1957, an unforeseen foreign policy event initiated a school reform movement in the United States that continues today. When the Soviet Union successfully launched the first satellite into space, the U.S. Congress maintained that the country needed to rapidly raise the degree of science and technology through education in order to revamp national defense. For this reason, the schools were expected to enhance remodernization in the country by providing experts capable of functioning effectively in a technologically sophisticated industrial society. There was a widely held view that essentialist and neo-essentialist education provided the best alternatives for achieving this goal. Despite the schools being an educational center with only limited connections to society, teaching was also directed toward nature and the community in order to enhance and enrich learning.

This explains why both the Ecological and Scientific-Technical Dimensions also started to become more significant features in the learning environments of community-based learning. The relationship between organisms and their environment became the key issue within environmental education, thus replacing traditional approaches focused on the ecological impact of environmental changes. Gradually, environmental education was expected to include "a socio-critical component that encourages students to question how their actions and those of their society impact on the environment" (Taylor, Littledyke, Eames, & Coll, 2009, p. 319).

Such a course of thinking is evidenced by examples such as students familiarizing themselves with the living organisms that inhabit a pond in a residential site, studying the well-being of the ecosystem in a mountainous area near a research station, or exploring the utilization of the sea and its problems on field trips (for one environmental education program, see, e.g., Butler & Roach, 1986, pp. 34–37). The following two programs show that these types of learning environments can offer students an opportunity to practice shared responsibility. The students have the chance not only to broaden their knowledge and develop their abilities, both of which are needed for studying ecological questions and evaluating alternative methods for resolving problems, but also for expanding their overall consciousness concerning environmental issues and values:

> In Beaufort, North Carolina, the environmental education program in Carteret County Schools for 1970 familiarized its students with marine ecology. The fourth to twelfth graders in the coastal schools made field trips to an open beach, an offshore island, a salty marsh, a port terminal, and a seafood-processing plant. With their teacher, the students examined the adaptation of animal communities, wave erosion, utilization of the sea, and consequent problems, as well as other conditions related to nature and life in coastal areas (Helgeson, Blosser, Howe, Helburn, & Wiley, 1972, pp. 35–37).

> At Dana Point, California, the resident outdoor education program for 1986 developed by the Orange County Marine Institute acquainted elementary and middle school students with nature's five ecosystems. During the three-day program, the students engaged in such activities as studying the ecology of the California foothills (*chaparral*), streamsides (*riparian*), and oak woodlands in the Santa Ana Mountains. They studied the interaction and interdependence of specific plants and animals, the supplies of natural resources, and the overall health of the ecosystem. In this manner, they also examined how the ecosystem shaped the local indigenous culture, such as the life and history of the *Juaneños*, an endangered tribe (Rigby, 1986, p. 20).

Despite the emphasis on ecological issues, a desire was also expressed in the learning environment to simultaneously maintain the Naturalistic Dimension when participating in such activities as the day camp program at the state park, or studying nature at the laboratory of the resident outdoor education center or along the shore of the nearby pond (for a resident outdoor education program, see, e.g., Taloumis, 1980, pp. 16–18). The following is a description of the resident outdoor education program at the environmental education center in the state of New York in the 1980s:

The resident outdoor education program of Geneva Area City Schools for 1982 offered science studies at the Rogers Environmental Education Center at Sherburne. The outdoor school program for sixth graders lasted for two and a half days, providing studies dealing with shores and forests. The students worked in groups and under the guidance of a nature scientist in the center's laboratory and on the shore of the nearby pond. A well-equipped laboratory afforded them the opportunity to study the pond and marsh's abundant plant and animal life in detail. They also acquainted themselves with the use of a map and compass as well as with the principles of forestry. Likewise, play and games during the evening program were associated with nature (Mitchinson, 1982, pp. 5–7).

The Sociocultural Dimension was also an essential component in instances when, for example, students helped at local centers for the elderly, nursing homes, and homeless shelters as part of their service-learning, or when they studied local history by gathering abstract and concrete material in the community as part of their outdoor education (for the service-learning project, see, e.g., Johnson, 1996, pp. 32–33). The following summary documents these practical efforts to enhance pedagogy at one school concerning the Sociocultural Dimension of its learning environment. In the early 1980s, the teachers and their students at a school in Rabun County, Georgia, were engaged in community-based fieldwork for the purpose of firsthand observation and study:

> The students of Rabun Gap-Nacoochee School became acquainted with their own community's past as well as its current economy and culture, special regional problems, and needs. The Appalachian Cookery Project for 1980 familiarized students with the cooking traditions of the community inhabitants. The students visited homes, where they observed cooking and discussed housekeeping and homemaking. They collected recipes by interviewing and photographing residents and also trying the recipes out. Later, the students wrote and published a cookbook of the Appalachian people (McKay, Adams, & Webb, 1991, pp. 165–172).

This study provides evidence that, especially since the 1990s, the Scientific-Technical Dimension was increasingly emphasized in many pedagogical programs of community-based learning. Outdoor education could include the application of mathematical and physical principles, as was the case with a bridge-building project at a resident outdoor school. Service-learning could cover a survey of the developmental needs of the community using modern methods of data collection. Environmental education could include the use of laboratory instruments to study impurities in the community drinking water (for the teaching procedures in one school, e.g., Boston, 1998–1999, pp. 68–69). Some programs made intensive use of computer-based systems during the investigation of the natural and built environments (for the teaching procedures used at some schools, see, e.g., Coulter with Litz & Strauss, 2003, pp. 55–61; Lauer, 2007, pp. 203–204; Thompson, Alibrandi, & Hagevik, 2003, pp. 47–54).

Despite attempts to teach various subjects outdoors, with other areas and entities also being explored, environmental education was nevertheless emphasized in the means, content, and settings of many instructional programs (for the teaching procedures in some schools, see, e.g., Corcoran & Pennock, 2005, pp. 20–23; Roberts, 2002, pp. 58–61, 98–99; Rulison, 2007, pp. 13–17). The following overview exemplifies the pedagogical application carried out at one school regarding the Scientific-Technical Dimension of its learning environment. It involves the teachers and their students at a middle school in Denver, Colorado, who were active in an environmental and community service-learning program:

> At the end of the 1990s, the environmental and community service-learning program at Cole Middle School aimed at identifying and solving environmental problems in the community. The program included creating a community environmental inventory, defining the problem, studying the policies to follow and the options available to the students for influencing policy and practice, and drafting and implementing a plan of action, along with reflecting on and assessing the research and action process. The seventh graders at Cole decided to study the poor quality of the community water supply. They interviewed experts in the community, conducted tests on the water's pH and chlorine content, and studied plumbing in houses. Finally, the students drafted an action plan recommending a cooperative venture with the weatherization project in low-cost housing. They expressed their hope that water-filtration components would be installed in homes with high levels of water impurities (Boston, 1998–1999, pp. 66–69).

4.2   *Indian Neocolonial and Postcolonial Schools*

In the mid-1960s, India implemented changes in pedagogy comparable to those taking place in the United States. This shift had a strong impact on the quality of the methods used in community-based learning. Starting specifically with the second five-year period (1956–1961), the new thinking about India's economic policy attempted to initiate a phase whose goal was to industrialize and urbanize the country, essentially following the model provided by the Soviet

Union (see Planning Commission, 1956, p. 51). Neocolonial and postcolonial forms of education were required to participate in accelerating a scientific and technological developmental path, in order to increase the productive capacity of the national economy. We could interpret this to mean that overcoming such an exceptionally difficult challenge required an effort to make schools into learning centers with only limited contact with society.

A firm belief developed that Indian society could become a modern industrial society only if students worked within an environment that applied technological processes, where they could become familiar with the use of modern tools, devices, and materials. This justified the manner in which the Scientific-Technical Dimension to community-based learning was also emphasized in the learning environment. For example, in work-experience education, the students could work in school workshops that made laboratory supplies and ink, or they could familiarize themselves with the latest techniques and scientific achievements at the community's experimental farm (for work-experience activities, see, e.g., Ministry of Education & Social Welfare, 1977, p. 10). The summary provided here demonstrates how teachers at Buharu School emphasized the Scientific-Technical Dimension in work-experience education programs in Ajmer District, Rajasthan:

> During the mid-1970s, the teachers of the Buharu village school encouraged their students to study characteristics of plant habitats. The students planted different species of trees in the area of the village, took care of them, and tried to protect them from damage caused by animals. They examined why certain trees did not grow in the area and what influence the trees might have on the climate. An expert visited the school and presented various techniques for testing the soil and water, demonstrating in practice the necessity of testing for agricultural production. The students brought samples of soil from the land that their parents were cultivating to be taken to the laboratory at Tilonia. They familiarized themselves with the latest agricultural techniques and scientific achievements, such as hybrid varieties of maize and millet (*bajra*) on the village experimental farm. The teacher and other experts guided them in a meticulous study of the reasons for Rajasthan becoming semiarid and the measures to be taken to arrest this development (Roy, 1980, pp. 369, 373–374, 376).

Additionally, the Sociocultural Dimension of the learning environment was significant in both approaches, as students became familiar through work-experience education with such functions as working at the community clinic, temple, or Village Council, as well as when helping in socially useful productive work at the community's special education institutes, nonformal educational centers, and slum areas, or in social service with construction projects and festivals (for the pedagogical activities in one school, see, e.g., Kumar, 1991, p. 122). The following summaries exemplify the pedagogical applications of work-experience education that were carried out at the Buharu village school in Rajasthan and social service that was carried out in Ramakrishna Mission Vidyalaya Secondary School in Tamil Nadu. These descriptions show two different ways in which the teachers emphasized the Sociocultural Dimension in their community-based educational programs:

> The students of Buharu School in Ajmer, Rajasthan, studied the structure and functioning of the Village Council (*Panchayat*). Aided by a teacher, the students sought information about the Village Council, including its structure, electoral terms, and voting procedures. They interviewed the Secretary of the Village Council, who visited the school and explained the Council's taxation practices, how it implemented decisions, and its general responsibilities and functions. Additionally, as a digression, the students became acquainted with historical changes in the administration of the village. They studied the pre-independence methods of local and regional administration used when Rajasthan was still governed by a king and its villages governed by his representatives. Finally, using this information, the students wrote a study in which they analyzed the number of representatives in their constituency, the number of adults eligible to vote in their own families, the strength of the particular group representation, and voting turnout. The study was later utilized in their own election process at school (Roy, 1980, pp. 374–375).

> In the mid-1970s at Ramakrishna Mission Vidyalaya Secondary School, located near Coimbatore, Tamil Nadu, the educational program emphasized social service. The Vidyalaya students participated in repairing the damage caused by storms and floods in the vicinity of the school. They built a new road as well as inexpensive housing for members of the casteless (*harijan*) colony inhabitants. They also dug a pond for storing rainwater that could percolate into the surrounding wells. Every year, the students participated in arranging and coordinating the Sri Ramakrishna Festival. Because this religious and social celebration attracted more than 30,000 visitors to the locality, it offered many kinds of work experiences and service activities for several months (Tillman, 1976, pp. 44–46).

Despite the emphasis on science and technology in the learning environment, the government's educational policy also favored the Productive Dimension.

This was particularly evident in socially useful productive work, such as undertakings for the school production centers, in scientific cultivation projects, or at the camps for work or social service (for a school-specific program, see, e.g., Singh, 1998, pp. 15–16). The following description illustrates the pedagogical applications of a scientific cultivation project carried out at one school in the late 1970s. The students at a village school in Kaira District, Gujarat, were involved in work within an environment that applied technological processes and that used modern tools, devices, and materials. The following description shows how the teachers created an authentic learning environment with work and production where students could cultivate plants using scientific processes:

> The educational program in the late 1970s at Vallabh Vidyalaya School in the village of Bochasan, near Borsad Taluka, emphasized work-centered education and community service. The core of the school's educational program comprised socially useful productive work that took up more than 25% of the teaching time. The secondary school students studied the cultivation of eggplant (*brinjal*) in their agricultural studies. They first set objectives for the eggplant-growing project, made plans for its various phases, and used the relevant literature to familiarize themselves with the different plant varieties. In the practical cultivation work, they applied scientific cultivation techniques for the 13 different varieties they grew from seed, utilizing modern fertilizers and pesticides to do so. In their notes, they documented the measures that they had taken and their experiences. The project ended with the students, under the teacher's direction, making an assessment of the degree to which the set objectives had been achieved (Buch & Patel, 1979, pp. 107, 109–113).

The camps for work and social service offer a different type of application of the Productive Dimension compared to what was previously described. The summary provided in the following exemplifies the activities of the camping program for work and social service in some urban schools in Rajasthan in the late 1980s. Here, the attempt was to link vocationally productive work experiences not only to socially useful productive work but also to the relevant curriculum content areas. The students made surveys and prepared reports, including such topics as handicrafts, home industries, and local agricultural products:

> In the late 1980s, the Ajmer city schools' camp program, which was based on work experiences and socially useful productive work, contained not only community service but also studies in the authentic environment

related to nature and culture. The Board of Secondary Education proposed a camp program for the schools with a specific schedule each day as well as detailed instructions for items such as materials, the campsite, and the formation of student groups. The ninth and tenth graders stayed at the camp for five days, in which the program's themes entailed community service, surveying and collection work, a national integration project, and cultural and recreational activities. In the survey and collection work, the students studied nature and culture in small groups or individually. They conducted surveys and prepared reports about issues concerning the environment, social problems, and the local sources of livelihood, such as handicrafts, home industries, and agricultural products. They collected many kinds of objects, such as plant leaves and roots, insects, and bird feathers and nests, as well as different types of stones to supplement the school's natural science collections (Srivastava, 1991, pp. 100–102).

This chapter has previously shown that programs familiarizing students with socially useful productive work outside the school most often included service-centered activities and emphasized the Sociocultural or Productive Dimension (for the service-centered activities in one school, see, e.g., Chowdhury, 2005, p. 3; Kuthiala, 2007, p. 3). However, since the 1990s, the science and technology-centered programs of socially useful productive work held an alternative dimension in their pedagogical procedures. These programs emphasized the Scientific-Technical Dimension when students worked in school shops repairing electronic devices and electrical equipment, doing electrical jobs, or producing computer-aided publications (for the Socially Useful Product Work [SUPW] programs in one school, see, e.g., Narayanan, 2001, p. 88). This overview provides an example of a program of socially useful productive work in Dehradun, Uttarakhand, in the early 21st century. The teachers and students of one boarding school worked with modern computers and computer-controlled devices in the new learning environment:

> The program in the early 2000s for socially useful productive work at Doon School contained a comprehensive alternative for publishing activities. The secondary school students participated in the entire publication process nearly independently: they wrote, reported, and published. Although only working two hours a week, they produced many types of printed matter using modern computers and computer-controlled devices. Computer programs enabled them to draw tables and graphic designs as well as to edit photographs. A desktop publishing program

allowed them to transform the layouts on the computer display into different types of publications, ranging from simple announcements to full books. In addition to producing a conventional yearbook, the students also produced other periodicals, such as the school's special publications: *The Doon School Information Review*, *The Academic Journal*, and the biannual scientific *Prayas*, *Arpan*, *The Echo*, and *Cosmos*. The school's weekly magazine, *The Doon School Weekly* (DSW), which has been published since 1936, now also appears in an international internet version (Dhillon, 2006, p. 1; *The Doon School*, n.d., pp. 2, 15–16, 19).

4.3   Chinese Postrevolutionary Schools

In 1977, after the Cultural Revolution, the 11th National Congress of the C.P.C. began a new phase for China's development policies called the Four Modernizations. Its new goal was to modernize agriculture, industry, and national defense through science and technology (Teng, 1978, p. 7). This development required educational reforms, and in 1978, the National Educational Conference drafted national education regulations (1978–1985) that restored educational policies that had been condemned during the Cultural Revolution. Basic curricula, teaching materials, textbooks, and teaching outlines were to be standardized. Primary and middle school instruction was to emphasize academic studies, particularly technology and science, in addition to political education and physical training. The teachers were to play a leading role in the classrooms. In addition to an academic orientation, integrating work and studies was still valued, for instance, the new teaching plan allocated a similar amount of time for manual labor as the 1963 regulations (Ministry of Education of the C.P.G., 1998c, pp. 1630–1632).

During the years of the Four Modernizations (1978–1982), the overall intention was to reform school pedagogics in the direction of formal teaching and methods in classrooms and out-of-school settings. The important principle was to integrate manual labor with studies in gardens, fields, and neighboring farms, providing learning environments where students could acquaint themselves and practice the prevailing skills and procedures. Although the emphasis was on productive processes in the learning environment, there was also a desire to prioritize the Scientific-Technical Dimension. This type of change in the nature of learning environments was especially seen when having students make test-based analyses of soil in the laboratory, perform experiments, and develop better varieties of rice and wheat, as well as when they created solutions for disease and pest problems. The students also shared their experiences with community members in order to benefit agricultural work (for pedagogical activities on agricultural work at some schools, see, e.g.,

Zhang, 1980, pp. 34–36). The following illustrates how students at one primary school in Zhejiang Province applied the subject matter to real-life scientific investigations:

> Shangyang Primary School in Suichang County had an experiment field in the Wang Cun Kou Commune in the late 1970s. In their field, the students plowed and improved soil by removing weeds and using fertilizers. They transplanted rice seedlings, cut rice crop, and beat rice into flat, light, and dry flakes. The students were keen to conduct experiments through the triple-cropping system for rice, wheat, and corn as well as interplanting sweet potatoes and soybeans. These methods enabled them to produce a far greater harvest on a small plot of land. Students also made field trips to the mountain area to pick traditional Chinese medicine for their pigs, based on advice given by the veterinarian (Liu & Rong, 1982, pp. 31–32).

According to the constitution of the P.R.C. of 1982 and the Sixth Five-Year Plan (1981–1985), the number of intellectuals would increase, since they would have an important role in contributing to socialist modernization (see China, 1983, Article 23; State Council, 1984, pp. 124–125). In 1981, the *Trial Draft of the Teaching Plan for Full-Time Primary and Middle Schools in a Ten-Year System* directed that work-based education should be implemented according to local situations and needs, the conditions of the school, and the interests and aspirations of the student (Central Educational Science Institute, 1990, pp. 317–318). This type of labor-related education was arranged in certain areas of handicraft production, agriculture, and industry that were established in conjunction with schools in addition to the classroom-centered school work. The students familiarized themselves with the vocational activities required on the school premises. They created scientific innovations in labor technique education, the results of which their school used to finance its functioning (for pedagogical activities on industrial work, see, e.g., Tong, 1986, p. 29; Wang, 1988, p. 22). The following exemplifies how the Productive and Economic Dimensions were stressed in the learning environments at the middle school in Yangjiang, Guangdong, in the early 1980s:

> Guangya Middle School in the District of Yangdong started to emphasize labor in its teaching procedures in 1958. The importance of labor rose and fell with the political climate of the times. In 1978, an academic emphasis returned, although the work-study procedures remained in the curriculum. Since the early 1980s, two school enterprises have supplemented the work-study concept and provided income for the school. One of the

factories produced a mixture of metalwork, especially small components for machines and other products, which could be manufactured with small lathes. This enterprise was housed in an old building of about 700 square feet with 15 lathes used for educational purposes for students. The enterprise offered many kinds of activities for students. They learned that they could perform various operations with lathes, such as cutting, sanding, knurling, drilling, and shaping (Fouts & Chan, 1997, pp. 39–40).

In line with socialist modernization efforts, Zhao Ziyang, the premier of the State Council, stressed at the Sixth National People's Congress that "economic reform, revolution of technology and economic construction all urgently need a great amount of qualified personnel who possess modern science, technology, and management knowledge" (Zhao, 1984/1998, p. 2184). The *Decision of the C.P.C. Central Committee* (1985/1991) emphasized that China needs a high-level workforce with qualified workers. The new direction for the education policy called for improving educational achievement and producing as many skilled people as possible (pp. 465–466). As a result, in 1987, the State Education Commission announced the *Teaching Plan for Full-Time Primary School and Junior Secondary School for Compulsory Education*. This curriculum, based on an academic model, reduced the time allocated to languages and mathematics but increased the time for social development, nature study, arts, and labor at the primary level and, for instance, labor technology at the secondary level. The curriculum provided a new impetus for combining academic education, productive labor, and technological education (Lewin, Little, Hui, & Jiwei, 1994, pp. 157–159). The intention was to transform the manual labor activities to those of science and technology in accordance with the students' individual abilities.

The Scientific-Technical Dimension was prioritized in the learning environment when the students produced fertilizers and pesticides and were taught by farmers how to prevent pests on a hybrid rice field, or when they installed electrical equipment, made technical drawings, and were involved in craft-based designing (for pedagogical activities, see, e.g., Liu & Dou, 1988, p. 16; Wang, Chen, & Wang, 1991, p. 53). The following illustrates the manner in which the Scientific-Technical Dimension was emphasized in the pedagogical processes at two junior high schools, one in Liaoning and the other in Zhejiang:

> Shiyan Junior High School in Fengcheng, Liaoning, had agricultural and industrial experiment facilities in order to combine theory with practice. At the beginning of the learning process, the school offered courses on work-based learning. The first graders studied basic agricultural skills

and tree growing; the second graders concentrated on crop plantation; the third graders learned about raising animals, carpentry, and sewing; and the fourth graders were to learn how to grow fruit trees and maintain home electrical appliances. After obtaining basic knowledge in class, the school's gardens, nurseries, greenhouses, farms, and factories provided spaces where the students could apply and practice the subject matter through agricultural and industrial experiments (Feng, 1988, p. 30).

Ge Yan Zhen Junior High School in Shaoxing, Zhejiang, cooperated with the No. 2 Automobile Factory. The students made excursions to the factory and the school invited factory employees to visit the school. The activities that took place in conjunction with the factory excursions were closely linked with relevant courses at the school. The students utilized the learned information about the technology of car manufacturing when they attended the school's technical drawing course. In 1989, this course introduced basic technical drawing skills and terminology. It familiarized the students with the specific skills of sketching, geometric construction, and auxiliary drawing (Gao, Wu, & Yuan, 1992, p. 15).

Since the turn of the 21st century, educational policies in China have increasingly emphasized modernization through science and technology. Fundamental transformations in the educational system have been focusing on equality, quality, efficiency, and revitalization (Li, 2017, p. 136), as the following quotation from the basic education curriculum issued by the Ministry of Education of the P.R.C. (2003) illustrates:

> Basic education is the foundational project for the rejuvenation of the country through science and education. It has a holistic, fundamental and leading role in improving the quality of the Chinese nation, cultivating talents at all levels and promoting socialist modernization. To maintain a moderately advanced education, basic education must be given priority and it should be effectively protected as a key area for infrastructure development and education development. (p. 908)

The curriculum reform for basic education in 2001 aimed to cover educational thinking, goals, content, and methods. The intention was to change teachers' professional orientation from transmitting knowledge to transforming knowledge. Tan and Reyes (2016) argued that this reform reflected neoliberal educational policies and practices such as "decentralization, school autonomy, student-centered teaching, critical and innovative thinking and real-life application" (p. 19). The emphasis of the reform is not only on increasing "scientific knowledge but developing a scientific spirit, attitude and method, as well as shaping one's worldview, value system and whole-brain ability" (p. 25). Cui and Zhu (2014) reported that the reform tried to draw attention to an integrated curriculum structure for the purpose of meeting the needs of schools and students. This reform intended to enhance active and problem-solving learning styles in order to improve such abilities as acquiring and processing information and cooperating with peers. It strove to change control of the centralized curriculum toward a joint effort between the central government, local authorities, and schools to enhance the relevance of the curriculum to local situations (pp. 2–3).

The 13th Five-Year Plan for education (2016–2020) also emphasized accelerating modernization, promoting innovation, and rejuvenating the Chinese nation. In the future, it will be central to Chinese education to implement such pedagogical methods as social investigations, productive labor, community service, scientific and technological labor education, and integrated practical activities (State Council, 2017, para. 13, 35). In 2017, the curriculum supplement on integrated practical activities was published to improve the quality of teachers' work in Chinese schools. This curriculum proposed to enhance students' ability to gain competences in doing research, using information and communication technology (ICT), designing products, and participating in social service. These pedagogical areas emphasize comprehensively understanding, analyzing, and solving real problems. The ultimate focus is on adapting the learned information to authentic social life and the world of work (see Ministry of Education of the P.R.C., 2017, Appendix 1, para. 4).

Integrated practical studies aimed to encourage teachers and students to do research on certain topics. The Sociocultural Dimension was stressed in this learning environment when some primary school students presented museum exhibits for visitors under the guidance of their teacher. These exhibits included local history and culture, and environmental issues (for pedagogical activities, see, e.g., Efird, 2015, p. 1147). The following shows how students of a rural primary school were involved in a community service-learning program in Yuncheng, Shanxi:

> The teachers of Guan Ai Primary School in Yongji organized a program of integrated practical studies for third to sixth graders. The goal was to investigate smoking problems in the villages around the school. First, the students talked with villagers in order to understand the smoking problem in rural areas. With their teacher's help, they decided to launch a public campaign that would focus not only on the hazards of smoking

but also on the difficulties of quitting and effective methods for quitting. Next, the students collected information and materials for their campaign. They interviewed a local doctor and looked up resources online. All students participated in designing materials such as posters and calendars, and some students prepared presentations. Finally, the students delivered PowerPoint presentations at meetings in the villages where they had conducted their studies and distributed the materials they had designed (Rural China Education Foundation, 2009, p. 9).

Innovative science and technology education was launched in 2015 for the purpose of accelerating the growth of innovation through education and training. Some researchers indicate that training students in science-related issues and helping them to keep up with the fast-paced progress of the intelligent technology era is a challenge for Chinese schools (see, e.g., Liu et al., 2017, para. 1). The Ministry of Education of the P.R.C. (2017) recommended topics for the Design and Production Activities module, which is a subcomponent of Labor Technology. For example, the topic Bionic Design in Life for ninth graders gives special importance to students' understanding of the practical meaning of bionics. Its main function is to identify structures and processes in biological systems that can be applied to engineering constructions. The topic includes such activities as visits to bionics exhibitions in museums, field trips to bionic buildings, and investigating the application of bionics in life. The learning focus is on biodiversity, biological characteristics for bionic design, and improving the spirit of innovation and the ability to solve problems (Appendix 5). The following illustrates how the Scientific-Technical Dimension was prioritized in the learning environment when the students of one high school implemented this topic in Qingdao, Shandong:

> The students of Qingdao Experimental High School carried out activities based on the Bionic Design in Life topic. These activities included visits to expeditions, field trips to community sites, and camps for generating new learning. During these activities, the students encountered the latest science and technology, brainstormed with their classmates, and had more chances to find, ask, and solve life-related questions. They were able to make use of community resources and generate economic and social benefits. The Bionic Robots project, for instance, was popular because it combined many ideas. Students could conceive, design, implement, and operate their own robotic fish swimming freely on the surface or underwater to undertake assignments such as detecting pollution or exploring undersea life (Liu et al., 2017, para. 24, 32).

5 Challenges

The essentialist and the neo-essentialist schools in the United States had access to considerably more economic, intellectual, and physical resources at the turn of the millennium than the progressive school had during the 1920s and 1930s. The Indian neocolonial and postcolonial schools, in turn, had access to more resources than the neo-traditional school had during the 1940s and 1950s. Despite this, when comparing the implementation of community-based learning in the two countries, these schools continued to be confronted with similar problems.

In American metropolises, a major migration toward the suburbs ensued after the Second World War. Poor inner-city areas inhabited primarily by minorities gradually increased and became areas where complex patterns of social and educational inequality became established. During the 1980s, a critical educational policy led to utilizing standardized school achievement tests to monitor the work performed by teachers. The early 2000s also saw environmental education and service-learning topics giving way to increased emphasis on curriculum standards and the tests based on them (for justifications for not teaching environmental or service-learning studies, see, e.g., McCrea & deBettencourt, 2000, p. 31; Scales & Roehlkepartain, 2004, p. 25).

Correspondingly, the turn of the millennium in India witnessed the most difficult contextual issues facing the country, specifically rapid population growth and persistent poverty. Even with the existence of large cities, the majority of the Indian population continued to live in the countryside, which was also reflected in huge disparities in education and income. Government guidelines for a new economic policy started to favor an urban way of life. This kind of thinking tended to marginalize work-experience education and socially useful productive work in the themes covered at school, with emphasis being placed instead on textbook-centered teaching, year- and term-end entrance examinations, and specific school levels (for the time allotted for work-based education, see, e.g., Yadav, 2011, p. 121).

Many American and Indian teachers felt that the new school reforms were incapable of supporting their work in the community-based parts of the curricula. They came to this conclusion because the teaching and learning process, which focused on academic knowledge and learning, actually emphasized the teacher-directed transmission of knowledge. In the United States, the preservice and in-service training of teachers was considered insufficient. The instructional material used in environmental education lacked an interdisciplinary and social approach, and there was a particular lack of material suitable for the urban environment. In India, the curriculum development for socially useful productive work proved to be inadequate because the schools lacked qualified teachers. Untrained teachers were also incapable of motivating students to engage in long-term activities. In both countries, insufficient economic resources limited practical efforts to develop community-based learning. The opportunities for acquiring teaching material or financing for field trips were limited. Many schools did not even offer the appropriate equipment, furniture, or work premises (for a closer examination of the barriers to teaching environmental education and work-experience education, see, e.g., Mastrilli, 2005, p. 24; Mayeno, 2000, p. 14; Ruhela, 2006, p. 98; Sehgal, 2001, pp. 212–213).

Since opening up its market economy policies in the early 1980s, China has experienced far more difficult challenges than the policies in the United States and India. Contemporary China faces difficult contextual issues, and especially suffers from urban and rural disparity, social inequalities and instability, environmental problems, and political and legal challenges. Much has been written about the profound changes in China's educational models, forms, and content. However, educational reforms have not yet been able to adapt to the needs of comprehensive human, economic, and social development. Imbalances and problems in coordinating education still exist, as the following quotation from the Five-Year Plan for education announced by the State Council (2017) depicts:

> The fundamental processes involved in integrating production and education and in integrating science and education have not yet been formed. Cultivating students' innovative and entrepreneurial ability needs to be strengthened. The gap between education in urban and rural areas and regions is still great. The total amount of quality educational resources is insufficient. The quality and structure of the teaching staff cannot adapt to the new requirements for improving the quality of education. (para. 11)

The central obstacle for educational reform is teachers' reluctance to give up traditional teacher-directed and book-centered teaching based on transmitting knowledge, which includes the testing of learned information. This approach, which views teachers' professional role and orientation as essentially knowledge transmitters, is in contradiction with the conception of learning and the nature of knowledge of the new curriculum of 2001 (see Tan, 2016, pp. 81–82). Its intention is to direct learning toward knowledge transaction. Rao (2013) argued that this curriculum reform emphasizes a view according to which "a teacher should not only impart knowledge, but also provide guidance, supervision, and evaluation for students in their learning lives. A teacher should be a designer who can establish a democratic, equal, and interactive relationship with students and create student-friendly learning environments" (p. 263).

Chinese teachers tend to reject the theory that all knowledge and moral values are subjective and, instead, believe that these are based on viewable or measurable facts (Tan, 2016, p. 84). An exam-oriented education system overemphasizes mastery of facts, patient listening, and teachers' authority, rather than attention that should be given to active learning pedagogics and integrated practical activities (see Bing & Daun, 2001, p. 22). Brown and Gao (2015) argued that the new philosophy of assessment would change teachers' thinking and practice. This led to policy pressures to manage, control, and hold schools accountable as well as to evaluate schools and teachers (pp. 14–15).

Changing teacher roles are bound to contemporary requirements for teacher education. The teachers' preservice and in-service training has to face the following fundamental issues, as Rao (2013) revealed:

> Most of the teaching practice in Chinese preservice teacher education programs has been regarded as the process of the application of theories. There is no interaction or mutual improvement between course studies and teaching practice. In such circumstances, the difficulty of cultivating practical competence and the ability to reflect teacher's work is not surprising. The inefficiency of in-service training programs is one of the main challenges regarding in-service training of teachers. Many teachers who have attended in-service teacher training courses have had difficulty putting their new skills into practice when they have returned to their teaching environment. (pp. 292–293)

The next section briefly discusses the properties of the activities of community-based learning in the United States, India, and China. The activities of the pedagogical approaches are compared from the perspective offered by the dimensions of the learning environment. In the United States, the primary focus is on experiential education, in India the focus is on vocationally productive education, and in China the focus is on productive labor education.

6   Conclusion

The approaches to community-based learning have placed varying degrees of emphasis on the dimensions of learning environments from the early 20th century to the early 21st century. This emphasis has been different as times changed with regard to particular pedagogical reforms in the United States, India, and China.

The present study demonstrates that community-based learning can take place in a variety of learning environments prioritizing the Naturalistic, Sociocultural, Productive, Economic, Martial, Ecological, or Scientific-Technical Dimensions, in accordance with the general direction of political, economic, and social development. By the mid-20th century, these socially different countries had intended to stress efforts to expand learning environments from schools to the reality outside of schools. The use of authentic learning environments was based on the idea that the subject matter could best be learned in real-life situations. Through the last five decades, pedagogical approaches and their learning environments have increasingly emphasized the use of technology-based applications. The following illustrates the development of community-based learning and its connections with the dimensions of learning environments in these countries.

6.1 Early Developments

The two decades following the First World War formed the most intensive period of progressive education in the United States. By emphasizing motor and sociomoral aims, educational policymakers attempted to familiarize students with the skills, current procedures, and principles needed in an early industrial society. The experimentalism-based progressive school strove to be part of the larger whole of social life. The activities in the school's workshops were closely connected with economy, sciences, arts, and communication. The students worked in the school's workshops, kitchen, and garden, studied in its library and science laboratories, and researched in local factories, laboratories, and institutes, in addition to participating in activities for the benefit of the school and the community.

Teaching gave special importance to the Sociocultural and Productive Dimensions of the learning environments, thus enabling the students to engage in such activities as helping compile a local housing program; renovating old buildings for the school's use; working in the school's farm maintenance shop, meat processing facilities, or transportation services; canning fruits and vegetables for sale; and doing electrical wiring on contract. The Naturalistic Dimension of the learning environment was prioritized during field trips and excursions in which students explored the formation of lakes and valleys by retreating glaciers as part of their studies, in school camping when they observed animals in fields and forests, or in school gardening when they took care of their plants from spring until fall.

In India, the neo-traditional school was created during the struggle for independence in the early 1940s and was most vigorous until the mid-1960s. By emphasizing physical and sociomoral aims, educational policymakers attempted to make students familiar with traditional vocational activities and the fundamentals of the various procedures and phases in the relevant working processes utilized in a preindustrial agricultural society. They practiced using craft equipment and raw materials and the ways of working offered by the community. At the neo-traditional school based on *satyagrahaism*, the students worked in the school's workshops, gardens, and cultivated areas and were engaged in various work-related activities for the advancement of the school and its community.

The Productive Dimension of the learning environment was emphasized in craft-related education in which the students engaged in such activities as participating in the process of spinning and weaving. They picked and cleaned cotton; ginned, carded, and spun it on a simple manual spindle (*takli*); and later spun it on a spinning wheel (*charkha*). The Sociocultural Dimension was stressed in social service within the framework of the village sanitation programs and construction projects. The students built compost pits in neighboring villages for preparing fertilizer and drainage pits for removing sewage. Moreover, they guided pilgrims at the Jagannathji fair and maintained general order.

Chinese policymakers attempted to acquaint students with the essentials of productive work and labor accompanied by the processes and procedures used in a revolutionary society. This was possible by stressing moral-political and intellectual aims in the late 1950s and, overridingly, moral-political aims from the mid-1960s to the mid-1970s. At the revolutionary school based on Maoism, the students worked in the school's workshops, factories, gardens, and fields, or at local cooperatives. The students also took part in different activities to improve the life of the school and the community.

The particular feature of the Chinese revolutionary school was to emphasize the Productive and Economic Dimensions of the learning environments, when students made school furniture, agricultural chemicals and tools, and drilling machines; when they grew local crops on farms on school premises; or when they worked in local cooperatives and their production units. Teachers gave special importance to the Social-Cultural Dimension of the learning environment, when students were involved in voluntaristic and social welfare work within contexts such as local construction projects and natural-disaster programs. The distinctive idea in achieving a moral-political education was that the school, factory, commune, and army should form a coherent whole.

Therefore, the Martial Dimension was also emphasized in the learning environment in which students took part in military activities and studied the principles of the People's Liberation Army.

6.2 *Impacts of Science and Technology*

In the late 1950s, the U.S. Congress experienced a profound change in its educational policies. Many people thought that the country needed to rapidly remodernize society by implementing education reform based on conservative functionalism. To achieve this goal, teaching at the realism-oriented essentialist school was to emphasize scientific investigation into the natural laws of the physical world. By focusing on intellectual aims, American policymakers endeavored to familiarize students with modern techniques and the underlying complex scientific principles needed for a technologically sophisticated industrialized society. Students were ultimately guided toward a new type of learning that was characterized by discovering and developing new principles and techniques. From the late 1970s onward, the neo-essentialist school also began to strive for scientific discipline and precision.

Besides classroom-centered instruction, teachers emphasized the Ecological Dimension in the learning environment of community-based learning. At the essentialist school, the students studied the well-being of the ecosystem in a mountainous area near a research station or explored the utilization of the sea and its problems on field trips. Teachers implemented the main objective of the American education policy in emphasizing the Scientific-Technical Dimension in the learning environment. At the neo-essentialist school, the students engaged with activities such as studying water impurities using computer-controlled devices at a river as part of their environmental education and charting the developmental needs of the community using modern methods of data collection as part of their service-learning.

In spite of the emphasis on the Ecological and Scientific-Technical Dimensions, a desire to maintain the Naturalistic Dimension was also expressed in the learning environment when the students studied nature at the laboratory of the resident outdoor education center or along the shore of a nearby pond. The Sociocultural Dimension was also an essential component when the students helped at local centers for the elderly, nursing homes, and homeless shelters as part of their service-learning programs.

In the mid-1960s, the government of India was convinced that the social function of the neocolonial school was to accelerate scientific and technological modernization in order to increase the productive capacity of the national economy. By emphasizing intellectual aims, the students were introduced to processes appropriate to the technological development required in a modern industrialized society. The students attended work-related lessons and activities within the school, in addition to going on field trips and staying at camps outside of school to supplement their academic studies. They received guidance in using the most up-to-date tools and devices and in methods of applying modern techniques and underlying scientific principles. A special effort was made to combine the application of science and technology in the teaching of productive processes. In the late 1970s, the postcolonial school also emphasized similar principles in the context of the Gandhian philosophy of basic education.

On this basis, teachers stressed the Scientific-Technical Dimension in the learning environments of community-based learning. The students at the neocolonial school familiarized themselves with the latest agricultural techniques and scientific achievements on the community experimental farm as part of their work-experience education. Apart from classroom-centered teaching, the students worked in school workshops, in the garden, in areas under cultivation, or, alternatively, in community-service activities outside the school.

The Sociocultural Dimension of the learning environment was especially significant in the postcolonial schools, where students helped in socially useful productive work at the community's special education institutes and informal educational centers, in slum areas, or in social service with construction projects and festivals. Teachers also emphasized the Productive and Scientific-Technical Dimensions in the learning environments, where students applied scientific cultivation techniques by growing different varieties of eggplant (*brinjal*) from seeds and utilized modern fertilizers and pesticides, or when they worked in school shops repairing electronic devices and electrical equipment, doing electrical jobs, or producing computer-aided publications.

In the early 1980s, Chinese policymakers announced their intention to emphasize intellectual aims appropriate for the purposes of a modern, technology-based socialist society. The important principle was to integrate manual labor with studies in out-of-school settings. Such sites as school gardens and their plots, as well as local cooperatives with farms and factories, provided learning environments for students in postrevolutionary schools. There they could familiarize themselves with the prevailing skills and procedures through practice. This type of labor-related education was arranged in certain areas of handicraft production, agriculture, and industry that were established in conjunction with schools.

In the late 1980s, the Chinese regime decided to give special importance to labor-related activities based on science and technology. The Scientific-Technical Dimension was especially evident in learning environments where the students produced fertilizers and pesticides and were taught by farmers how to prevent pests on a hybrid rice field, or when they installed electrical equipment, made technical drawings, and were involved in craft-based designing.

Since the turn of the 21st century, Chinese policymakers have increasingly emphasized modernization through science and technology. Besides traditional instruction, the Scientific-Technical Dimension played an important role in learning environments where the students carried out such integrated practical activities as being involved in comprehensive themes like Bionic Design in Life. Teachers also stressed the Sociocultural Dimension in learning environments in which students presented museum exhibits for visitors in community-service projects or when they investigated smoking problems in the villages around the school.

6.3   *Future of Learning Environments*

It is possible that future learning environments will increasingly emphasize technology-based learning. Thus, in the coming years, students will use more technological applications when participating in various activities of community-based learning. The advancement of information and communication technologies has promoted various learning paradigms, from free-tech learning to electronic technologies (e-learning), and from e-learning to mobile learning (m-learning), and on to ubiquitous learning (u-learning). U-learning aims at accommodating learners and their learning style by providing appropriate information anytime and anywhere they wish. Ubiquitous learning environments make it possible to carry out educational activities in several places at the same time, from any device, and adapts to the user's situations and needs (Yahya, Ahmad, & Jalil, 2010, p. 120).

However, recent technological developments cannot replace human interaction between a school and a community. Smith and Sobel (2010) argued that the real world for many young people is what happens on their computer monitors. Due to this alienation of students from the real world directly outside their schools, many of them are nature- and community-deprived. Approaches to community-based learning could provide a way for teachers and communities to prepare students to become participants in local problem solving (p. viii). Prast and Viegut (2015) suggested that it is important for community-based learning to increase curricular partnerships within the community, to research and use instructional techniques that help students obtain meaning from the content and improve student engagement (p. 111).

References

Arends, R. I. (2009). *Learning to teach* (8th ed.). New York, NY: McGraw-Hill.
Arunachalam, G. A. (1949). Periyanayakanpalayam basic school: An experiment in Tamil Nad. In *Two years of work: Report of the Second Basic Education Conference,*

Jamianagar, Delhi, April 1941 (3rd ed., pp. 102–105). Sevagram, India: Hindustani Talimi Sangh.

Bei jing shi di shi san zhong xue dang zhi bu. (1975). Kai men ban xue, yue ban yue hao [A school combined with a society, a society becomes better]. *Hong qi, 18*(12), 40–43.

Bing, L., & Daun, H. (2001). *Gender and school inequalities in China: Case study in five Beijing schools.* Stockholm, Sweden: Institute of International Education, Stockholm University.

Bo, Y. (1998). Guan yu 1958 nian du guo min jing ji ji hua cao an de bao gao (jie lu) [The report of a draft plan for the national economy in 1958 (extract)]. In D. He (Ed.), *Zhong hua ren min gong he guo zhong yao jiao yu wen xian: 1949–1975* [The important educational documents of the People's Republic of China: 1949–1975] (Vol. 1, pp. 797–799). Haikou, P.R.C.: Hainan Publishing. (Original work published 1958 in *Xin hua*)

Boston, B. O. (1998–1999). "If the water is nasty, fix it." *Educational Leadership, 56*(4), 66–69.

Braund, M., & Reiss, M. (2004). The nature of learning science outside the classroom. In M. Braund & M. Reiss (Eds.), *Learning science outside the classroom* (pp. 1–12). London, U.K.: Routledge Falmer.

Brown, G. T. L., & Gao, L. (2015). Chinese teachers' conceptions of assessment for and of learning: Six competing and complementary purposes. *Cogent Education, 2*(1), pp. 2–19.

Buch, M. B., & Patel, P. A. (1979). *Towards work centered education: A programme of socially useful productive work in education.* Ahmedabad, India: Gujarat Vidyapith.

Butler, V. R., & Roach, E. M. (1986). Coastal studies for primary grades. *Science and Children, 24*(2), 34–37.

Central Educational Science Institute. (1990). Middle school education (D. Luo & X. Yang, Trans.). In *Education in contemporary China* (pp. 258–329). Ghangsha, P.R.C.: Hunan Education Publishing. (Original work published in Chinese)

Chen, T. H. (1981). *Chinese education since 1949: Academic and revolutionary models.* New York, NY: Pergamon Press.

China. (1983). *Constitution of the People's Republic of China, adopted on December 4, 1982 by the Fifth National People's Congress of the People's Republic of China at its fifth session.* Beijing, P.R.C.: Foreign Languages Press.

Chowdhury, S. (2005, October 15). Residential project. *Doon School Weekly*, p. 3.

Chu xiong zhuan shu bian. (1958). *Qin gong jian xue di yi mian jing zi: Da yao zhong xue jian chi de fang xiang shi yi qie xue xiao de fang xiang* [A mirror on a work-study program: The orientation Dayao High School takes is the one for all schools]. Yunnan, P.R.C.: Yunnan People's Publishing.

Clarke, J. M. (1951). *Public school camping: California's pilot project in outdoor education.* Stanford, CA: Stanford University Press.

Corcoran, P. B., & Pennock, M. (2005). Democratic education for environmental stewardship. In T. Grant & G. Littlejohn (Eds.), *Teaching green: The elementary years. Hands-on learning in grades K–5* (pp. 20–24). Gabriola Island, Canada: New Society.

Coulter, B., with Litz, N., & Strauss, N. (2003). Investigating an urban watershed: How healthy is Deer Creek? In R. Audet & G. Ludwig (Eds.), *GIS in schools* (pp. 55–61). Redlands, CA: ESRI Press.

C.P.C. Central Committee. (1998a). Zhong gong zhong yang guan yu wu chan jie ji wen hua da ge ming de jue ding [The decision of the C.P.C. Central Committee on the Great Proletarian Cultural Revolution]. In D. He (Ed.), *Zhong hua ren min gong he guo zhong yao jiao yu wen xian: 1949–1975* [The important educational documents of the People's Republic of China: 1949–1975] (Vol. 1, pp. 1406–1408). Haikou, P.R.C.: Hainan Publishing. (Original work published 1966 in *Hong qi*)

C.P.C. Central Committee. (1998b). Zhong gong zong yang, guo wu yuan guan yu bao zheng xue sheng, jiao shi shen ti jian kang he lao yi jie he wen ti de zhi shi [The directive of the C.P.C. Central Committee and the State Council on guaranteeing students and teachers are healthy and have proper work]. In D. He (Ed.), *Zhong hua ren min gong he guo zhong yao jiao yu wen xian: 1949–1975* [The important educational documents of the People's Republic of China: 1949–1975] (Vol. 1, p. 989). Haikou, P.R.C.: Hainan Publishing.

Cremin, L. A. (1968). *The transformation of the school: Progressivism in American education, 1876–1957*. New York, NY: Knopf.

Cuban, L. (1993). *How teachers taught: Constancy and change in American classrooms 1890–1990* (2nd ed.). New York, NY: Teachers College Press.

Cui, J. (1959). Bu bu shen ru, bi bi luo shi [Make a further step and make sure it will happen]. *Ji lin jiao yu, 4*(6), 21.

Cui, Y., & Zhu, Y. (2014, June). Curriculum reforms in China: History and the present day. *Revue Internationale D'éducation de Sèvres*. Retrieved from http://journals.openedition.org/ries/3846

Decision of the C.P.C. Central Committee on the reform of the educational structure. (1991). In *Major documents of the People's Republic of China: December 1978–November 1989* (pp. 465–484). Beijing, P.R.C.: Foreign Languages Press. (Original work in Chinese published 1985 in *Xin hua*)

de Lima, A. (1944). *The little red school house*. New York, NY: Macmillan.

Devi, S. A. (1940). The Segaon village school. In *One step forward: The report of the First Conference of Basic National Education, Poona, October 1939* (pp. 179–186). Segaon, India: Hindustani Talimi Sangh.

Dewey, J. (1950). *Democracy and education: An introduction to the philosophy of education*. New York, NY: Macmillan. (Original work published in 1916)

Dewey, J. (1953). *The school and society*. Chicago, IL: University of Chicago Press. (Original work published in 1899)

Dewey, J., & Dewey, E. (1915). *Schools of to-morrow*. London, U.K.: Dent.

Dhillon, M. (2006). *The Doon School Weekly: Computer aided SUPW programme* (Unpublished project work). Dehra Dun, India: Doon School.

D'Souza, A. A., & Chaudhury, K. P. (1965). *The multipurpose school: Its theory and practice*. Bombay, India: Allied.

Efird, R. (2015). Learning places and 'little volunteers': An assessment on place- and community-based education in China. *Environmental Education Research, 21*(8), 1143–1154.

Feng, Z. (1988). Tan tan gai ge nong cun chu zhong de ke cheng jie gou [On the improvement of the course schedule of a rural junior high school] [Special issue]. *Ren min jiao yu, 39*(Z1), 30, 32.

Fouts, J. T., & Chan, J. C. K. (1997). The development of work-study and school enterprises in China's schools. *Journal of Curriculum Studies, 29*(1), 31–46.

Freeberg, W. H., & Taylor, L. E. (1963). *Programs in outdoor education*. Minneapolis, MN: Burgess.

Freeman, D. (1938). The print shop. In R. W. Merritt, Community education in Ellerbe, North Carolina. *Progressive Education, 15*(2), 123.

Gandhi, M. K. (1962a). *Basic education* (B. Kumarappa, Ed.). Ahmedabad, India: Navajivan. (Original work published in 1951)

Gandhi, M. K. (1962b). *True education*. Ahmedabad, India: Navajivan.

Gan su lan zhou ge ming wei yuan hui. (1969). Chang ban xiao, liang gua gou [Cooperation between a factory and a factory-run school]. *Hong qi, 12*(2), 30–35.

Gan su lan zhou ge ming wei yuan hui. (1998). Hong qi za zhi dui diao cha bao gao de an yu [Comments of the Red Flag regarding the investigative report of "A factory sets up a school: The school is cooperating with a factory"]. In D. He (Ed.), *Zhong hua ren min gong he guo zhong yao jiao yu wen xian: 1949–1975* [The important educational documents of the People's Republic of China: 1949–1975] (Vol. 1, pp. 1440–1442). Haikou, P.R.C.: Hainan Publishing. (Original work published 1969 in *Hong qi*)

Gao, W., Wu, F., & Yuan, H. (1992). Yi xiang ju you shen yuan yi yi de jiao yu gai ge shi yan [An educational reform test in the Keqiao area of the County of Shaoxing, Zhejiang]. *Ren min jiao yu, 44*(1), 13–18.

Gauvain, M., & Parke, R. D. (2010). Socialization. In M. H. Bornstein (Ed.), *Handbook of cultural development science* (pp. 239–258). New York, NY: Psychology Press.

Gong qing tuan. (1998). Zhong gong zhong yang pi zhuan gong qing tuan zhong yang shu ji chu guan yu zu zhi cheng shi zhi shi qing nian can jia nong cun she hui zhu yi jian she de bao gao [Report by the Central Secretary Division of the Communist Youth League on organizing urban youth to participate in the rural socialist construction]. In D. He (Ed.), *Zhong hua ren min gong he guo zhong yao jiao yu wen xian: 1949–1975* [The important educational documents of the People's Republic of China: 1949–1975] (Vol. 1, pp. 1274–1276). Haikou, P.R.C.: Hainan Publishing.

Green, R. L. (1936). Developing a modern curriculum in a small town. *Progressive Education, 13*(3), 189–197.

Guang xi nan ning shi di er zhong xue dang zhi bu. (1976). Kai zhan jiao yu ge ming da bian lun de yi xie ti hui [Some ideas based on discussions about educational reform]. *Hong qi, 19*(2), 40–43.

Guang ya zhong xue. (1959). Sheng chan lao dong tong jiao xue jie he de yi xie zuo fa [Some practices of combining productive work with teaching]. *Guang dong jiao yu, 4*(9), 9–10.

Hammerman, D. R. (1961). *A historical analysis of the socio-cultural factors that influenced the development of camping education* (Doctoral dissertation). Retrieved from the ProQuest Dissertations and Theses database. (UMI No. 61-2370)

Han, D. (2000). *The unknown Cultural Revolution: Educational reforms and their impact on China's rural development*. New York, NY: Garland.

Har bin shi an guang xiao xue. (1971). Hen zhua lu xian dou zheng, shang hao she hui zhu yi wen hua ke [Pay attention to the correct way, use socialist cultural lessons]. *Wen hua da ge ming, 5*(4), 19–22.

Harisalo, R. (2008). *Organisaatioteoriat* [Organizational theories]. Tampere, Finland: Tampere University Press. [in Finnish]

Helgeson, S. L., Blosser, P. E., Howe, R. W., Helburn, N., & Wiley, K. B. (1972). *Environmental education programs and materials* (PREP Report No. 33). Washington, DC: National Center for Education Communication, Office of Education, U.S. Department of Health, Education, and Welfare.

Holland, B. (1955). About our outdoor school. *Journal of Health, Physical Education, Recreation, 26*(5), 16–18.

Holland, B., & Lewis, J. (1950). The outdoor education curriculum at the secondary school level. *The Journal of Educational Sociology, 23*(9), 539–540.

Holmes, B., & McLean, M. (1989). *The curriculum: A comparative perspective*. London, U.K.: Unwin Hyman.

Hong, Y. (1975). The educational revolution. *Prospects: Quarterly Review of Education, 5*(4), 481–484.

Huang, S. (1959). Ben xue qi wo ban sheng chai lao dong de an pai [The work schedule of our class for this semester]. *Guang dong jiao yu, 4*(7), 17.

Jarvis, P. (2009). *Learning to be a person in society*. Abingdon, U.K.: Routledge.

Jensen, C., & Burgess, R. C. (1952). *An analysis of the school and community camping program in Highline, King County, Washington* (Unpublished master's thesis). University of Washington, Seattle, WA.

Jia ding xian di er zhong xue. (1959). Ba sheng chan lao dong an pai de geng hao [Make better arrangements for a work schedule]. *Shang hai jiao yu, 3*(6), 13–14.

Ji lin sheng shi yan zhong xue. (1959). Gao ju jiao yu yu sheng chan lao dong xiang jie he de hong qi qian jin [Go ahead and hold high the red flag of combining education with productive work]. *Ji lin jiao yu, 4*(1), 17–21.

Jin, Y. (1965). Yang yuan xian nong cun xiao xue jiao yu jian wen [Educational information about primary schools in the rural County of Yangyuan]. *Ren min jiao yu, 16*(3), 24–26.

Jiu tai xian shi yan xiao xue. (1960). Guan che jiao xue gai ge yuan ze, shi dang zeng jia lao dong [Carry out the principle of teaching reform, provide reasonably more work]. *Ji lin jiao yu, 5*(14), 23.

Johnson, J. L. (1996). The benefits of service learning: Student perspectives. *Thresholds in Education, 22*(2), 32–33.

Kauppi, A. (1996). Mistä nousee oppimisen mieli? Kontekstuaalisen oppimiskäsityksen perusteita [The foundations of the contextual learning conception]. In A. Kajanto (Ed.), *Aikuisten oppimisen uudet muodot: Kohti aktiivista oppimista* (pp. 51–109). Helsinki, Finland: Aikuiskasvatuksen tutkimusseura. [in Finnish]

Ke, R. (1958). Jie shao qin xian yi zhong de jiao xue gai ge gong zuo [Introducing the teaching reform of No. 1 High School in the County of Qin, Shanxi]. *Ren min jiao yu, 9*(8), 30–31.

Kimonen, E. (2015). *Education and society in comparative context: The essence of outdoor-oriented education in the United States and India.* Rotterdam, The Netherlands: Sense Publishers.

Kulkarni, G. R. (1940). A few practical problems in correlation: The experiment in the basic school at Rajpipla. In *One step forward: The report of the First Conference of Basic National Education, Poona, October 1939* (pp. 126–131). Segaon, India: Hindustani Talimi Sangh.

Kumar, R. (1991). Work experience/community service programme in Springdales Schools, New Delhi. In *Learning by doing: Report of the National Review Seminar on Work Experience* (pp. 116–131). New Delhi, India: Department of Vocationalization of Education, National Council of Educational Research and Training.

Kuthiala, S. (2007, April 21). Building lives. *The Doon School Weekly*, p. 3.

Land, S. M., & Hannafin, M. J. (2009). Student-centered learning environments. In D. H. Jonassen & S. M. Land (Eds.), *Theoretical foundations of learning environments* (pp. 1–24). New York, NY: Routledge.

Lauderdale, W. B. (1981). *Progressive education: Lessons from three schools.* Bloomington, IN: Phi Delta Kappa Educational Foundation.

Lauer, T. (2007). Mapping and sharing field trips on the Internet. In K. Carroll (Ed.), *A guide to great field trips* (pp. 203–204). Chicago, IL: Zephyr Press.

Lewin, K. M., Little, A. W., Hui, X., & Jiwei, Z. (1994). *Educational innovation in China: Tracing the impact of the 1985 reforms.* Essex, U.K.: Longman.

Li, J. (2017). Educational policy development in China for the 21st century: Rationality and challenges in a globalizing age. *Chinese Education & Society, 50*(3), 133–141.

Lian, F. (1958). Yi suo pu tong zhong xue de dao lu [The road of an ordinary middle school]. *Ren min jiao yu, 9*(8), 6–10.

Liao ning sheng ge ming wei yuan hui. (1968). Yi suo pin xia zhong nong zhang quan de min ban xiao xue [One local school managed by farmers]. *Hong qi, 11*(5), 46–51.

Liu, J. (1998). Liu jiping tong zhi zai quan guo jiao yu ting ju zhang hui yi shang de jiang hua [Comrade Liu Jiping's speech at the National Conference of the Bureau Directors of Education]. In D. He (Ed.), *Zhong hua ren min gong he guo zhong yao jiao yu wen xian: 1949–1975* [The important educational documents of the People's Republic of China: 1949–1975] (Vol. 1, pp. 1250–1255). Haikou, P.R.C.: Hainan Publishing.

Liu, J., & Rong, G. (1982). Shang yang xiao xue kai zhan lao dong jiao yu huo quan mian feng shou [Shangyang Primary School achieved a lot through a work-based education system]. *Ren min jiao yu, 33*(3), 31–32.

Liu, K. (1956). Liao ning shi yan zhong xue deng san xiao kai she jin mu gong shi xi zuo ye he ji qi xue shi xi ke de qing kuang [Starting to work with metal, wood, and machinery in three schools like Liaoning Shiyan High School]. *Ren min jiao yu, 7*(10), 31–36.

Liu, S. (1998). Ban hao ban gong ban du xue xiao [Running schools well with part-time work and part-time study]. In D. He (Ed.), *Zhong hua ren min gong he guo zhong yao jiao yu wen xian: 1949–1975* [The important educational documents of the People's Republic of China: 1949–1975] (Vol. 1, pp. 1369–1371). Haikou, P.R.C.: Hainan Publishing. (Original work published in 1993)

Liu, S., & Dou, K. (1988). Nong cun xiao xue zen yang wei ben di jing ji fa zhan fu wu [How a rural primary school serves a local economy]. *Ren min jiao yu, 39*(9), 15–16.

Liu, X., Gong, X., Wang, F., Sun, R., Gao, Y., Zhang, Y., ... Deng, X. (2017, June). *A new framework of science and technology innovation for K–12 in Qingdao, China.* Paper presented at the American Society for Engineering Education Conference, Columbus, OH.

Mao, T. (1990). Remarks at the Spring Festival. In *Selected works of Mao Tse-tung* (Vol. 9, pp. 36–53). Secunderabad, India: Kranti. (Original work in Chinese published 1969)

Mao, Z. (1998a). Gong zuo fang fa (cao an) (jie lu) [The work method (draft) (extract)]. In D. He (Ed.), *Zhong hua ren min gong he guo zhong yao jiao yu wen xian: 1949–1975* [The important educational documents of the People's Republic of China: 1949–1975] (Vol. 1, pp. 796–797). Haikou, P.R.C.: Hainan Publishing. (Original work published in 1991)

Mao, Z. (1998b). Zai chun jie zuo tan hui shang de tan hua [Talk at the seminar of the Chinese Spring Festival]. In D. He (Ed.), *Zhong hua ren min gong he guo zhong yao jiao yu wen xian: 1949–1975* [The important educational documents of the People's

Republic of China: 1949–1975] (Vol. 1, pp. 1249–1250). Haikou, P.R.C.: Hainan Publishing. (Original work published in 1967)

Mao, Z. (1998c). Zai hang zhou hui yi shang de jiang hua [Speech at the Hangzhou meeting]. In D. He (Ed.), *Zhong hua ren min gong he guo zhong yao jiao yu wen xian: 1949–1975* [The important educational documents of the People's Republic of China: 1949–1975] (Vol. 1, p. 1383). Haikou, P.R.C.: Hainan Publishing. (Original work published in 1967)

Mastrilli, T. (2005). Environmental education in Pennsylvania's elementary teacher education programs: A statewide report. *The Journal of Environmental Education, 36*(3), 22–30.

Mayeno, A. S. (2000). *Environmental education needs and preferences of an inner city community of color* (Unpublished master's thesis). San Francisco State University, San Francisco, CA.

Mayhew, K. C., & Edwards, A. C. (1966). *The Dewey school: The Laboratory School of the University of Chicago 1896–1903.* New York, NY: Atherton Press. (Original work published in 1936)

McCrea, E. J., & deBettencourt, K. (Eds.). (2000). *Environmental studies in the K–12 classroom: A teacher's view.* Washington, DC: North American Association for Environmental Education.

McKay, K. H., Adams, D. H., & Webb, R. C. (1991). "Kim: When we were in Foxfire ...." In E. Wigginton and his students (Eds.), *Foxfire 25 years: A celebration of our first quarter century* (pp. 165–172). New York, NY: Doubleday.

Merritt, R. W. (1938). Community education in Ellerbe, North Carolina. *Progressive Education, 15*(2), 121–125.

Ministry of Education. (1956). *Experiments in primary and basic education.* New Delhi, India: Government of India.

Ministry of Education of the C.P.G. (1998a). Jiao yu bu dang zu guan yu quan guo shi fan jiao yu hui yi de bao gao [The report by the Ministry of Education of the Central People's Government at the National Teacher Education Conference]. In D. He (Ed.), *Zhong hua ren min gong he guo zhong yao jiao yu wen xian: 1949–1975* [The important educational documents of the People's Republic of China: 1949–1975] (Vol. 1, pp. 1079–1081). Haikou, P.R.C.: Hainan Publishing.

Ministry of Education of the C.P.G. (1998b). Jiao yu bu guan yu shi xing quan ri zhi zhong xiao xue xin jiao xue ji hua (cao an) de tong zhi [Notification from the Ministry of Education of the Central People's Government on implementing the new teaching plan (draft) of the full-time primary and middle schools]. In D. He (Ed.), *Zhong hua ren min gong he guo zhong yao jiao yu wen xian: 1949–1975* [The important educational documents of the People's Republic of China: 1949–1975] (Vol. 1, pp. 1202–1205). Haikou, P.R.C.: Hainan Publishing.

Ministry of Education of the C.P.G. (1998c). Jiao yu bu guan yu shi xing quan ri zhi zhong xue zan xing gong zuo tiao li (shi xing cao an), quan ri zhi xiao xue zan xing gong zuo tiao li (shi xing cao an) de tong zhi [Notification of the Ministry of Education of the Central People's Government on the trial of provisional regulations of the work of full-time secondary and primary schools (trial draft)]. In D. He (Ed.), *Zhong hua ren min gong he guo zhong yao jiao yu wen xian: 1976–1990* [The important educational documents of the People's Republic of China: 1976–1990] (Vol. 2, pp. 1630–1639). Haikou, P.R.C.: Hainan Publishing.

Ministry of Education of the C.P.G. (1998d). Jia qiang si xiang jiao yu, lao dong jiao yu, ti chang qun zhong ban xue, qin jian ban xue [Strengthen ideological education, work education, and recommend masses run schools and, furthermore, do it economically]. In D. He (Ed.), *Zhong hua ren min gong he guo zhong yao jiao yu wen xian: 1949–1975* [The important educational documents of the People's Republic of China: 1949–1975] (Vol. 1, pp. 799–802). Haikou, P.R.C.: Hainan Publishing.

Ministry of Education of the C.P.G. (1998e). Zhong yang wen jiao xiao zu guan yu 1961 nian he jin hou yi ge shi qi wen hua jiao yu gong zuo an pai de bao gao [The report of the Ministry of Education of the Central People's Government on the cultural and educational work arrangement in 1961 and the future period]. In D. He (Ed.), *Zhong hua ren min gong he guo zhong yao jiao yu wen xian: 1949–1975* [The important educational documents of the People's Republic of China: 1949–1975] (Vol. 1, pp. 1027–1029). Haikou, P.R.C.: Hainan Publishing.

Ministry of Education of the P.R.C. (2003). Ji chu jiao yu ke cheng gai ge gang yao (shi xing) [Outline of the curriculum reform for basic education (trial)]. In D. He (Ed.), *Zhong hua ren min gong he guo zhong yao jiao yu wen xian: 1998–2002* [The important educational documents of the People's Republic of China: 1998–2002] (Vol. 4, pp. 907–909). Haikou, P.R.C.: Hainan Publishing. (Original work published 2001 in *Ren min jiao yu*)

Ministry of Education of the P.R.C. (2017). Jiao yu bu guan yu yin fa "zhong xiao xue zong he shi jian huo dong ke cheng zhi dao gang yao" de tong zhi [Notification of the Ministry of Education on printing and distributing the outline of the curriculum for comprehensive practical activities in primary and secondary schools]. Retrieved from http://www.moe.gov.cn/srcsite/A26/s8001/201710/t20171017_316616.html

Ministry of Education & Social Welfare. (1977). *Work-experience in schools: Third all India educational survey*. New Delhi, India: Government of India.

Ministry of Higher Education of the C.P.G. (1998). Gao deng jiao yu bu guan yu zan ting yi jiu liu liu nian, yi jiu liu qi nian yan jiu sheng zhao sheng gong zuo de tong zhi [Notification of the Ministry of Higher Education of the Central People's Government on suspending the enrollment of post-graduate students in 1966 and 1967]. In D. He (Ed.), *Zhong hua ren min gong he guo zhong yao jiao yu wen xian: 1949–1975*

[The important educational documents of the People's Republic of China: 1949–1975] (Vol. 1, p. 1403). Haikou, P.R.C.: Hainan Publishing.

Mitchinson, D. F. (1982, October). *Outdoor education residential programs: "Where we've been, where we are, where we're going."* Paper presented at the Workshop Session of the New York State Outdoor Education Association Conference, Buffalo, NY.

Narayanan, M. (2001). Live skills: Learning by doing. In *Navchetna 2001* (p. 88). New Delhi, India: Mother's International School.

National Defense Education Act of 1958, 20 U.S.C. § 101. (1958).

Nei meng gu wu yuan xian min zu gong she. (1973). Jian ku fen dou, qin jian ban xue [Work hard, build a school diligently and thriftily]. *Hong qi, 16*(6), 75–78.

Ong, E. K. (1970). Education in China since the Cultural Revolution. *Studies in Comparative Communism, 3*(3–4), 158–176.

Palese, A. (2009). *The Great Leap Forward (1958–1961): Historical events and causes of one of the biggest tragedies in People's Republic of China's history.* Lund, Sverige: Språk- och Litteraturcentrum, Lunds Universitet.

Parikh, N. (1940). The basic syllabus in practice. In *One step forward: The report of the First Conference of Basic National Education, Poona, October 1939* (pp. 172–179). Segaon, India: Hindustani Talimi Sangh.

Planning Commission. (1956). *Second five year plan.* New Delhi, India: Government of India.

Prasad, P. J. (1949). Basic syllabus at work: Two years of correlated teaching in the basic schools of Bihar. In *Two years of work: Report of the Second Basic Education Conference, Jamianagar, Delhi, April 1941* (3rd ed., pp. 133–149). Sevagram, India: Hindustani Talimi Sangh.

Prast, H. A., & Viegut, D. J. (2015). *Community-based learning: Awakening the mission of public schools.* Thousand Oaks, CA: Corwin Press.

Rao, C. (2013). The reform and development of teacher education in China and Japan in an era of social change. In E. Kimonen & R. Nevalainen (Eds.), *Transforming teachers' work globally: In search of a better way for schools and their teachers* (pp. 261–301). Rotterdam, The Netherlands: Sense Publishers.

Ren min ri bao she lun 1967–1–22. (1989). Wu chan jie ji ge ming pai da lian he, duo zou zi ben zhu yi dao lu dang quan pai de quan [Uniting fully with proletarian revolutionaries, taking power from the power holders who use the capitalist road]. In D. He (Ed.), *Zhong hua ren min gong he guo zhong yao jiao yu wen xian: 1949–1975* [The important educational documents of the People's Republic of China: 1949–1975] (Vol. 1, pp. 1411–1412). Haikou, P.R.C.: Hainan Publishing.

Rice, J. M. (1969). *The public-school system of the United States.* New York, NY: Arno Press and the New York Times. (Original work published in 1892)

Rigby, J. A. (1986). California treat: Three days in five ecosystems. *Science and Children, 23*(4), 20–23.

Roberts, P. (2002). *Kids taking action: Community service learning projects, K–8*. Greenfield, MA: Northeast Foundation for Children.

Roy, A. (1980). Schools and communities: An experience in rural India. *International Review of Education, 26*(3), 369–378.

Ruhela, S. P. (2006). *Work experience education*. New Delhi, India: Diamond Books.

Rulison, L. L. (2007, September). Student "experts" in community character: An interdisciplinary unit for middle school grades. *Green Teacher, 28*(82), 13–17.

Rural China Education Foundation. (2009). *Service learning handbook*. New York, NY: Author.

Salamat, U. (1970). *The school and the community*. New Delhi, India: Ministry of Education and Youth Services, Government of India.

Scales, P. C., & Roehlkepartain, E. C. (2004). *Community service and service-learning in U.S. public schools, 2004: Findings from a national survey*. St. Paul, MN: National Youth Leadership Council.

Schoen, L. (2013). Supporting teachers' work: Insights from a study of differentially improving schools in the United States. In E. Kimonen & R. Nevalainen (Eds.), *Transforming teachers' work globally: In search of a better way for schools and their communities* (pp. 3–34). Rotterdam, The Netherlands: Sense Publishers.

Sehgal, G. C. S. (2001). *Work education*. New Delhi, India: APH.

Shang hai shi jiao yu yu sheng chan lao dong xiang jie he zhan lan hui. (1958). *Qin gong jian xue zai shi dong zhong xue* [The work-study program of Shidong High School]. Shanghai, P.R.C.: Shanghai Education Press.

Singh, M. (1998). *School enterprises: Combining vocational learning with production*. Berlin, Germany: UNEVOC.

Si ping shi yi ma lu xiao xue. (1959). Sheng chai you ji di, lao dong you ji hua [There are places for production, there are plans for work]. *Ji lin jiao yu, 4*(6), 19–21.

Smith, G. A., & Sobel, D. (2010). *Place- and community-based education in schools*. New York, NY: Routledge.

Smith, J. W. (1955). Adventure in outdoor education. *Journal of Health, Physical Education, Recreation, 26*(5), 8–9, 18.

Smith, J. W. (1970). Where we have been, what we are, what we will become. *Journal of Outdoor Education, 5*(1), 3–7.

Spears, H. (1940). *The emerging high-school curriculum and its direction*. New York, NY: ABC.

Srivastava, J. M. (1991). The camp life in the implementation of S.U.P.W./W.E. programme. In *Learning by doing: Report of the National Review Seminar on work experience* (pp. 100–102). New Delhi, India: Department of Vocationalization of Education, National Council of Educational Research and Training.

State Council. (1984). *The Sixth Five-Year Plan of the People's Republic of China for economic and social development 1981–1985*. Beijing, P.R.C.: Foreign Languages Press.

State Council. (2017). Guo wu yuan guan yu yin fa guo jia jiao yu shi ye fa zhan "shi san wu" gui hua de tong zhi [Notification of the State Council on printing and distributing the 13th Five-Year Plan for the development of national education]. Beijing, P.R.C. Retrieved from http://www.moe.gov.cn/jyb_xxgk/moe_1777/moe_1778/201701/t20170119_295319.html

Stein, D. (1998). Situated learning in adult education. *ERIC Digests*. Retrieved from http://www.ericdigests.org/1998-3/adult-education.html

Subbarao, C. S. (1958). *Basic education in practice*. Secunderabad, India: Ajanta.

Sun, J. (1957). Lin xian yi zhong shi zen yang jin xing lao dong jiao yu de [How No. 1 High School in the County of Lin, Henan, started a work-based education program]. *Ren min jiao yu, 8*(10), 41–45.

Taloumis, T. (1980). Overnight camping with fourth-graders. *Science and Children, 18*(1), 16–18.

Tan, C. (2016). *Educational policy borrowing in China: Looking west or looking east?* London, U.K.: Routledge.

Tan, C., & Reyes, V. (2016). Neo-liberal education policy in China: Issues and challenges in curriculum reform. In S. Guo & Y. Guo (Eds.), *Spotlight on China: Changes in education under China's market economy* (pp. 19–33). Rotterdam, The Netherlands: Sense Publishers.

Taylor, N., Littledyke, M., Eames, C., & Coll, R. K. (2009). Environmental education in context: Observations, conclusions, and some recommendations. In N. Taylor, M. Littledyke, C. Eames, & R. K. Coll (Eds.), *Environmental education in context: An international perspective on the development of environmental education* (pp. 319–326). Rotterdam, The Netherlands: Sense Publishers.

Tchen, Y. (1977). Education and productive work in China. *Prospects: Quarterly Review of Education, 7*(3), 413–416.

Teng, H. (1978, May 5). Speech at the National Educational Work Conference. *Peking Review*, pp. 6–12.

The Doon School: Information handbook. (n.d.). Dehra Dun, India: Doon School.

Thompson, A., Alibrandi, M., & Hagevik, R. (2003). Historical documentation of a culture. In R. Audet & G. Ludwig (Eds.), *GIS in schools* (pp. 47–54). Redlands, CA: ESRI Press.

Tian jin shi si shi er zhong ge ming wei yuan hui. (1970). Wo men shi zen yang kai zhan "xue gong" huo dong de? [How do we carry out school activities?]. *Hong qi, 13*(8), 58–60.

Tillman, M. (1976). Non-formal education and rural development: A historical sketch and selected case studies. *New Frontiers in Education, 6*(1), 29–49.

Wang, D. (1958). Chang ge san zhong de xin qi xiang [New atmosphere in Changge No. 3 School]. *Ren min jiao yu, 9*(4), 19, 34–37.

Wang, J., Chen, Y., & Wang, Z. (1991). Jiang su sheng tai xian liang xu xiang kai zhan zhong xue yu she hui shuang xiang fu wu [The township of Liangxu in the county of Tai, Jiangsu, starts two-way service between a high school and society] [Special issue]. *Ren min jiao yu, 43*(Z1), 52–53.

Wang, R. S. (1975). Educational reforms and the Cultural Revolution: The Chinese evaluation process. *Asian Survey, 15*(9), 758–774.

Wang, S. (1988). Nan kai zhong xue de zheng ti gai ge [General reform in Nankai High School]. *Ren min jiao yu, 39*(11), 21–23.

Wang, Y., Wang, C., Bai, R., Sun, Z., Chen, W., Yu, S., ... Fu, L. (1996). Qin gong jian xue [A work-study program]. In M. Xia (Ed.), *Ning bo shi jiao yu zhi* [Educational memorandum of Ningbo, Zhejiang] (pp. 290–295). Hangzhou, P.R.C.: Zhejiang Education Publishing.

Wegner, F. R., & Langworthy, H., Jr. (1936). Roslyn, N. Y., moves toward integration. *The Clearing House, 11*(2), 84–87.

Wilson, B. G. (1998). What is a constructivist learning environment? In B. G. Wilson (Ed.), *Constructivist learning environments: Case studies in instructional design* (pp. 3–8). Englewood Cliffs, NJ: Educational Technology.

Wu yuan xian ge ming wei yuan hui. (1968). Yi suo li lun he shi ji yi zhi de xin xing xue xiao [One new-type school combining theory with practice]. *Hong qi, 11*(4), 24–31. (Original work published 1968 in *Jiang xi ri bao*)

Yadav, S. K. (2011). *National study on ten year school curriculum implementation*. New Delhi, India: Department of Teacher Education and Extension, National Council of Educational Research and Training.

Yahya, S., Ahmad, E. A., & Jalil, K. A. (2010). The definition and characteristics of ubiquitous learning: A discussion. *International Journal of Education and Development Using Information and Communication Technology, 6*(1), 117–127.

Zakir Husain Committee. (1938). *Basic national education: Report of the Zakir Husain Committee and the detailed syllabus with a foreword by Mahatma Gandhi* (3rd ed.). Segaon, India: Hindustani Talimi Sangh.

Zhang, K. (1980). Ban hao non zhong, wei nong ye xian dai hua fu wu [Start an agricultural high school to serve agricultural modernization]. *Ren min jiao yu, 31*(11), 34–36.

Zhao, Z. (1998). Zheng fu gong zuo bao gao (jie lu) [Government work report (extract) in 1984]. In D. He (Ed.), *Zhong hua ren min gong he guo zhong yao jiao yu wen xian: 1976–1990* [The important educational documents of the People's Republic of China: 1976–1990] (Vol. 2, pp. 2184–2185). Haikou, P.R.C.: Hainan Publishing. (Original work published in 1984)

Zhao yuan he sui hua ge wei hui. (1971). Jian chi qin jian ban xue, wei wu chan jie ji zheng zhi fu wu [Continue a work-study program, serve proletarian politics]. *Hong qi, 14*(6), 47–51.

Zhou, E. (1998). Lun zhi shi fen zi wen ti [About the intelligentsia]. In D. He (Ed.), *Zhong hua ren min gong he guo zhong yao jiao yu wen xian: 1949–1975* [The important educational documents of the People's Republic of China: 1949–1975] (Vol. 1, pp. 1081–1085). Haikou, P.R.C.: Hainan Publishing. (Original work published in 1984)

Zuo, Z. (1986). Wo men chang dao le jian chi lao dong ji shu jiao yu de tian tou [Benefits of continuous labor technique education]. *Ren min jiao yu, 37*(10), 28–29.

Afterword

Eija Kimonen and Raimo Nevalainen

The main idea of this book is to describe the features of community-based learning in schoolwork around the world. The chapter authors present numerous approaches to community-based learning that are designed to meet the challenges of contemporary education. This book shows how learning is connected with authentic community environments, where learning is linked to life, experiences, and practical problems. It also demonstrates how teachers can make learning more functional and holistic so that students have the ability to work in new situations within the complex world around them.

Modern society is difficult to govern. It is apparent that overcoming the existing social, economic, and environmental problems requires an understanding of new values, goals, and procedures in order to manage the globalizing world. The articulation of entities can create the basis for understanding even a complicated society. The best context for profoundly conveying human action is social reality and life, in which people also learn to assess individual and communal choices. A person develops into a socially functional human being only in relation to other people and communal work and activity.

This book demonstrates that the pedagogical approaches to community-based learning have many positive influences on the school culture and the surrounding community. However, implementing these approaches into daily school life requires further development of school teaching and learning practices in the following ways:

– *Learning through participation.* An ideal curriculum emphasizes life-centered environmental issues. To achieve this, the school's educational aims should be planned jointly and include the participation of students and their parents. Instruction should stress outdoor projects in small groups based on cooperative learning. The students must be shown how to access information from various sources using different methods. American progressive schools in the late 1930s, for example, were intended to connect teaching with real life and the surrounding society. The learner-centered teaching and learning process emphasized mastery of cooperative learning and working, information acquisition and processing, and problem solving. Relating to this, a group of high school students in Kansas took part in drawing up a housing program with the city housing committee. In this work, they made use of a survey carried out earlier by students on housing conditions.

- *Making schools into community learning and activity centers.* Ideal school facilities are used in activities that meet the needs of community members of all ages, including evenings and weekends. The activities must be based on initiative, cooperation, and voluntary action. In the late 1930s, Indian basic and post-basic schools, for example, intended to make the school a center for comprehensive social service and reconstruction for the community. The aim was to make the school as self-sufficient and communally functioning as possible. This is illustrated by the case in which the students at one school in Rajasthan took part in various kinds of postal services, such as acquiring postcards, envelopes, and money order forms for the public, writing letters for the villagers who were illiterate, and ensuring that everything was taken to the city post office.
- *Strengthening the cooperative process between schools and the community.* Ideal schoolwork creates organic relations with all interest groups in the surrounding community. Outcomes of schoolwork must also be utilized in areas other than facilitating learning. Teachers can, if they want, act as animators in helping community members to achieve common goals and solve problems. One village school in Hebei, China, in the early 1960s, for example, was engaged in production so that they could attain self-sufficiency. The school helped the villagers and, in turn, the villagers helped the teachers to run the school. Students assisted the peasants by collecting lime, a natural substance that improves growth, and burning it to make fertilizer. The school received economic support from peasant families for schoolbooks and tuition.
- *Actively engaging with community members and partners.* The ideal activities taking place in schools and communities are planned and evaluated in voluntary teams, so that needs can be met and compromises in problem situations can be reached. Likewise, the teachers can actively work to maintain the school by cooperating with members of the community while, at the same time, breathing life into the neighborhood. In the early 21st century, teachers practicing place-based learning with native Hawaiians in Hawaii, for example, integrated community partners as important parts of the school, which drove the curriculum and programming. Such community partners can include libraries, local museums, county health departments, transit authorities, youth and family services, and sports clubs as well as organizations focused on life skills and artistic and technological fields.
- *Arranging activities based on the needs of the school and community members.* Community members of various ages should have the opportunity to be involved in mapping communal needs and identifying the resources that can satisfy these needs. Teachers could coordinate these activities, if they

are willing. One middle school in Colorado, for example, aimed at identifying and solving the community's environmental problems in the late 1990s. The students decided to perform a study of the poor quality of the community water supply. They interviewed community members, conducted water quality tests, and studied plumbing in homes. With their teacher, the students drafted an action plan recommending a cooperative venture with the weatherization project in low-cost housing.
- *Creating learning networks and using resources.* Education must use all the human, physical, and financial resources of the community's learning networks. Different groups within the community can utilize the learning networks to develop various cooperative partnerships. In the late 2010s in Texas, students in one middle school, for example, participated in social action projects and advocacy campaigns. They researched information via the Internet and newspaper articles in addition to contacting community members, local organizations, and support networks. Working collaboratively, students developed an advocacy campaign to showcase their issue and proposed solutions.

The ideal school offers the opportunity to articulate reality in such a way that teaching and education are connected with situations of social reality, and learning is connected to the student's life, experiences, and particular problems. This view holds that problem solving requires an understanding and awareness of the whole, which can be achieved through activity. Applying a holistic approach to work and activity allows for a level of action that does not merely repeat previously learned knowledge and skills, but that teaches the ability to function in new situations. Therefore, previous knowledge helps to express an increasingly broad and complicated reality. The activities taking place in all of the subcomponents of an ideal society also enhance education and instruction. In this manner, learning is linked to its natural context, with ideal instruction being actively problem-oriented, holistic, and life-centered.

Index

absolute idealism   13–14, 31, 42
academic achievement   126, 155
academic expertise   44, 56
academic model   233
academic orientation   231
academic-oriented learning   56
academic schools   214
action   10–11
action civics   154–157, 167, 183–186
action-oriented education   181
active learning   21, 47, 64, 66, 73, 239
active-learning pedagogics   64, 66, 73, 239
active-learning projects   47
activism   105
activity   10, 14, 20, 36, 40, 261
activity-based class   200
activity-pedagogical approach   200
activity-pedagogical processes   201
Addams, J.   96
agriculture education   204–205
Agyeman, J.   181
ahimsa   23, 69, 207
aims of community-based learning   6, 15, 27, 37, 57, 63, 67, 74–75
aims of education   6–8
   functionalist approach   6–7
   global approach   7–8
   intellectual   37, 47, 50, 63
   moral-political   37–38, 54–55, 63, 65, 74 76, 214, 217, 241
   motor   15–16, 45, 74, 240
   physical   26–27, 29, 32, 37, 47, 50, 54–55, 63–65, 74, 129, 241
   pragmatistic approach   6–7
   sociomoral   15–16, 27, 29, 45, 50, 74, 240–241
   traditional approach   7
Allport, G. W.   8
Alsbury, T. L.   vii, xii, xv, 95–145
American dream   16
American school   44
Analects   12
animator   6, 260
Apple, M. W.   115
army   215–216, 219, 241–242

Ash, S. L.   173
ashrama   22, 25
Asia   20, 49, 56
assessment   57, 60, 66, 154–155, 163, 173, 187–188, 229, 239
asset-based   102
at-risk behaviors   124, 127, 139
authentic   x, 18, 96, 116, 136–137, 151, 184–185, 259
   environment   199, 229
   experience   10, 18
   learning   130, 186, 199
   learning environment   xiii, 197–198, 229, 240
   social life   235
Avis, J.   129

Bagley, W. C.   44
balanced   26, 55, 95–96, 115
basic education, Gandhian   29, 66–68, 72, 243
basic schools   27, 29, 205–206, 260
basic school system   23
Battistoni, R. M.   102
Beason-Manes, A. D.   176
Bennett, J. V.   128, 130–133, 138–139
Berg, A. C.   173
Betti, E.   4
Blank, M. J.   173
Blonsky, P.   20–21, 41–42
boarding schools   22, 24, 218, 230
Boggs, G.   188
Bomer, R.   174
book-centered learning   215
borrowing and lending educational ideas   4, 19, 60
Briody, J.   185
Britain   22
British raj   24
British rule   23
British socialism   49
Bronfenbrenner, U.   104, 115–116
Brown, V. A.   163

California Regional Occupational Centers   105

camp   16–18, 203–204, 224, 229–230, 236, 243
camping education movement   16, 44
camping program for work and social service   229
camps for work   229
capitalist society   45
career interests   127–128, 139
Carney, T. M.   137
change process   8–9
character-building   17, 26–27, 29, 158
Chi, B.   155
Chicago Laboratory School   202
Chilcoat, G. W.   158
child-centered education   15, 44, 71–72
child-centered pedagogy   15
China   3–4, 8, 12, 14, 20, 22–23, 30, 32–34, 38–43, 49, 52–55, 60, 62–67, 70–76, 197–198, 200, 209, 216, 219–220, 222–223, 231–234, 236, 238–240, 260
Chinese curriculum reform of 2001   61
Chinese educational reforms   221
Chinese philosophical tradition   3, 33–34, 71
Chinese socialist modernization   54
Chinese socialist revolution   31
Chinese view of nature   12
civic engagement   99, 130–131, 138–139, 156–158, 167, 173, 185–186, 190
civic issues   131, 156–157
civil resistance   23–24
classical liberal society   16, 58, 73
classical liberalism   60
classroom-centered schoolwork   232
classroom-centered teaching   242–243
Clayton, P. H.   173
co-agency   77
Coalition for Community Schools   150
cognition   11, 35, 40
Cold War   43, 45, 72, 76
collapse of the progressive trend   19, 45
collective education   42
Collins, M.   152
communal needs   260
Communist Party of China   23
community   vii, 5–6, 15, 18, 25–30, 59, 63–65, 98, 102–103, 107–110, 112, 115, 130, 150–152, 155–156, 159–161, 173, 179–180, 220, 226, 260–261
community-based fieldwork   225
community-based learning
    definitions of   98–100
    reformist   5–6
    radical   6
    universal   5
community camp program   204
community-centeredness   75, 206
community integration   107
community learning and activity centers   260
community outcomes   101
community partners   102, 107–110, 112–113, 230
community purposes   101–103
community service   58–59, 61, 98–103, 130–134, 184–185, 226, 229–230, 235
community service-learning program   134, 226, 235
community-specific practices   181
community work   67
community's experimental farm   227
comparative education   xiii, xvi, 3–4, 197–198
comparative educational method   4
complex method   21
computer-based systems   226
computer-controlled device   230, 242
concepts   6, 34–36, 163, 167, 186
Cone, R.   102
conflict-theoretical view   24, 34
conflict theory   24
Confucianism   11–13, 22, 34, 37
Confucius   12
Conlon, S.   162
consciousness   10, 34–37, 132, 158, 224
conservation   204–205
conservation movement   44
conservatism   56–57
conservative functionalism   56, 242
constructivist learning environment   199
constructivist teaching approach   98
contexts outside the school   199
    personal   199
    physical   199
    sociocultural   199
contextual learning environment   199
convergent thinking   175
Cooley, E. G.   114
cooperative learning   61, 259
cooperative partnerships   261
cooperative process   260
correlated craft-related processes   206

INDEX

correlation-based teaching 221
craft 26–26, 28–30, 205–206, 241, 243
craft-related
    activities 202
    courses 209
    education 28–29, 208, 221, 241
    process 206
    productive work 30
    work 30, 71
creative behaviors 176
creative problem solving 172–178
critical reflection 103, 158
critical thinking 97, 116, 136, 159, 175, 184, 188
Crowley, K. 165
Csikszentmihalyi, M. 100, 152
cultural competence 137, 140, 156
Cultural Revolution 38–39, 54, 214–217, 220–221, 231
culturally diverse 136
culture-based education 111
Culwick, C. E. 164
curriculum 5, 28, 32, 40, 46–48, 52, 59–61, 64–66, 70, 73, 97, 99, 107–108, 110, 158, 174, 180, 200, 207, 212, 215, 217
    academic 56–57, 59, 99–100, 233, 235, 259
    comprehensive 200
    core 200
    correlated 200, 206
    experience-based 200, 202
    experiential 61
    fused 200
    integrated 184, 217, 235
    local 173, 235
curriculum-focused approaches 200
curriculum framework, four-level 180
curriculum planning 221
curriculum reform in China 61, 63–64, 66, 234–235, 238
curriculum standards 97, 237

Dalton Plan 20–22
Danner, H. 4
Darling-Hammond, L. 60, 73
Darwin, C. 13–14, 22
decentralization 25, 234
decentralized economy 25, 43, 73
Delcourt, M. A. B. 152
Delli Carpini, M. 156
democracy 16, 28, 49–50, 115, 130

democratic society 18, 27, 30, 46, 48, 52, 60, 70, 96, 133
Deng, X. 52–54
Dewey, J. 5, 7, 9, 13–16, 18–19, 21–22, 40, 60–61, 96–97, 98, 103, 114–115, 155–156, 183, 201–203
Deweyan
    activity-pedagogical methods 61, 200–201, 203
    activity-pedagogical work 202
    ideas of progressivism 40, 103
    progressive school 5
dialectical and historical materialism 31, 34, 49–50, 71
dialectical change in society 13, 31
dialectical materialism 3, 31–35, 37, 39–40, 54, 61, 63, 71–72, 74
dialectical process 75
Dietz, T. 182
Diffily, D. 152
dimensions of learning environments xiii, 197, 200, 211–212, 217, 223, 232, 239–243
discipline-specific practices 181
discovery learning 46
divergent thinking 175
Doctrine of the Mean 12
Doon School 230–231
Dorval, K. B. 176
Durkheim, E. 6–7

early industrial society 16, 18, 74, 203, 240
eclectic approach 50, 61
Ecological Dimension 57, 242
ecological systems theory 104, 115, 116
Economic Dimension 212, 220, 232, 241
economic values 28, 39, 54, 57, 65, 68, 76
ecosystem 224
education
    aims 6–8, 15, 26, 45, 50, 54, 57, 62, 67, 74–77
    goals 7, 15–16, 27, 31, 38–39, 42, 44–46, 48, 50, 56, 58, 60, 63, 75, 158, 180, 212, 215–216, 220, 223, 226, 242
educational change 8–9, 40, 62, 66
educational pendulum 42
educational program
    academic 49, 55, 59, 72
    student-centered 15, 21, 44, 61, 71–72, 124, 181, 198–199, 234, 259
    subject-centered 48, 55–56, 59, 72

educational reform   7–9, 32, 43, 49, 62, 70, 72, 96, 209, 217, 221–222, 231, 238
education through school camping   16–17
education through school gardening   201, 240
educator's role   5
Ellis, G.   164
Engels, F.   22, 31–33, 53
England   24
English-language learners   60, 107–108, 124
enrichment   150–151, 158
environmental action   48, 180
environmental awakening   44, 57–58
environmental education   44, 47–48, 57–59, 172–173, 179–183, 223–226, 237–238, 242
environmental education center   224–225
equity   69, 102, 114, 116, 130, 132, 140, 165–166, 188
Erbstein, N.   156
essential academic knowledge   48, 60
essentialism   43–44, 48–49, 56–57, 59
essentialist activity education   48, 56–57, 59–60, 72, 223, 242
essentialist education   44, 49, 56–57, 72–73, 223
essentialist school   45, 56–57, 74, 223, 237, 242
Europe   20–22, 24, 31, 49, 56
European colonial policy   22
evaluation   66, 99, 178, 180, 238
evolution theory   13
Ewart, M.   vii, xii, xv, 95–145
exam-oriented education   239
experience   10, 13–15
experience-based curriculum   200, 202
experiential curriculum   61
experiential education   18, 74, 187, 197, 200, 239
experiential learning   21, 156
experiential pedagogics   125
experimentalism   13, 18, 240
experimentalism-based progressive school   240
experimentalist pragmatism   15
experimental school   14, 22, 96–97
experiment field   232
extracurricular activity   98, 155
Eyler, J.   101, 116, 125, 127

factors in society   71, 74–75

factory school   21
farms   209–213, 216–217, 219–220, 231, 234, 241, 243
festival   22, 152, 166, 207–208, 228, 243
Feuerbach, L.   31
field-based education   180
field-based environmental education   173, 179–181
field excursions   211
field trip   105, 200, 202, 207, 224, 232, 236, 238, 240, 242–243
firmness of truth   24
firstness   10
Fitzpatrick, C.   46
Forbes, C. T.   180
Ford, R.   174
forest of the school   205, 210
Four Books   12
Four Modernizations   54–55, 231
Freedom Schools   158–160, 162, 167
Freeman, N.   184
free-market economy   31, 60
Freire, P.   6, 160
French Revolution   50
Fröbel, F.   20
Fullan, M. G.   8
functionalism   3, 7, 14, 56, 71, 242
functionalist approach   6–7
functionalist tradition   6
fundamental educational change   9, 62, 66

Gandhi, M.   23–30, 32, 206–208
Gandhian basic schools   23, 26–27, 205–208, 260
Gandhian philosophy of basic education   66–68, 72, 243
Gandhian reformist-pedagogical ideal   26
Gandhian tradition   26–28, 30, 66–67, 71–72, 74, 205–207, 209
Garcia, E.   174
Gardner, H.   183
Germany   20
Gibson, H.   17
global approach   7–8
global education reform   76
globalization   8, 68, 70, 76
Goree, K. K.   152
graduation requirement   98, 107
Great Leap Forward   37, 43, 56, 209, 212–214, 221

INDEX

Guagnano, G. A.   182
Guomindang   23, 41
Gutek, G.   6, 14, 31, 44, 49, 52, 56, 66

Haensly, P.   174
Hammerman, D.   46, 203–204
Hammerman, E.   46
Hammerman, W.   46
handicraft production   26–27, 29, 205, 232, 243
Hargreaves, A.   x
Hargreaves, L.   vii–ix, xv
harmony   12–13, 25, 37
Harris, J. A.   162
Hayes, K.   132
Hawaii   xvi, 110–112, 260
Hawley, J. D.   127, 138
Head, B. W.   165
Hébert, T. P.   152
Hegel, G.   13–14, 31, 33, 42
Hiller Connell, K. Y.   163
Hindu   23–24
Hindu nationalist ideology   68, 70, 73
historico-hermeneutical approach   3–4, 197–198
Hlebowitsh, P.   18, 20, 30, 40, 48, 51, 55, 59, 65, 69
holistic approach   261
holistic integration   26, 37, 46, 63–64
Hopkins, D.   9
Hoyle, E.   x
Hull House   96
human work   37
Hungerford, H.   48, 180, 183

iCivics   xvii, 154–155
idealism   13–14, 31, 42
Illich, I.   6
inclusion   96, 101, 115, 156, 179, 212
incremental adaptation   8
independence struggle of India   24
independent investigations   149–153, 166
India   3–4, 8, 11, 22–30, 43, 49–52, 54, 60, 62, 66–76, 197–198, 200, 205–208, 220–222, 226–227, 237–242, 260
Indian Modernization   49, 73
Indian Tradition   22, 27
Indo-European culture   11
industrialism   25
industrialization   42–43, 50–51, 72, 213

industrialized society   13–14, 200, 203, 226, 242
Indus Valley culture   11
inequities   130, 132–133, 157
information and communication technology   8, 235, 244
information technology   61, 64, 199
innovation   xviii, 19, 64, 68, 162, 207, 221, 232, 235–236
inquiry-based instruction   162, 165, 167, 172, 182–186
in-service teacher training   237, 239
instruction   21, 27–29, 31, 46, 61, 64, 67, 103–105, 116, 135–136, 151, 183–184, 187–189, 199, 205, 221, 230–231, 242, 244, 259, 261
instructional practice   124, 127, 135–136, 181
instrumentalist pragmatism   15
integrated curriculum   217, 235, 260
integrated labor-related activities   211
integrated practical activities   61, 64, 235, 239, 244
integrated practical studies   235
integrated teaching   28–29, 32, 54, 58, 64, 68, 111, 216
integration   18, 26, 29, 37, 45, 46, 63–64, 74, 163, 184
integration of school education   18
intellectual development   62, 126
interdisciplinary   163, 174, 237
interest groups   xi, 260
internalization   16, 26, 36–37, 39
interrelationship   xi, 163, 212
Isaksen, S. G.   175, 176
Islamic rule   22

Jacoby, B.   187–189
James, W.   10, 13
Jensen, B. B.   181
John, P. D.   x
Johnsen, S. K.   viii, xii, xv–xvi, 149–171, 151–152, 172–194, 174
Johnson, K.   151–152
Jones, S. R.   101, 113, 138
justice-oriented citizenship   149–150, 158–162, 167

Kahne, J.   155, 159–160, 162
Kalof, L.   182
Kanaʻiaupuni, S.   110–111

Kaye, C. B.   184
Keeter, S.   156
Kerschensteiner, G.   20–21
key competence   163
Khrushchev, N.   43
Kilpatrick, W. H.   19, 21
Kimonen, E.   vii–viii, xi, xiii, xvi–xvii, 3–91, 197–257, 259–261
Klein, E.   179, 180
knowledge   10–11, 14, 20, 26, 31–32, 34–36, 40, 44–45, 48, 50–51, 60, 66–67, 74, 77, 101, 111, 116, 163–164, 182, 239, 261
Kobashigawa, S.   vii, xii, xvi, 95–123, 124–145
Kollmuss, A.   181
Kothari, D. S.   50–51
Kothari Education Commission   50
Krupskaya, N. K.   32–33

labor and productive work   210, 212
labor and technical education   61, 63–64, 233
labor and technology-related programs   65
laboratory of life   17, 46
laboratory school   14, 202
labor-related activities   39, 61, 210–211, 243
labor-related education   31, 39, 54–55, 213, 218, 232, 243
labor-related out-of-school activities   63, 65
labor-related programs   72
labor-related technology projects   54, 63
labor-related work   216
labor school   21, 32–33, 42
labor technology   233, 236
language learning curriculum   136
Latin American   49
learner-centered education   181
learner-centered environments   199
learner-centered teaching   61, 259
learner differences   174
learning centers   227, 260
learning environment   10, 17, 28, 54, 61, 63, 198–204, 208, 211–213, 217–219, 222–233, 235–236, 239–244
learning networks   6, 261
learning process   21, 39, 54, 56, 59, 61, 67–68, 111, 210, 237, 259
learning through participation   259
LeCompte, K. N.   viii, xii, xvi, 149–171, 172–194
legitimation   37

Lenin, V. I.   22, 32–34, 42, 53
Levine, P.   155
Levinson, M.   154–156, 184
liberalism   60, 65
life-centered community-based learning   5
life-centered community school movement   5
life-centeredness   28, 261
Ligon, J. A.   158
Lin, A.   155
Lindzey, G.   8
literacy   47, 97–98, 108, 158, 172–173, 186–189, 207, 209
local craft   28, 205
Lunenburg, F.   184

Makarenko, A.   42–43
Mallinson, V.   75
Maloch, B.   174
mandatory service-learning   113, 130–131, 138
manual labor   38–40, 210, 231, 233, 243
manual skills   16
Mao, Z.   9, 23, 30–40, 54, 209, 213–215, 218
marine ecology   224
Marinova, D.   163
market-based educational policy   53, 73
market economy   31, 45, 52, 55, 60–61, 73, 238
Marks, H. M.   100–101, 103, 127, 138
Martial Dimension   219, 242
Marx, K.   22, 31–34, 36, 50, 53
Marxism   31, 49
Marxism-Leninism   33–34, 49
Marxist   21–22, 32–34, 36, 40, 42
Marxist polytechnical education   21, 42, 71
materialism   31, 34, 40, 49–50, 53, 65, 71
materialistic view of history   32–33
Maxim Gorky Colony   42
McGrath, N.   163
Mead, G. H.   13
meaning   10–11, 203, 207
meaningful learning   155, 173–174, 184
Melaville, A.   173, 180, 188
mentalistic education   18
metacognition   58–59
Metz, E.   130–131
microsystem   104, 115
Middaugh, E.   155, 169
Milner, H. R.   187
mimamsa school   11
modernization   9, 29, 43, 49–56, 60–66, 69,

INDEX

71–74, 76, 208, 223, 231–234, 242, 244
multiculturalism   137, 158
multidisciplinary   64, 163
multipurpose higher secondary school   208–209
multipurpose school   208
museum   61, 108, 163, 165, 204, 235–236, 244, 260
Musgrove, S. L.   163

National Defense Education Act of 1958   44–45, 221
Native Americans   24, 176
naturalism   20
naturalistic conceptions of the human   14
Naturalistic Dimension   201, 203–204, 224, 240, 242
nature study   22, 201, 233
Nehru, J.   49–50
neocolonial approach   43, 50–51
neocolonial education   71, 227
neocolonial educational policies   66
neocolonial school   50, 74, 226–227, 237, 242–243
neocolonial work education   49, 51
neo-conservatism   57
neo-conservative ideology   56
neo-Darwinism   14
neo-essentialism   56–57, 59
neo-essentialist education   57, 223
neo-essentialist educational theory   56, 73
neo-essentialist movement   49
neo-essentialist school   57, 74, 223, 237, 242
neo-evolutionary theories   203
neoliberal educational policies   66, 234
neoliberal social change   68, 70, 76
neoliberal social doctrine   56, 70, 73
neoliberal thinking   56, 70
neoliberalism   65
neo-traditional education   3, 27–28, 30, 67, 71, 221
neo-traditional school   74, 200, 205–207, 220–221, 237, 241
neo-traditionalism   30
Nesmith, S. M.   viii, xii, xvii, 149–171, 172–194
Nevalainen, R.   iv, vii–ix, xi, xiii, xvi–xvii, 3–91, 197–257, 259–261
newcomer programs   95, 107–110, 113, 127
No Child Left Behind Act   60, 97, 114
nondogmatic socialism   50

nonformal educational center   228
nonviolence   23–25, 69, 207
normative thinking   164

Olarte, A. C.   173
Olszewski-Kubilius, P.   151
open economy   73
organized camping   16–17
Osborn, A. F.   175
outdoor education   44–48, 204, 224–225, 242
outdoor laboratory   46
outdoor school program   204, 225
outline of curriculum reform   61
out-of-school activities   46, 61, 63, 65
out-of-school context   200, 207
out-of-school environments   47
out-of-school setting   231, 243
out-of-school site   48, 53, 112, 204, 236, 243

Parker, F.   14
Parkhurst, H.   19–22
Parnes, S. J.   175
Patel Review Committee   66, 69
pedagogical progressivism   13, 16, 18, 40, 42, 44, 60, 200, 203
pedagogical reform   14, 19, 21, 23, 26, 43–45, 71–72, 200, 205, 221, 240
pedagogical strategies   150–165, 174–187
Peirce, C. S.   10
People's Republic of China   23, 34, 43, 52, 54, 72, 75
Perlstein, D.   158
Pestalozzi, J. H.   20
Peyton, R. B.   48, 180
philosophy of education   9, 11, 13, 31
Phoenix Settlement   24
place-based learning   107, 110–113, 173, 179–181, 260
place-based programs   110–113
planned economy   23, 52, 73
Plekhanov, G. V.   32
policy borrowing and lending   4, 19
political education   231, 241
polytechnical education   21, 31–33, 50, 71
polytechnical labor school   32
Porfilio, B. J.   132, 140
positive youth development   152
postcolonial pedagogical approach   67–69, 72
postcolonial school   67, 74, 226–227, 237, 243

postcolonial work education   67, 70
post-Mao era   54
postrevolutionary education   54, 63, 73–74, 231, 243
postrevolutionary labor education   54, 62–63
postrevolutionism   55, 65
practical activities   10, 34–35, 61, 64
pragmatism   3, 10–11, 13–16, 31, 71
pragmatistic tradition   6–7
Prast, H. A.   4, 150, 244
preindustrial agrarian society   27–28, 74, 207, 241
preindustrial handicraft   71
preservice teacher education   172, 174, 176–179, 184–191, 237, 239
problem solving   15–16, 18, 21, 41, 46, 57–59, 61, 63, 67–69, 97, 116, 129, 136, 156, 159, 172, 174–178, 199, 202, 235, 244, 259–261
production center   229
Productive Dimension   202–203, 208, 211, 213, 217–218, 228–230, 240–241
productive labor   37, 39–40, 42–43, 62–63, 67, 71, 75, 209–210, 212, 217, 233, 235
productive labor education   55, 200, 217
productive labor-related projects   54–55
productive work   28–30, 32, 36, 38, 51–53, 217, 219, 229
professional identity   x
professional orientation   x, 198, 234
program variation   138–139
progressive education   3, 5, 13–22, 40–44, 71, 73, 200, 221, 240
progressive pedagogical approach   15
progressive pedagogy   14–15, 19, 42, 45
progressive school   5, 15–16, 18–19, 74, 200–203, 220, 237, 240, 259
progressive teaching procedures   61, 221
project method   21
public school camping   16–17
public school forestry program   204

Rabun Gap-Nacoochee School   225
radical social theory   3, 71
radical theory of social development   31
Raju, P.   11
Ramirez, L. M.   173
rationalism   67, 72
realism   17, 44–46, 57, 72
realism-oriented essentialist school   45, 56–57, 73, 242

reality
    cultural factor   198
    evolutionary   14
    mental factor   198
    objective   31, 44, 66
    outside the school   15, 198, 240, 259, 261
    physical factor   44, 198
    subjective   10
real-life situations   17–18, 64, 99, 240
real-world problems   97, 156, 162–164, 191
reconstruction   13, 15, 23, 27, 29, 41, 43, 260
reconstructionism   5
Red Guards   216
Redman, C. L.   163–164
reflection   99–100, 103, 132, 136–137, 154, 158, 179, 187, 189–190
reflective thinking   15, 59
reform
    community-based learning   63, 135–136, 237
    curriculum   61, 63, 234–235, 238
    educational   7–9, 20–21, 30, 32, 43, 49, 52, 55–56, 62–63, 66, 70, 72, 76, 96, 209, 217, 219, 221–222, 231, 238, 242
    pedagogical   9, 21, 23, 26, 41, 43–45, 71–72, 200, 205, 221
    pedagogy   9, 13–14, 20–21, 42, 51, 221, 231
    school   8–9, 18, 22, 42, 45, 97–98, 101, 215, 221, 223, 237
    social   6, 8, 12, 23, 25, 30, 40, 49, 52, 54, 209, 212, 216
    technological   66–67, 70, 73, 76
reform-pedagogical ideals   19, 26, 44
reform-pedagogical movements   44–45, 221
Reis, M.   199
Remington-Doucette, S. M.   163–164
remodernization   56, 223, 242
Renzulli, J. S.   151–152
resident outdoor education   204, 224–225, 242
resident outdoor school   204, 225
resources   6, 46, 107, 109–110, 112–113, 156, 173, 198–199, 222, 260–261
    community   63, 152, 236
    cultural   53
    economic   53, 152, 221, 237–238, 261
    educational   174, 238
    human   129, 261
    intellectual   237
    local   55, 173–174
    mental   221

INDEX

natural 38, 224
pedagogical 45
physical 237, 261
revolutionary education 3, 38, 71–72, 212, 216, 222–223
revolutionary era 222
revolutionary labor education 31, 36, 39, 54
revolutionary movement 30, 39, 53
revolutionary pedagogics 37
revolutionary schools 74, 209, 220, 241
Riordan, M. 179–180
Rizvi, F. 6–8
romantic naturalism 20
Rooted School 98
Rousseau, J. J. 20, 22
Rousseauean child-centered education 21, 44, 71–72
Roxas, K. 108–109
rural school xv, 38–39, 41, 110, 181, 210, 213, 215, 218, 235–236, 238
Ruskin, J. 24
Russia xvi, 21, 23, 32, 53
Russian Revolution 21, 32, 49, 52
Russell, J. Y. 163
Ryser, G. 174

Saltmarsh, J. 113, 156
satya 23, 69, 207
satyagraha 3, 23–26, 67, 71
satyagrahaism 28, 241
school behavior 126
school camping 16–17, 201, 240
school-centered community-based learning 8, 36, 54, 58, 62, 67, 75–76
school community 134, 198
school culture x, 9, 113, 198–199, 259
school enterprises 232
school factories 211, 217
school farm 203, 205, 210, 213
school gardening 201, 240, 243
school organization 8, 198
school production center 229
school reform 8–9, 18, 21–22, 42, 45, 52, 97, 101, 116, 215, 221, 223, 237
school shop 202, 230, 243
school workshop 202, 227, 243
schools' camp program 229
Schwartz, S. H. 8, 75
science- and technology-based work education 50, 76

science- and technology-centered program 51, 62
scientific cultivation project 229
Scientific-Technical Dimension 197, 200, 223, 225–227, 230–231, 233, 236, 240, 242–244
Scott, L. M. viii, xii, xvii, 149–171, 172–194
Second World War 18, 45, 220, 237
secondness 10
secularism 50, 52, 70
Seitsinger, A. M. 99, 101, 127, 135–136
self-sufficiency 23–28, 75, 207, 212, 215, 220–221, 250, 260
self-sufficient village community 25, 30
senior project 100–101, 114
service-centered activity 230
service-learning 57–59, 95–101, 105–107, 112–114, 125–127, 130–135, 139–140, 155, 159, 172–173, 176, 184–189, 225–226, 235, 237, 242
Shantiniketan Brahmacharya Ashrama 22
Sharkey, J. 173
Sharp, L. 17–18, 45–46
Shirley, D. x
Short, D. 107–109
Shulman, L. 6
situated learning environments 199
slum area 228, 243
Smith, G. A. 107, 110–111, 244
Smith, J. 46, 204
Snedden, D. 115
social action 156, 158, 162, 167, 261
social change 4, 6, 8–9, 45, 68, 70–71, 75–76, 100, 132, 197–198, 221
social consciousness 132, 158
social education 33
social equality 34, 50, 52, 70
social justice 25, 50, 69, 95, 100–101, 113, 115–116, 129–130, 132, 158, 188
social reality 15, 259, 261
social responsibility 64, 130
social service 29–30, 64, 67, 70, 207–209, 228–229, 235, 241, 243, 260
social transformation 5, 11, 207
socialism 38, 43, 49–50, 54–55, 63–64, 72
socialist market economy 55, 60–61, 66
socialist modernization 54, 60, 62, 232–234
socialist society 31, 38–40, 43, 54–55, 63, 65–66, 73–74, 76, 210, 212, 217, 243
socialist theory 31, 36, 61, 63
socialization 6, 17, 199–200

socialization environment 199–200
socially useful labor 31–32
socially useful productive work 67–70, 229–230, 237–238, 243
socially useful work 29
society-centered community-based learning 15, 26, 29, 38, 54, 74–76
Sociocultural Dimension 200, 208–209, 211, 213, 225, 227–228, 235, 241–244
South Africa 23–24
Soviet school curriculum 32
Soviet school system 21
Soviet Union vii, xi, 4, 14, 20–22, 32–33, 40–44, 49, 53, 223
spare-time schools 213–214
special education institute 228, 243
Spencer, H. 20, 22
spinning wheel 25, 241
spiritual awakening 26
Spranger, E. 8
Sputnik 44
Stalin, J. 42
Stalinist school 42
standardization 46, 56–57, 59, 73, 97, 215, 231
standardized school achievement tests 60, 237
standardized tests 66, 133–135
Starko, A. J. 151–152
Stern, P. C. 182
strategic competence 164
student perspectives 138
study project 200
study visit 201–202, 207
subject-centered 48, 55, 59, 72
subject-centered curriculum 56
Subotnik, R. F. 151
summer camp 203–204
SUPW program 230
Sutherland, C. 164
Swick, K. 184
symbolic universe 37
syncretistic view 61, 67

Tagore, R. 22
Tähtinen, U. 24–26
takli 206, 241
teacher, agent of change 5–6, 111, 125, 195
teacher-centered instruction 221
teacher-centeredness 49

teacher-directed teaching 56, 238
teacher-directed transmission of knowledge 237
teacher education 221, 239
teacher educator 188
teacher preparation xii, 98, 116
teacher professionalism x, xvii
teacher training 41, 239
teaching practice 158, 182–183, 239
teaching procedures 221, 226, 232
teaching profession 6
technical schools 21
technology-related values 3, 51, 62, 76
Terry, A. W. 176
textbook-centered teaching 237
theoretical values 45–47, 50, 54, 57, 62, 67, 76
thinking 10, 15, 35, 101, 103, 163–164, 175
thirdness 10
Tinkler, A. 188
Tinkler, B. 188
Tolstoy, L. 21–24
Tolstoy Farm 24
traditional crafts 30
traditional education 57, 111
traditional society 24, 27
traditional values 29, 37, 57
transaction of knowledge 238
transdisciplinary learning 149–150, 162–165, 167
transforming knowledge 234
transmitting knowledge 19, 234, 238
Treffinger, D. J. 175–176
truth 3, 10–11, 14, 23–27, 30, 35, 69, 71, 207
truthfulness 25
types of citizens 159

ubiquitous learning environments 244
Ukraine 42
Union of Soviet Socialist Republics 32
United States 3–4, 8, 10–11, 13–16, 18, 20–22, 24, 31, 43–47, 54, 56–58, 62, 67, 70–76, 95–97, 101, 105, 107–110, 113–114, 125–127, 133, 137, 159, 166, 179, 197–198, 200, 205, 221–223, 226, 237–240
universal pedagogical approach 16
universal structure of values 75
universal values 3, 5, 17, 29, 46–47, 75
university faculty 162, 165
University for Young People 150

INDEX

Upanishads 11
urbanization 221

value(s)   164, 198–199, 207, 211, 214, 217, 220, 224, 239, 259
value dimension   3–4, 8, 16, 38, 58, 62, 68, 70, 75–76
value education   69
value theories   8
Van de Kerkhof, M.   165
Vedas   11
Vernon, P. E.   8
Viegut, D. J.   4, 150, 244
Vinal, W.   17
village community   25, 27, 29–30, 41, 206
Village Council   227–228
village industry   25
village school   208, 215, 218, 227–229, 260
vocational activities   26–27, 206, 232, 241
vocational education   28, 221
vocationally productive education   26, 30, 50, 74–75, 197, 200, 239
vocationally productive units   52, 70–71, 73
vocationally productive work experience   52, 68, 229
Vogel, E. F.   53
voluntary teams   260
volunteerism   95, 98–99, 104, 113, 124–125, 160, 187

Wade, R. C.   98, 100, 103, 126, 185
Washburne, C. W.   19
Weah, W.   102
Weible, J. L.   181
Western parliamentary democracy   49–50

Westheimer, J.   159–160, 162
Wiek, A.   163–164
Wilke, R. J.   48, 180
Wilson, P.   46
work and service activity   207
work- and service-centered activities   230
work-based learning   95, 99–100, 104–107, 114, 126–130, 133, 139, 210, 233
work-centered education   229
work education   32, 49–50, 67, 69–70
work-experience education   51, 69, 227–228, 237–238, 243
work-experience programs   50, 52
work-related activities   5, 16, 32, 210, 241
work-related lessons   206, 242
work-related pedagogy   15, 69
work-study procedures   232
work-study schools   34, 37, 43, 72, 209, 214, 217, 220
work-study students   213
workers-peasants-soldiers   222
World Bank's structural adjustment program   70, 73

Xiao Zhuang Normal School   40–41
Xing-zhi, T.   20, 40–41
Xu, D.   20, 41

Yamauchi, L. A.   111–113
Yates, M.   131–132
Youth Service America   107

Zakir Husain Committee   28, 205
Zimmerman, H. T.   181
Zint, M.   180

Printed in the United States
By Bookmasters